PRIMITIVE PEOPLES TODAY

PRIMITIVE PEOPLES TODAY

BY

EDWARD WEYER, JR.

Dolphin Books
Doubleday & Company, Inc.
Garden City, New York

Printed in the United States of America

CONTENTS

ACKNOWLEDGMENTS

The author wishes to thank Dr. Conrad M. Arensberg of Columbia University for his helpful comments on the manuscript.

He is also grateful to the staff of the Firestone Library of Princeton University for their courtesy in permitting him to consult the Human Relations Area Files and other source material.

PRIMITIVE PEOPLES TODAY

INTRODUCTION

The World of Primitive Man

The modern interest in primitive peoples had its beginnings in the golden era of exploration when travelers of the fifteenth and sixteenth centuries brought back to Europe descriptions of native tribes in the newly discovered continents. The accounts told mostly of strange customs. The "savages," as they were called, were sometimes described quite well but often fancifully, and as for their origin, folklore offered the only clues.

A new era was introduced when archeologists excavated relics indicating that man had been on earth much longer than had been suspected, and that some primitive tribes were still using implements that had changed little since prehistoric times. The idea that living aborigines might provide a mirror to the past, and that civilized and primitive man might have shared a common origin, stimulated new interest in native tribes. Soon scholars began to wish that methods could be developed for measuring the unrecorded reaches of time.

Such methods have now been developed, and others are likely to follow. Evolutionary science and genetics have solved some of the riddles of racial differentiation; and modern archeology, with new techniques for dating specimens, is putting together the story of man's migrations and cultural development.

The social anthropologist is also approaching his studies with new techniques and attitudes. Instead of specializing in bizarre customs, he looks for the whole pattern of life and thought in a primitive tribe. He analyzes the arts of life in relation to environment and the evolution of such institutions as marriage and the family, religion and government. The time factor has begun to figure prominently in his thinking, for he is continually dealing with practices that lose much of their meaning if considered without knowledge of their roots.

All these studies promise to help clarify the mysteries surrounding man's development, and they may help us to understand some of the enigmas of our nature. The efforts of people to adjust to nature, to adapt to an immense range of environments, to get along with their fellow men—all these adventures along man's rough road must be studied if we are to profit from experience. For the future is like a corridor into which we can see only by the light coming from behind.

THE WORD "PRIMITIVE"

The word "primitive" has many meanings. In this book we use it to describe tribal groups living close to nature and showing definite roots in the prehistoric past. The word has long been used in this way, but anthropologists do not consider it an ideal term, for it may unintentionally suggest low intellect, crude habits, or brutish impulses.

A better word in some ways is "pre-literate," which says only that a people do not use a written language. Yet it, too, does not completely serve our purposes here. Even the Incas, with their highly developed arts and elaborate governmental organization, lacked a written language, and to call them pre-literate would be to bracket them with the lowliest of aborigines.

When one meets, say, a band of wild Chavante Indians in the jungle of Brazil, as the writer did a few years ago, the fact that they are pre-literate is hardly one's first thought. Other lacks are much more obvious; they are wearing no clothing; they have no metal of any kind; and the arrows and spears with which they defend themselves are tipped not with stone points but with sharpened bamboo or bone. Their long hair hangs loosely behind their necks. They have no eyebrows, having plucked them in accordance with tribal custom, which in our view adds a macabre touch to faces already grim. Using no utensils, they have just devoured the haunch of an animal, which they roasted on a triangle of sticks tied half-way up the legs of a simple tripod. They have been sleeping on the ground without any covering; a large patch of ashes shows where they have scraped the embers aside to take advantage of the warmth. They have no huts, except for some tiny tunnels of leafy saplings, each barely large enough for one man to crawl into in case of rain.

At first glance, we might suppose that these people were living about as close to the original state of man as anyone on earth today, and our inclination might be to describe them as very low in the primitive scale. However, an airplane flight over their territory reveals that the Chavantes have large villages of spacious thatched huts. The clearing in the center of one of them is large enough to contain four athletic fields. Far from exhibiting anything like subhuman intelligence, the people have troubled to lay their community out in the form of a perfect circle, which they could do only by knowing how to use a string several hundred feet long to form the radius.

Flying just high enough to avoid their ever-ready arrows, we see that they are growing corn and that the women are mixing food in pottery bowls. Though the Chavantes on the trail seemed to lack even some of the tools of the early Stone Age, here in their village they possess two things that came in only in the New Stone Age, or Neolithic period—agriculture and pottery. We therefore realize that the band we met in the forest was a hunting party detached from the rest of their tribe and limited in material possessions to what they could carry.

More difficult even than measuring the material achievements of a people is evaluating their intellectual, aesthetic, or moral level. These Chavantes exhibited marked distrust in dealing with us. A bow-and-arrow man stood on each side of the chief, and the other men also remained on their guard. Their suspicion bore out what the nearest civilized settlers had told us regarding their unfriendliness. Cruelty and deceit, we had been warned, were the only methods the Chavantes used in dealings with others; their history had been a long series of massacres. In short, they were the worst of savages.

Granting that the Chavantes are terrible fighters when aroused, it does not follow that they are innately more vicious than other people. Until recent times, it was customary to call all aborigines "savages." Actually, among their own kind, they are apt to be as agreeable and affectionate as the rest of mankind. They respect the rights of others and observe well-developed rules of behavior. The husband may be as pampered or as henpecked as his civilized brother, the wife as loyal or as shrewish. Like many "civilized" peoples, the "savage" is savage only toward his enemies.

Contact between primitive and civilized people has involved much conflict, and the word "savage" expresses well the side of the native that is often most evident to the white man. But the term is not otherwise generally appropriate. Fortunately, it has almost gone out of use.

Though their hostility has as yet prevented us from learning much about the Chavantes, the study of other tribes shows that a life in the wilderness does not necessarily prevent the development of a distinctive art or music, a "literary sense," or complex spiritual beliefs and observances. To appreciate this, however, and to arrive at anything like a valid evaluation of unfamiliar cultures, we must abandon any assumption that our own standards are the only ones.

The anthropologist does not consider whether a custom is attractive or repugnant, or morally good or bad. He is cautious about imputing motives to primitive peoples, for he realizes that any interpretations must be grounded in aboriginal standards rather than civilized ones. Like a coin collector who is more interested in the coins themselves than in how much they will buy, he values the facts according to how useful they prove in a process of scientific reasoning. The fact that two widely separated tribes may subscribe to the same belief is far more important to him than whether the belief is true or good by his own standards. Indeed, he may be pleased that it is out of the ordinary, for this may help to establish its origin.

STAGES OF CULTURE

It was formerly thought that a people's advancement could be gauged simply according to whether they lived by hunting, herding, or farming. The assumption was that any tribe, in order to rise from an animal-like existence, must pass through these three successive stages. This is no longer accepted in all respects.

The earliest stage of human existence, to be sure, was one that depended on hunting and the gathering of wild products from nature. The people of that stage did not domesticate animals or plant crops. However, some hunting peoples, such as the Eskimos, have evolved techniques far more complex than those of some purely herding peoples such as the Todas of southern India. In the agricultural arts, primitive peoples show such a range of development that it has been found useful to recognize two divisions. The simplest farming techniques are those performed only with a hoe or a pointed stick. Many tribes in the tropics exploit rudimentary techniques of this sort along with hunting. The more elaborate agriculture employs the plow drawn by a domestic animal.

It is not known whether the domestication of herd-animals came before or after the development of agriculture. It is also uncertain whether the pastoral mode of life arose chiefly as a single invention and spread, or whether various peoples independently hit upon such practices as the taming of male animals through castration and the prolonging of lactation through continued milking. The herding cultures of the world show considerable diversity, depending upon whether cattle, sheep, reindeer or other animals predominate, and on local cultural peculiarities.

The lack of herding cultures in aboriginal America suggests that the basic techniques may have spread from one or a few centers in the Old World and had not yet reached the New. Reindeer herding had spread through northern Asia as far east as the Chukchees near Bering Strait, but it had not reached the Eskimos, even though they hunted the caribou, an animal amost identical with the European and Asiatic reindeer. The Lapps and Asiatic reindeer herders may have learned some of their techniques from cattle herders and horsemen to the south.

Climate, vegetation, and other environmental factors have helped to determine whether a people can best concentrate on hunting, fishing, herding, or farming. The natural resources of a region generally have much to do with the pattern of primitive life. Dependence on large herds for food and clothing is a development that generally occurs where there is not enough rainfall or a warm enough season for tillage.

Perhaps the most serious fallacy in rating people according to their mode of food procurement is the fact that this is only one of the many aspects of primitive life. Art, music, religion, family organization, tribal government, and other aspects of life contribute to the total culture, and they rarely show uniform development.

THE RACES OF MAN

It is as difficult to grade peoples in the physical scale as in regard to their mode of life. The gorilla, orangutan, and chimpanzee all have either dark brown or blackish skin. The lighter skin of the Caucasian race might therefore appear to place it further up the evolutionary ladder. But the fact that Caucasians have more hair on face and body would put them closer to the apes. The extent to which the jaws protrude in profile beyond the rest of the face, known as prognathism, has been cited as a measure of primitiveness, for the lower animals show this feature more pronouncedly than man. Negroes exhibit more prognathism than other races, and the Caucasians are at the opposite end of the scale. Yet in the development of the lips, the Negro is further removed from the archaic types than any other race. The Mongoloid peoples have the thinnest and therefore the most anthropoid lips, and also perhaps the shortest legs in proportion to stature. In other respects, however, they are the least "ape-like" of peoples.

Racial pride has long caused people to consider themselves better than others, and language itself has become a party to the prejudice. Though we strive to use colorless and relatively objective words like "archaic" and "early" instead of "primitive," people are so sensitive that it remains difficult to discuss these matters scientifically. Partly because of such complications and partly because the problem itself is extremely complex, few satisfactory formulas have been devised for determining racial status or evolutionary rank.

Unfounded assumptions of mental superiority have also clouded the racial issue. It was once assumed that the "lower races" were deficient in mental capacity and childlike in their psychology. While we have no reason arbitrarily to deny the possibility of mental differences paralleling the physical ones that seem to have resulted through evolutionary processes, tests have not revealed that one race is notably superior to the others in the sum total or average of its capacities. Every sizable group of people, whatever their race, shows wide variation in aptitudes. It is quite unscientific to try to use race as an index of intelligence. Culture and upbringing strongly influence an individual's patterns of thought and the ways in which he uses his mental faculties.

The simplest classification of mankind distinguishes three main divisions: Black, White, and Yellow. The Yellow includes not only the Mongoloids of Asia but also the Indians of North and South America, and it is sometimes called the Yellow-red race. Though these three divisions are frequently referred to as races, it may be better to call them "stocks," for they are further subdivided. The anthropologist considers a race a division of mankind that possesses enough constant inherited traits to set it apart as a distinct group within the three basic divisions, Black, White or Yellow, or outside of them. The traits must be physical, not cultural, historical, or political. Within a race there may be a tremendous range of variability, and there is no completely pure race. But modern anthropologists recognize as many as thirty races, aside from a number of less conspicuous subdivisions.

Africa has so long been spoken of as the home of the Black race that it is well to remind ourselves that the northern third of the continent has been inhabited by Caucasian peoples probably since aboriginal times. Most of Africa south of the Sahara is inhabited by Bantu Negroes. Between these lies a zone in which the two racial types have intergraded. In parts of the Sudan and East Africa, a number of tall and very slender dark peoples have been given various names, such as Hamite, Half-Hamite, or Nilotic. The last term is the best, since it refers to their place of concentration, along the upper Nile and south of it, whereas the word Hamite is best reserved for people speaking Hamitic languages. Skeletally, these East Africans of Nilotic type appear to be closer to the Caucasians than to the true Negroes of West and Central Africa, with whom, however, they share dark skin, sometimes thick lips, and curled or woolly hair. The Abyssinians are more clearly Caucasian in type than some of the others and are believed to have come from across the Red Sea so long ago that there is no record of their migration.

Neither the Bushmen of South Africa nor the Pygmies of Central Africa are classed as true Negroes. The Pygmies are the smallest people on earth (the men average 4 feet 11 inches). They look enough like Negroes in miniature to have been called Negritos, or "Little Negroes," though we are ignorant of what racial connection, if any, exists between them. The Pygmies most commonly pictured live in the Ituri Forest of eastern Belgian Congo. Others are found locally as far west as the Cameroons in western Africa; and Negritos live in the interior of the Malay Peninsula, the Philippines, and New Guinea, where again their connections, if any, with far-off Africa raise interesting unsolved questions of race and migration. All of them have dark brown skin and spirally curled hair.

The spotty distribution of the Negritos suggests they may be the modern remnants of a once widely distributed race, now crowded by stronger peoples into isolation in tropical forest regions. The alternative theory, currently supported by several authorities, is that in two or more different places, full sized Negroid peoples with frizzly hair and dark skin independently produced a small version of themselves either through an abrupt hereditary change, that is, by mutation, or through long-term natural selection. Proof or disproof must await further development in archeology or in genetics.

The Bushmen in southern Africa are somewhat larger than the Negritos. Their skin, however, is yellowish brown and much wrinkled in old age. They have very broad noses, pointed chins, and flat ears. Their hair is tightly coiled in tufts generally termed "peppercorns." Some Bushmen are hollow-backed, and some even possess the enlarged buttocks known as steatopygia, a condition seen in its most extreme form among Hottentot women in South Africa. The Hottentots may represent Bushman and Nilotic or "Hamite" inheritance with an admixture of the extinct African type known as Boskop.

A great many other dark peoples live outside of Africa. The largest group are the Oceanic Negroids. Most of those in this category are Melanesians ("Black Islanders"), who inhabit the islands of the South Pacific eastward from New Guinea to Fiji (see map, page 241). The Melanesians have frizzly hair and their skin is very dark. The casual observer might take a Melanesian for an African Negro, and the two groups are, in fact, physically similar. Yet there are differences which, together with the wide geographical separation, precludes the Oceanic Negroids from being considered a recent African offshoot or a simple blend of African Negro with some other strain. The lips of the Melanesian are thinner than those of typical African Negroes, and the nose, though generally broad, may be thin and almost beaklike. The people of New Guinea, though somewhat different, are often classed with the Melanesians.

The Australian aborigine belongs in a separate group. He is definitely further removed from the Negro than are the Melanesians, for he has abundant straight or wavy hair. His dark brown eyes are deep-set beneath heavy, jutting brows, and his forehead is sloping. The Australian is generally regarded as an ancient type, preserved against intermixture by geographic isolation. He also shows evidence of Caucasian relationship, at least in some of his features, as will be explained in the chapters on the Ainu and Arunta tribes.

Another distinctive dark people inhabited the island of Tasmania when it was discovered in 1642, but they bebecame extinct in 1876. This race differed from the Australian aborigines in having woolly instead of wavy hair. Some anthropologists have classed them as Negritos with an admixture of a nearly extinct aboriginal people of southeastern Australia known as the Murrayians. The latter were stocky in build, had brown skin, wavy abundant hair, and features somewhat similar to those of Europeans. The early ancestors of the Tasmanians may have migrated from the island of New Caledonia in Melanesia and acquired some of the Murrayian traits on the way.

North of Melanesia, from the Marianas to the Gilberts, live the Micronesians. They get their name from the word Micronesia ("small islands") applied to these and nearby archipelagoes. Some of the Micronesians are as tall and sturdy as western Europeans. Their skin is predominantly brown, and some show considerable intermixture with Malayan, Indonesian, Melanesian, and Polynesian strains.

The Polynesians occupy the innumerable islands within a triangle formed by Hawaii, New Zealand, and Easter Island. They are a tall people with straight or wavy hair and light brown skin. Their lips are fairly full, and their noses moderately thick, but not flat. By our standards they are handsome and well-proportioned. The anthropologist Ernest Hooton classed them as mostly brunette White with Mongoloid and Melanesian admixture. The Polynesians can generally be distinguished from other Pacific groups by their more Caucasoid appearance. Some do not look very different from American Indians. Their name refers to the "many islands" they inhabit.

The Indonesians are a varied brown-skinned people, smaller than the Polynesians and darker than the Mongoloids, to whom they show some relationship. As a national group, the Indonesians are identified with Java, Sumatra, Celebes, Borneo, and a number of smaller islands. But racially they resemble some other groups scattered elsewhere in southeast Asia. This region is undoubtedly a home of early man and an ancient ethnic crossroads. Where to draw the line between the Indonesians and various other composite groups such as are found in eastern Tibet, southwestern China, northern Burma, Thailand, Malaya, and parts of the Philippines is difficult to say. All probably represent a blending of aboriginal south Asiatic peoples with later Mongoloids from the north. People resembling American Indians are also sometimes encountered in Southeastern Asia.

From India to the East Indies (but only in small, scattered groups) are found the Veddoid peoples, named after their typical representatives, the small-bodied Veddas of interior Ceylon. Other Veddoids are the Dravidian and the Munda tribes of India, the Nicobar Islanders in the Bay of Bengal, some of the Moi of south-central Vietnam, the Sakai of the Malay Peninsula, the Toala of Celebes, and, according to some students, certain tribal peoples in southeastern Arabia. The typical Veddoid is of slight build, with dark skin, broad nose, and straight black hair. The eyes are deep-set, the mouth large, the beard moderate. On the one hand, the Veddoids resemble the Caucasian; on the other, they show a similarity to the Australian aborigines. So it is not surprising that they should sometimes be called Indo-Australoids. Their ancestors have probably contributed to the darkness of skin seen in many of the people of the otherwise basically Caucasian population of India.

Mongoloid peoples are characterized by "oblique" eyes, caused by the epicanthic fold, which is a lapping-over of the flesh of the eyelid so that it conceals the inner corner of the eye. Their skin has a yellowish tinge, and their hair is straight and black. The Mongoloids are now extremely numerous over much of eastern and central Asia but were probably far less plentiful only a few thousand years ago. They may have spread by an almost "explosive" expansion of population and reached their present concentrations only in recent millennia. They now occupy almost every climatic environment in that part of the world—arctic, tropic, and desert.

An extreme type of Mongoloid face, such as is seen in the Tungus of eastern Siberia, in the Amur River country and to the north, has been interpreted as a possible evolutionary response to extreme cold. Carleton S. Coon, Stanley M. Garn, and Joseph B. Birdsell have suggested that the slit-shaped, heavy-lidded eyes and the over-all flatness of the faces of these people give them better protection against frostbite than is possessed by people with thin, bony features and a prominent nose. In the course of time, they reason, the evolutionary process might have eliminated the less fit, producing a people exhibiting this type of face. It is a provocative theory, but like others in this branch of human ecology, it is hard to prove. The issue is somewhat clouded by the fact that other Siberian tribes inhabiting the cold arctic fringe of Asia do not exhibit this extreme development.

The Eskimos and Indians reveal their relationship to the Mongoloid peoples of Asia by their straight black hair, the Mongoloid eye-fold (especially in childhood), and to some extent their skin color. When we realize that the earliest inhabitants of America came from Asia as much as 20,000 to 30,000 years ago, it is not surprising that the American

Indians do not resemble the Asiatic Mongoloids more closely. It seems likely that other racial strains not conspicuous now in northeastern Asia contributed to the ancestry of the earliest Asiatic migrants to North America.

Lastly, the Caucasians, or white peoples, occupy parts of Europe, Asia, and Africa. They have also spread into many new lands during the past few centuries and have mingled with the other races locally. Many Caucasian peoples are far darker than most Mongoloids, as in India and in some of the Asiatic and African lands bordering the Mediterranean, for, as we shall see, hair and form of face are better criteria of race than color of skin.

Considering their isolation, the most surprising representatives of the white race are the Ainus (see chapter on, pp. 189–208), an aboriginal Caucasoid people living on the northern Japanese island of Hokkaido and nearby Sakhalin.

RACIAL TRAITS

The color of the skin has long been one of the basic criteria in racial classification. Skin color is easy to measure by means of standard guides, such as a small disk-shaped top with adjustable "pie slices" of color. The percentage of red, yellow, black, and white can be adjusted by sliding the color disks one over another. Several surprising facts are revealed by this color top: To match the skin color of a white person, for instance, more than 30 per cent of the area of the disk must be black; the average Negro's skin contains only about twice as much black as this. The American Indian, though he is called a "redskin," actually has only about 17 per cent of red in his skin. The Chinese, belonging to the Yellow race, have only five per cent more yellow than Caucasians do.

Hair texture is also an important criterion in classifying races. Human hair is described as being straight, wavy, curly, frizzly, and woolly. The extremely woolly type we have referred to as "peppercorn" is bunched in isolated tufts between which the scalp is visible. The texture of the hair is determined by the straightness or curvature of the root sac and apparently also by the cross section of the hair, which is nearly circular in straight hair and more oval in the curly types.

Other important characteristics in racial classification are the color of the hair and the eyes, the presence of the epicanthic fold in the "oriental" eye, the shape of the nose, the form of the teeth and the lips, and stature. Even beyond these, however, the anthropologist notes a number of less obvious points, which, while not contributing separately to a diagnosis in the racial sense, appear to have a statistical bearing on the study of racial differences.

One of these is the sacral or Mongolian spot, a blotch of bluish coloring which some persons have at birth near the base of the spine. It usually disappears within a few weeks or months. The Mongolian spot was first observed among members of the Yellow race, but other races also show it with varying frequency. The sacral spot is therefore no proof of Mongoloid ancestry; nor is its absence disproof.

Another characteristic of the Yellow race on both sides of the Pacific is an unusual tooth formation, described as "shovel-shaped." Instead of being almost flat, the inner surface of the upper front teeth shows thickened edges that almost appear to have been folded over. Almost all American Indians have this sort of teeth; many Chinese and Japanese also do. Shovel-shaped teeth are rare among Negroes and practically absent among Europeans. They are therefore not a test of Mongoloid extraction. However, when the sacral spot and shovel-shaped teeth appear together, the statistical likelihood increases. Add to this combination the eye-fold, and all reasonable doubt is dispelled. Since a glance at the face would probably have revealed just as much, the utility of this method is not great.

From the point of view of heredity, it is unscientific to speak of a person as having a certain percentage of Indian, Negro, or other blood. Blood is not the carrier of heredity; nor can a person's race be determined by his blood. Nonetheless, there are interesting peculiarities of the blood that are inherited and have some statistical value in anthropology. One of these is the grouping of the blood into the types O, A, B, and AB. Owing to the importance of using the right type of blood in transfusions, almost a million persons have been typed in widely scattered parts of the world. Public attention has also been drawn to the question of the inheritance of the blood types because of their use in paternity suits. Although blood typing does not establish who the father of a child is, it does sometimes establish that a certain person is *not*. Similarly, since most racial groups show all four types, blood grouping has only limited usefulness in racial classification. In only one tribe do all individuals have the same type of blood, and they are part of a larger tribe: the Polar Eskimos, a small isolated branch living in northern Greenland, all of whom have type O. It is also worth noting that 91 per cent of some American Indian groups have type O. The more usual thing is to find substantial percentages of two or more types. Blood group percentages sometimes cut across racial lines. The highest frequency of type B on earth, for instance, is exhibited by three groups that seem to differ in other respects about as much as people can: the Congo Pygmies, the Hindus, and the Mongols. Furthermore, the Mongoloids on the western side of the Pacific show different percentages from the Indians on the American side.

Another characteristic that has been much studied is the so-called "sickling" trait. About fifteen years ago it was noticed that a considerable percentage of Negroes, both in American and Africa, had sickle-shaped red blood corpuscles among the normal disk-shaped ones. This was found to be caused by an unusual type of red coloring matter, or hemoglobin. The condition proved to be hereditary. Tests performed on about 29,000 individuals show that throughout the tropical portion of the bulge of Africa one person in seven or eight, on the average, possesses this trait.

Because of the absence of sickling among other races, it began to be referred to as a race-linked trait restricted to persons of Negro or Hamitic ancestry. Then it was reported among the Yemenite Jews and in various countries bordering the Mediterranean. Also difficult to explain was its presence among three aboriginal tribes of India; but even there, Negro crossings might have occurred at an early date.

However, high frequencies among certain Greeks and Turks broke the theory that race was the important factor. Scientists began to suspect that the sickling trait might carry an evolutionary advantage that caused those who had it to reproduce faster. This advantage appears to have been discovered: persons possessing sickle-cell blood enjoy a special resistance to malaria. The reason for this is not known, but the regions where it is common are ones where malaria is a serious killer. In the United States, the sickling trait is apparently a carry-over from African days, and the number of persons possessing it may diminish with succeeding generations. The percentage of those with the sickling trait in a given locality is apparently held below a certain level because inbreeding of such persons produces a special form of anemia in the offspring.

Color blindness occurs more frequently among some tribes than others. It differs from the sickle-cell trait in being a recessive characteristic and sex-linked; that is, it is inherited by males but transmitted by females who themselves have normal color vision. Eight out of 100 American males have red-green color blindness, whereas only one out of 100 Eskimos or Indians are afflicted with it. Its rarity among these people may be due to the value of good color vision in hunting, especially in detecting the shape of an animal against its background. One of the highest frequencies of color blindness, thirteen per cent, prevails among the buffalo-tending dairymen of the Toda tribe of southern India.

The width of the head divided by the length provides the important ratio known as the *cephalic index*. Because it is clearly hereditary and does not vary materially with age or sex, or in response to environmental influences, the cephalic index is considered one of the most valuable standards for distinguishing otherwise similar peoples. It is by no means uniform for the primary divisions of mankind and is therefore most useful in differentiating smaller racial groups, such as the Nordic and Alpine subdivisions of the whites.

A number of diseases occur much more frequently among some races than others. Cancer, for example, appears to afflict Caucasian peoples oftener than others. The Eskimo may not have had it prior to the European period; but today in Greenland, where there has been strong European influence for a number of generations, cancer is frequent. Whether change of diet, racial mixing, or some other factor is at work is not known. Again for unknown reasons, the Navaho Indians of today show a very low incidence of cancer. Diabetes is more common among people of Jewish extraction than in many other Caucasian groups. Where differences of this sort can be shown to result from hereditary factors, they are of interest to the student of human evolution as well as to the medical man.

The people of nature show enough peculiarities in regard to specific diseases to warrant a great deal more research than has been undertaken. The fact that they live on radically different diets and under diverse climatic conditions makes these people a "living laboratory," which medical science is only beginning to utilize. Much benefit to all mankind may come out of such investigations, but the time remaining is limited because the spread of civilization is rapidly eliminating many differences.

EVOLUTION AND RACIAL TYPES

Three factors are thought to control the evolutionary process through which the various racial types have developed: variation, selection, and heredity.

Variation is the factor that causes every individual in a tribe or family (except for identical twins, triplets, and so on) to differ from his brothers and sisters.

Sudden variations, called mutations, are believed to play a part in normal evolution. Ordinarily, mutations are rare.

It is estimated that each person possesses something like 44,000 pairs of heredity carriers, or genes; in all this number, only about one mutation per individual can be expected on the average. Furthermore, there is only about one chance in thirty that a mutation will affect a characteristic that is visible.

The animal breeder selects his breeding stock so as to stress traits that he considers desirable. In nature, environmental conditions affect the possibility that a given animal will live to reproduce its kind. Thus one animal survives because it can run faster than another or conceal itself better from an enemy. When its traits possess more "survival value" than those of its brothers, selection, operating through heredity, may favor perpetuation of those traits. Variation itself produces random differences; but selection and heredity produce a systematic trend. It is believed that mental as well as physical traits may be inherited. If this is so, they too may be selected and become statistically more prominent through the evolutionary process.

In the early days of Darwinian evolution, undue emphasis was sometimes given the role of natural selection in the purely anatomical sense. Increased knowledge of genetics and physiology indicates that the process involves a number of other factors besides the obvious environmental ones. In any case, there does not always appear to have been a steady increase in the efficiency of each organism. Many outworn characteristics are retained: for example, the human appendix. In other words, evolution does not move forward with anything like the efficiency of machine production, where each new model may represent an improvement. It is infinitely slow and very complex. If we liken the variations that distinguish individuals to the ripples that chase across the surface of the sea, the underlying hereditary pattern can be compared to the broad currents and ground-swells. Variations add variety to the surface; heredity perpetuates the basic pattern.

In man, because he is a creature of choice, selective factors sometimes operate that have nothing to do with climatic or other environmental conditions or the practical need to survive. Instead, social or psychological preferences may influence the evolutionary trend. If, to take an arbitrary example, the men of a certain community preferred blondes to brunettes generation after generation, an increase in the percentage of blond people in the population could be expected. The selective force at work here would not result from man's relation to his environment but would merely reflect a current vogue. Animals in their mating habits also sometimes express this sort of "sexual selection."

Still another type of evolutionary selection is illustrated by the Rh factor in the blood. When a woman lacking the Rh factor carries a child by a man who is Rh positive, the embryo sets up antibodies in the mother's blood. These react destructively and often fatally on the embryo's blood and may also injure the mother. Therefore, under natural conditions, Rh negative individuals tend to disappear from a population that is primarily Rh positive. The selective factor here is physiological incompatibility. If, by chance, other traits are associated with a trait of this sort in significant amounts, their disappearance along with the incompatible trait may influence evolution in other ways.

Innumerable efforts have been made to show that extreme climatic conditions have produced different types of physique and physiognomy. The fact that Eskimos have very narrow noses has been cited as an adaptation to the breathing of cold air, and so has the very flat, fat-padded and slit-lidded Mongoloid face of coldest Siberia. However, early anthropological writings contain numerous environmental arguments that have not stood the test of time.

A familiar example of this is the fact that peoples native to the tropics generally have a darker skin than those of the temperate or arctic regions. But in reality, a darker suit is hotter in the sun than a light one, and one would suppose that a dark-skinned person would feel hotter in the sun than a light one. We therefore must search elsewhere for an explanation of the abundance of dark-skinned peoples in the tropics; and as a matter of fact, no altogether satisfactory theory has been offered. Skin that becomes tanned through exposure acquires better resistance to sunburn; thus, we assume that the individual can adapt himself to life in the sun. But there is no direct evidence that generations of sunburn can produce a dark-skinned breed of men. And again when we plot the distribution of the dark-skinned races, we find that some of them live in forested regions and pass much time in the shade. Sunburn-producing rays are strongest in the desert, in the rarefied atmosphere of high mountains, and on the dazzling snowfields of the far north, where the sun seasonally shines long hours. These regions have not always produced dark-skinned peoples. The Eskimo's face and hands are dark from exposure, but the rest of his body remains almost as light as a European's. Perhaps the Eskimo and other arctic peoples have not lived long enough under the northern glare to have evolved dark skins; or their clothing may have provided sufficient protection. And this reminds us that man, unlike the beasts of the field, short-cuts the evolutionary process by all manner of devices such as clothing, fire, shelter, eye-shades, and disguises.

Soviet thinking differs from Western thinking on the subject of whether acquired characteristics can be inherited. Most European and American scientists do not believe that they can. The son of a blacksmith, or even generations of blacksmiths, do not inherit a stronger right arm, they argue. Nor does a descendant of people who practice some sort of bodily mutilation generation after generation show the effect. But some Soviet scientists subscribe to the belief that modifying the individual can modify the race. They argue that skills acquired through training can be inherited. The famous Russian scientist Ivan Pavlov, who made his name in the field of conditioned responses, subscribed to this belief in 1923. He based his opinion on some vaguely documented experiments which purported to show that rats trained to respond to a bell could produce, through successive generations, a breed that learned the trick more and more quickly. But the best evidence indicates that Pavlov himself later doubted that the experiments had proved this point. Considering how readily experiments of this sort should be able to demonstrate transmission of acquired characteristics, it is significant that so long a time has passed without proof. It is quite a different question whether a more intelligent breed of rats can be produced by breeding only from the smartest ones in each litter.

The physical differences evident among the various races remain unimportant in comparison with the similarities. It is estimated that between 90 and 99 per cent of the approximately 44,000 pairs of genes in each individual are shared by all other groups of men. This means that the human organism is basically similar the world over. Thus, all races can mate with all others and produce fertile young.

It is easy to overestimate the rate at which evolution can take place in the human species. When occasionally a mutation that has survival value occurs, one small step may have been taken in the direction of change. But each individual is an almost illimitable combination of attributes, some advantageous, some not, and even in an aboriginal society the unfit are often preserved. We need not wonder then that evolutionary trends are not more clear-cut. In the million years or so that man has walked upright, he has lost or gained relatively few physical characteristics in comparison with the ones he has retained. The great change has taken place in his mode of life.

CULTURAL EVOLUTION

The anthropologist uses the word "culture" not in the sense of refinement and good taste but to designate all the techniques, implements, customs, beliefs, attitudes, artifices and arts by which a people live. Culture to an anthropologist includes almost everything about a people that is not physical or instinctive. The idea that cultures evolve somewhat as do physical organisms was introduced shortly after the turn of the century. However, it was found that cultural evolution proceeds in a different way from evolution of the organic body.

Three primary factors (corresponding to variation, selection, and heredity in organic evolution) determine cultural evolution, but they work through learning processes that do not involve heredity in the genetic sense. That is, although a child will *look* like an Eskimo or a Zulu depending entirely on whether he is born one, he will grow up *acting* like an Eskimo or a Zulu depending on the culture in which he is raised.

Ideas are not inherited; they are passed down through the generations through teaching, planned or "unconscious." Animals live primarily by instinct, man by learning. Instinct begins for a chicken before it is hatched: a warning sound from the mother hen will cause the chick to react while it is still in the egg. From the moment it hatches, the bird will pick up a worm and hurry away with it. Human babies show some instincts at birth, but the vast majority of reactions needed to carry them through life must be learned. Among animals, learning plays some part in the preparation of the young for life, but between the highest apes and man there is a tremendous rise in the ratio of learning to instinct.

In cultural evolution, invention plays the part of variation. A hunter changes the design of his harpoon or the manner in which he stalks his prey. If the new way seems to succeed better, he and others may break with tradition and adopt it.

Primitive people rarely employ conscious or orderly experimentation; they have no well-ordered method for evaluating a new tool or taboo. Their lack of written records hampers them in trying to build foresight out of hindsight. They have no statistical methods or principles of science; and they only occasionally hit upon a radically new way of doing things. The Eskimos alone among all the northern peoples, indeed among all primitive peoples around the world, discovered a way to build a dome. Presumably, they had been accustomed to using snow blocks for making a windbreak long before they discovered how to build a whole house. Just how they hit upon the idea of carrying a curved and in-sloping wall full-circle we shall probably never know. But when they discovered how to spiral inward and roof themselves over, they had the key to the invasion of a new realm—the floating ice beyond the Arctic shore. Once discovered, the invention of the snow house enabled the Eskimos to range much more widely in their hunting, and it probably proved vital to survival among some of them.

The snow house is an example of a culture element that may have helped to determine the general course of evolution. People who lacked it no doubt sometimes perished. Most culture traits do not have so clear-cut a survival value as the snow house, but several inventions in combination may determine the strength or weakness of a given culture in its struggles against the forces of nature or in competition with neighboring peoples.

In both physical and cultural evolution, many variations have been adopted that do not appear to possess obvious value. Some clearly impose a handicap, as for example the blood-letting rites of the inhabitants of the Australian desert, where every drop of moisture counts. As the late Dr. Robert H. Lowie put it, culture is a thing of shreds and patches. To survive, a society or an organism need not be perfect; it must only be better than its competitors.

In cultural evolution, tradition plays the role heredity plays in organic evolution. Tradition is the balance wheel that sustains momentum through the vicissitudes of trial and error. It is often in error. Yet without tradition there could be no cultural evolution, any more than there could be organic evolution without heredity.

Despite the remarkable knowledge that primitive people often have of their natural environment, there is much that they cannot understand. These unexplained happenings are the foundation of primitive religion. Whatever the man of nature cannot explain and predict—sudden storm, sickness, the failure of food supply—becomes the object of religious observances. Thus the hunter's weapons may be scarcely more important than his rituals and amulets; and he may fail to recognize any sharp line between what we could call accurate information and the supernatural. Whenever the practical arts can do no more and supernatural aid may better the prospect, the tools of religion take over—sacrifice and masked dance, sacred charm and vision-rousing herb. And then the medicine man is master.

Evolution occurs in primitive religion as in other phases of culture. But religion is generally conservative. A stone knife, for example, may be retained for religious rites long after metal ones have come into use for other purposes. Some of the most rapid changes in native religion have occurred under the shock of contact with an alien culture. One instance of sudden change was the Ghost Dance cult, which began in 1869 among the Lake Paiute Indians of Nevada and spread to many other tribes. Its cause lay in the westward movement of the white man's economy. Its typical features were prophecies of cataclysm, promises that the tribal lands would be returned to native ownership, and revelations that the ancestral heroes would come back to earth. The Ghost Dance cult went through several phases and continued into the twentieth century, leaving lasting changes in the culture of the people affected.

Another case is the recent Cargo Cult in the South Pacific, which also sprang up in reaction to European culture. In typical form, it features predictions that shiploads of white man's goods and gadgets will miraculously be landed where the people can enjoy them freely, and that all the disadvantages of being a "native" will be wiped out. We have a much less clear understanding of what took place in primitive religions before the European era.

MEASURING TIME

The efforts of archeologists to piece together the story of man's past were long handicapped by the lack of any method of dating events among people who did not keep a historical record. The *order* or *sequence* in which different implements or styles of art came into use in a specific locality could be told from the relative depth at which the remains were excavated. But the *dates* at which they had come could not be determined. It was thus not possible to ascertain what was going on at the same time in two different places. And since prehistoric migrations could not be plotted on any except the broadest lines, the question of how the various tribes and cultures got where we find them today remained clouded.

Archeologists borrowed some of the methods of measuring time used by geologists, principally those based on the rate of deposit and erosion. One promising method for estimating the duration of physiographic and climatic changes during the decline of the last glacial epoch proved to be the counting of varves, the yearly layers of silt laid down in lakes or other still water. A more precise approach to events within the last two thousand years is the counting of tree rings. A master curve is plotted from the growth rings of many old trees; the rings show considerable variation in thickness in accordance with climatic changes. By matching the growth rings of a sample of wood from an ancient settlement against the master curve, the sample could be placed in its proper chronological position. Tree-ring chronology helped to prove that around the beginning of the eighth century irrigation was introduced in the Southwestern United States, a development of no small consequence, since about 150 miles of large canals were constructed by the tribespeople. Tree rings also showed that pottery designs in the Southwest changed every 75 to 100 years during one period. However, the tree-ring method could not be applied in many parts of the world, and the oldest date that it yielded was about 217 A.D. It remained for the Carbon-14 method to carry the chronological torch back into the really dim past.

No one doubted that America's earliest inhabitants had come from Asia and by the Bering Strait route, but the question was: how long ago, and in how many migrations? Specialists knew that the story of racial and cultural movements between Asia and America could not be worked out without a more far-reaching chronology. The solution came in a quite unexpected way.

It was discovered that streams of neutrons from outer space constantly bombard the earth, creating a radioactive element known as Carbon 14. All living beings take this element into their systems, in the proportion of only about one atom to every trillion of normal earth-type carbon. The atoms of Carbon 14 "burn out" like sparks struck from a nuclear anvil, and because they burn out at a known rate, the percentage of Carbon 14 in a prehistoric sample of charcoal, bone, shell, or other organic material gives a direct measure of the length of time that has passed since the specimen was living. The Carbon-14 method gave a new time-scale of unimagined scope and ushered in a new era in archeology.

While not precise to the year like the tree-ring method, the Carbon-14 method pushes back the working time-scale of archeology many thousands of years. Hundreds of key specimens have been tested since the method was worked out in 1949, and critical events in primitive man's migrations and cultural evolution are rapidly coming into sharp focus.

One famous sample, charcoal found with a piece of chipped obsidian and the bones of extinct animals at a prehistoric campfire site in Nevada, established that man was in North America more than 23,800 years ago. This was four or five times as far back as some scientists would have thought possible a few decades earlier. That date represented the maximum range of the Carbon-14 method. However, refinements in the laboratory techniques are lengthening the scale.

Comparison of related languages has also provided a workable time-scale. Study of European and other languages whose evolution is a matter of historical record has revealed that the simple words of everyday speech have changed at a fairly uniform rate. Scientists applying this principle to aboriginal languages claim that vocabulary change is not materially influenced by such things as density of population or the variability of cultural change. By using a list of only a few hundred words, they can compute how long it has been since two given languages or dialects were one. This method, known as glottochronology, has proved useful in estimating the date at which two tribes or nations became separated through emigration, warfare, or other causes.

The potential utility of vocabulary analysis can be appreciated by the fact that the number of different languages is often greatest where written records are lacking. The American Indians, when discovered, were speaking from 40 to 200 or more different languages, depending on how one classifies the dialects. A comparable situation existed among aboriginal tribes of South America, and many of these languages are still in use.

For more distant estimates of time, other types of language analysis are sometimes used. Grammar is generally more stable than vocabulary, and specialists get a hint of very old relationships by comparing the ways in which two languages inflect their words to express gender, number, case, tense, mood, and so forth, and by noting how words are put together in sentences. However, the principles used here have not afforded the statistical nicety of vocabulary comparison.

Through these methods, anthropologists specializing in the various branches of their science are piecing together the ravelled strands that link us all physically and culturally with the past. Their purpose is to understand the manifold ways of man and to trace his progress from chipped flint and magic charm to the threshold of his adventure with metals and miracle molds.

Field anthropologists are pressing their inquiries among aboriginal peoples today as never before, and with far better training than their predecessors. The present-day student generally undergoes four years or more of graduate study before becoming a qualified anthropologist, and he normally does a year or more of research in a single tribe. He must often endure the hardship and perhaps danger of life beyond the fringes of civilization. But it is difficult to find a profession whose devotees are more deeply interested in their work.

The tribes chosen for presentation here have been selected to give the reader as wide a sampling as possible in regard to race, environment, and cultural distinctions. The photographs have been gathered from many sources both in America and abroad; in many parts of the world it is already too late to take other pictures of this sort, for modernization is rapidly shattering the aboriginal pattern of life. Similarly, time is running out for field research among truly aboriginal tribes. So, while the masked dancer still performs his rites in a forgotten forest and a lonely Eskimo on the floating ice stakes his life on an ingeniously carved harpoon, we offer this view of the primitive present.

AN ARCTIC HUNTING PEOPLE

The Eskimos

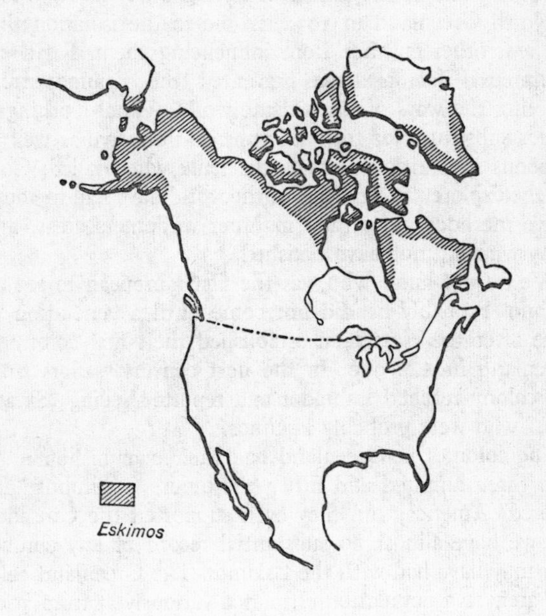

Eskimo culture gives us our best opportunity to observe what life was like in the Ice Age, for the Eskimos are Stone Age people living under climatic conditions resembling those of the glacial period. Their way of life, moreover, illustrates more strikingly than that of any other people the use of ingenuity in solving the problems of human survival.

The Eskimo has shown himself resourceful enough not only to survive on the northernmost fringe of the earth but to enjoy a fairly comfortable life. Most surprising, in a zone that epitomizes hardship, hazard, and hostility as far as human life is concerned, he proves himself to be as generous, friendly, and good-natured as any man on earth.

The possibility of studying these "prehistoric people" while they still maintain their ancient ways, as the writer was able to do in the region of Bering Strait in 1928 and in North Greenland in 1932, is due to the isolation that has kept other cultures from influencing them. Rigid environmental factors have prevented the Eskimos from adopting the ways of the outside world: Wool clothing is a poor substitute for fur, and guns do not serve as well as harpoons in hunting animals that sink when killed. Conversely, explorers in this part of the world have had to adopt native methods more than in other wilderness areas, and many who did not have perished.

We do not know who was the first European to see an Eskimo. Probably he did not come until a generation or more after the Norsemen established their first colony in Greenland in A.D. 986. In the next century, sailors from this colony reached Labrador and reported seeing "Skraelings," who were probably Eskimos.

The colonies in Greenland had their own bishop more than three hundred and fifty years before Columbus "discovered" America, and they even supported the Crusades. But we have almost no substantial record of any contact they may have had with the Eskimos. The Greenland colonies grew to a population estimated variously at from 3000 to 10,000 and then vanished sometime around 1410, either succumbing to physical hardship or blending with the Eskimos through intermarriage.

In 1721 Greenland was reoccupied by Europeans under the leadership of the missionary Hans Egede.

Exactly one hundred years later, William Edward Parry on his second voyage (1821–1823) discovered the Iglulik Eskimos at the head of ice-choked Foxe Basin, seven hundred miles west of Greenland. His expedition found the tribe living in a state of flexible monogamy, freely exchanging wives under certain circumstances and showing little evidence of marital jealousy. They may not even have understood the "facts of life," including conception, as Vilhjalmur Stefansson, the celebrated Arctic explorer and student of Eskimo life, later reported concerning some of the Coronation Gulf Eskimos.

All groups of Eskimos either lend or exchange their wives under special circumstances, as when a man's own wife is less able to make a difficult journey. In addition, before missionaries discouraged such customs, some tribes had a ceremonial game in which the lamps in an igloo were blown out and a general exchange of wives occurred. Questions of paternity did not seem to bother them—which is what we might expect if the Eskimos did not understand the father's role in procreation.

During certain seasons almost all Eskimos get their food, clothing, and fuel from seals and other sea mammals. These animals usually sink when shot or speared. The Eskimos solve this problem by using a weapon that enables them to strike down and yet retrieve their prey. This weapon is the harpoon.

Primitive people many centuries ago invented this remarkable implement, which can at once kill an animal and secure it on the end of a line. The head of the harpoon, upon entering the body, becomes detached from the shaft and turns crossways beneath the skin like a toggle. The hunter holds the other end of the line, and as the animal dives he is able to check it. He does so by snubbing the line around a shaft stuck into the ice, or, if he is in a kayak, he uses one or more blown-up skins attached to the line, the buoyancy of which keeps the animal from diving or swimming as freely as it might.

Walrus as well as seal are caught in this way around Bering Strait and in the Greenland–Baffin Island area. In northern Alaska the Eskimos, using a large skin boat (*umiak*) manned by a team of hunters, even catch whales with this equipment.

It is not possible to understand the way the Eskimo lives

without also understanding his kayak. Sitting in a round opening in this small, decked-over "canoe" with his gut rain jacket tied tightly around the hole and around his face and wrists, he can make himself one with his boat. Even if capsized, the kayaker can right himself and continue the chase. On the precipitous coast of King Island south of Bering Strait, when the surf cuts the hunter off from the seals and walruses in the sea below, companions lift the man in his kayak, swing him like a pendulum, and at a signal let him fly right over the breaking waves. To get back home, he has to land on the sheltered side of the island or wait for the waves to abate.

Considering the climate, it is not surprising that few Eskimos learn to swim, and despite their skill with the kayak, many drown. In parts of Greenland, one death in every four or five among men of hunting age results from drowning in a kayak. And as a result, among people over sixty, there may be only five or six men for every ten women.

The hunter works from a kayak when he is hunting seals in the sea. But when the seals have come out onto the ice to bask in the sun, he hunts them by crawling over the ice on his belly, scratching the ice with seal claws attached to a wooden handle so as to pass himself off as another seal. When within range, he throws his harpoon, holds his animal from escaping, and knifes it as soon as he can get to it.

A third method of hunting seals is through the breathing holes they make in the ice. This is practiced only where the sea is covered over in winter with continuous ice, particularly in the central Arctic of northern Canada. The dog is important in this type of hunting. By scent, it locates beneath the snow the hole to which the seal must come for air. When it has found the hole, the dog withdraws, and the hunter stations himself in readiness.

The breathing hole may be only about an inch in diameter, but beneath it the seal will have gnawed out a cigar-shaped space large enough for its body. In order to know when a seal has come, the Eskimo sticks a wand somewhat larger than a knitting needle into the snow as far as the water. This "indicator" is usually fitted with a crosspiece to keep it from slipping down, or he may attach a feather to it as a more sensitive indicator. When the indicator moves, the Eskimo knows the seal has come and thrusts his harpoon straight down. To get the seal out he must enlarge the hole by chipping.

The harpoon was perhaps the most important of the many ingenious inventions in clothing, transportation, and house design that enabled the Eskimos to survive in a climate reminiscent of the Ice Age.

If you look at "Inuk"—meaning "man"—as he comes home from the seal hunt, you will see why he is classed with the Mongoloid peoples of Asia. The color of his skin, his straight black hair, and his wide cheekbones remind you somewhat of an Indian. The Mongolian fold at the inner corner of each eye is fairly prominent in the children who greet him as he enters the hut, but becomes much less so with age.

Unfortunately we do not know enough of the archeology of Siberia to piece together the early chapters in his racial history. In Alaska, archeologists who have dug up dozens of ancient villages have shown that the Eskimos have occupied their present territory no more than a few thousand years. During this time, however, several subcultures have evolved and spread or declined.

Some students have reasoned that the Eskimos are descended from Indians living near Hudson Bay. Inland-dwelling Eskimos in that region and also in northern Alaska do look more like Indians than other Eskimos, and there has doubtless been intermixture. The Eskimos in these parts do not depend on sea hunting, and their culture shows more ties with the Indian.

But Inuk, belonging to the Polar Eskimos of North Greenland, lives hundreds of miles from any Indians. He has a broad, "six-sided" face, and being a typical Eskimo, he has the narrowest nose in the world. His clothing and speech, of course, distinguish him from all other people.

Inuk's language has not been found to resemble any other in North America except that of the Aleutian Islanders. Eskimo is spoken from Bering Sea to East Greenland, a distance as great as that from Maine to the Amazon. The most divergent dialects, at opposite ends of this 3400-mile Arctic span, show a "correspondence" in 65 per cent of the words. Most of the difference is concentrated among dialects at the western extreme, so that those of the southern part of Bering Sea differ more from those of northern Alaska than do those of the Greenland Eskimo. In fact, the greatest extremes differ almost as much as English and German and could be regarded as separate, though related, languages; but over most of this vast extent, a person who knows one dialect of Eskimo well can make himself understood. Indeed, it has been computed statistically that all Eskimos spoke one language perhaps a thousand years ago.

Among the Indians of North America, on the other hand, there are some seventy-five different languages.

Stefansson has said that it is harder to acquire idiomatic and fluent mastery of Eskimo than of Hebrew, Greek, Latin, and Russian in succession. Whereas in English we have only four forms for "man" (man, men, man's, and men's), there are a thousand different forms of the word in Eskimo, depending on the associated thoughts. Eskimo is deficient in general terms. For instance, there is no word for "color," but only words for the separate colors, and special words must be used for different kinds of dying, as "to die of thirst" and "to die of longing." The number of such specific words or terms is thus immense.

The process of expressing complex thoughts by adding many prefixes and suffixes to a single word enables the Eskimo to compress long statements into a few spasms of the vocal organs. The Danish Eskimologist William Thalbitzer gives an example of two Eskimo words that said what it took nineteen in English to convey, and another of an Eskimo passage of 100 words that required 666 words in English.

The word "Eskimo" means "eaters of raw meat" and was originally applied by certain Indian tribes, but the Eskimo himself has a different word for his people, *Inuit;* it is the plural of his word for "man" and means "the people."

Inuk is dressed from head to foot in furs. Alone among the peoples of the world, the Eskimos have made full use of the principle that the warm air in one's clothing or in a house cannot escape downward. Result: on a hunting trip a mere ten pounds of clothing will keep Inuk comfortable through a blizzard. Using the air-capture principle, he wears a hooded jacket that is loose around his thighs. He doesn't let the warm air escape at the top—except when exertion makes him too hot and he pulls the fringe of fur away from his chin.

Inuk's face is a ruddy brown. But on entering the dwelling, he immediately strips to the waist, and we see that the parts of his skin that have not been reached by the sun and wind are much lighter and are comparable to the skin of the Chinese and other Mongoloids. He has to get his furs off or he will swelter in the heat of the dwelling, which is partly below ground level and is built of stone and sod. No cold air can enter through the ten- to twenty-foot entrance tunnel, for it slopes upward toward the living quarters, where all the warm air is captured. You can hardly crawl through the doorway, because it is only about two feet high. A small vent in the ceiling closed by a fur "stopper" can be opened if the house must be cooled off. If you are outside when this "stopper" is removed, you will see a plume of steam pour skyward. In the frigid month of February, a hand withdrawn from a mitten steams like a cloth soaked in boiling water.

Inuk of the Polar Eskimos will use a snow house—the word "iglu," by the way, does not mean "snow house" but any house—only on the trail. Three-fourths of the Eskimos have never even seen one. But this is no reason to minimize the importance of an invention that has been hit upon by no other people in the world—the construction of a dome by laying an ascending spiral of blocks. The importance of this most remarkable device is that it gives the Eskimos freedom to travel on land or sea in the winter. Tents would be too cold, and men could not carry other building materials. The snow house is not only indispensable to those Eskimos who live and hunt in winter on the floating ice but is preferred by many who stay on land.

The snow blocks are tilted farther and farther in as the circular wall rises, and a single block of the right shape closes the hole in the top. The doorway is cut after the wall has been built, and, as has been pointed out, the Eskimo takes advantage of the upward-sloping entrance tunnel. The window is a piece of clear ice or a framed piece of translucent gut.

At 30 degrees below zero Fahrenheit, the occupants can raise the temperature to 40 degrees, 50 degrees, or even 60 degrees above, near the roof of the house. Yet the ceiling does not melt; the cold outside neutralizes the heat inside in the layer of air next to the snow. And skins are pegged to the ceiling to protect it from the heat of the three or four seal-oil lamps that warm the room. It is colder near the floor.

The advantage of seal oil is that it is much easier to carry than wood. Further, it requires no chimney, and a lamp burning it will go all night—like an automatic "oil-burner" —if a lump of blubber is hung above it to drip as the wick becomes more exposed and burns brighter.

Inuk's wife, also bare to the waist, takes his clothes and beats the snow out so the furs will dry quickly. Husband and wife do not rub noses, but the woman might nuzzle a baby upon returning from an absence. There is a great deal of guttural chatter as news is exchanged.

Inuk's broad smile shows the typical worn-down teeth of an Eskimo. The chewing of many tough or gritty substances has ground a flat edge on both rows. The teeth are worn down almost to the gums, yet Inuk has no cavities. If he begins to eat white man's food, decay will soon set in. Like many Eskimos, Inuk happens not to have grown any wisdom teeth. The inside surfaces of his upper front teeth, like those of many Indians, are shovel-shaped. His jaws are broad and powerful, and his head rises high above the ears, sloping up more sharply and less roundly than ours.

Natural selection, the process that is assumed to bring about the survival of the fittest, may have made the Eskimo a somewhat special creature in the physical or physiological sense. For example, it has been suggested that his narrow nose has evolved in response to the cold. But the Eskimo's ingenious mode of life, and especially his diet, is the important thing in his survival. It was once thought that only an Eskimo could live on meat alone, but Stefansson has disproved this by living on such a diet. Nor would the scores of white men have died of scurvy in the Arctic if they had adopted the Eskimo diet of raw or slightly cooked meat, balanced by a sizable percentage of fat.

Civilization has actually dealt the Eskimos a severe blow through the introduction of diseases to which they seem to have little resistance. Numerically, however, most groups seem to have "hardened up" after the first heavy losses, which are apparently almost inevitable when an isolated people come into contact with civilized man. In some regions the population is on the increase. It should be added that a disconcerting recent development is the appearance of trichinosis among the Eskimos. This disease is ordinarily carried by pork but is now found in some of the marine animals of the north. It can be prevented by cooking the meat, but that unfortunately decreases the vitamins in the food.

Both Inuk and his wife have very little body hair. Nature has not begun to provide them with extra protection against the cold. Seeing them only in their bulging clothes, you might imagine them fat, but they aren't.

Inuk takes an enormous drink of water, collected from a dripping piece of ice, and lies down on his back on the bed platform. His wife begins to drop one piece of dripping meat after another into his mouth. He belches appreciatively.

He is only five feet two inches tall (two inches shorter than the average of all the Eskimo men that have been measured). His wife, of average height, is four inches shorter than he is. His facial hair is fortunately sparse or he would have trouble with the ice that might gather on it.

Four to eight pounds of meat a day is not unusual for this little man to consume. It has been claimed that on occasion Eskimos have eaten up to ten and fifteen pounds.

Inuk, bulging with the meat he has eaten, rolls over. The stores of walrus meat and seal have lasted through the dark season, and he is once more eager to be out regularly to hunt. With the approach of summer, thousands of birds will arrive. Younger members of the tribe will catch them by swinging small nets into the passing flocks.

Inuk is fortunate to have lived long enough to have a grandchild. His daughter-in-law, now tending the lamp on the platform, reached puberty at the average age for a Greenland girl–fifteen and a half years. She is now in her early twenties and has had two trial marriages. There was no wedding ceremony when she settled down with her present husband, who carried her off by force. She considers monogamy the normal thing but knows of a few cases of women with more than one husband or men with more than one wife. She may have from four to ten children. The ones that survive she will suckle until they are three or four years old, but several will probably die young, and if hard times come to the clan she will have to kill some at birth.

If she had not borne a child, divorce and remarriage would have been natural. No one attaches any stigma to the child her sister bore out of wedlock. The relatives love the child for itself, and someone is always ready to adopt a child who is too much of an economic strain on its parents.

Although the little boy is mouthing a sharp knife and might hurt himself, the adults do not take it away from him. They love the child, but he has been named after a wise and heroic relative who died recently, and they think the youngster is endowed with all the skill and wisdom of his namesake, though he may still be too small to show such endowments. He is in fact thought to have the dead man's soul. Spanking or scolding might drive it out, causing him to sicken and die, so they are gentle with him.

Though some Eskimos live as far south as the latitude of central England, Inuk's tribe, as Polar Eskimos, lives farther north than any other people on earth—within 13 degrees of the North Pole. Here in Smith Sound, the temperature will average about 20 degrees Fahrenheit below zero in the coldest month. Eskimos five hundred miles farther south in the region west of Hudson Bay will get colder weather; for them, the average will be 25 degrees to 30 degrees below, and there will be extremes of minus 40 degress, 50 degrees, or more.

For 112 days the sun has not been seen, but ever since the latter part of January there have been one or more hours of bright twilight each day. This has made it possible to travel freely over the snow-covered surface a good deal of the time, and to hunt and make camp without difficulty. The twilight hours are brightened by the reflecting power of the snow and by the very clear air. Also, the moon in such high latitudes is in the sky longest and highest during the two weeks each month when it is more than half full, and this helps the hunter. Now, at the middle of February, a trace of bright light shows through the translucent window of the hut, for the sun has begun to appear above the horizon a little each day.

Summer will come with great speed in this land. Except in sheltered spots, the snow will vanish by June. Under the long hours of sunlight, myriads of flowers will burst into bloom. Inuk's people will then live in tents. The sleds and most of the other things that were essential in winter will be useless. And the Polar Eskimos will for a few brief months enjoy the pleasures that for inhabitants of the temperate zone are spread through spring, summer, and autumn.

The Eskimos do not have chiefs, but in Alaska during whale-hunting there may be a captain of the large skin boat, and he will be influential in other ways. Toward the center of their territory, among the islands of the Canadian Arctic archipelago, the settlements thin out, and an encampment may consist of only a few related families.

The territory in which the Eskimos live is eight hundred miles broader than the United States, but you could put all of the Eskimos into a football stadium and many seats would still be empty. In recent decades, the total population has ranged between 35,000 and 40,000. Alaska and Greenland each have about 15,000. Recent counts give Canada about 9000, of which over 6000 are in the region of Hudson Bay, Baffin Island, and Hudson Strait. The Atlantic coast of Labrador has about 1000. Approximately 1200 live on the Asiatic side of Bering Strait. The southern limit of the Eskimos in the west is around the base of the Alaska Peninsula, and in the east in the neighborhood of Hamilton Inlet, Labrador.

The Eskimos can be divided into about a dozen cultural subdivisions, each embracing numerous permanent villages and seasonal camps. There is much trading and visiting over wide areas. The Eskimos themselves identify more than a hundred tribal groups, each designated by a word ending in "-miut," meaning "the people of." Inuk's Polar Eskimos, totaling only 271, have four such subdivisions: "The Northerners," "The Leeward People," "The Middle People," and "The Southerners."

The Eskimos have an elaborate system of rituals and taboos for bringing good hunting, curing sickness, and otherwise coping with crisis and misfortune. The religious leader, called an angakok, is a wizard capable of being tied up and then presumably journeying to the realm of the spirits in order to foresee the future and bargain for better times. In the darkened room, when he "flies" about with his trousers on his arms for wings, and his falsetto voice reaches out to the sphere of the supernatural, one can sense some of the fearful intimacy that links these people with the unknown forces that are said to control human misery.

In the central part of the Eskimo region, the angakok

confers with a goddess who apportions the sea mammals to the Eskimos. In Alaska, a moon deity occupies a prominent position, and there are innumerable other deities and spirits. Good-luck charms and magic phrases are important. Dancing and singing to the rhythm of a large tambourine is frequently a feature of religious gatherings, and in Alaska there are elaborate ceremonies with complex masks.

The Eskimo does not fear punishment in the afterlife but dies confident of another existence, one that may be less burdensome than this. Therefore he fears the dead but not dying. Presumably to confuse the ghost and prevent it from returning, the mourners take the corpse out through the roof, and they sometimes plug its nostrils with moss to keep the spirit in the body. The realm to which the dead go depends more on the manner of dying than on the breaking of religious taboos, which is punished in life by scarcity and sickness.

The Eskimo worries about the souls of the animals he kills and always gives a drink of water to the seal so that its spirit will carry a good report to the seal heaven—whence come all future seals that he can hunt. Many of the taboos, particularly in the central Arctic, are intended to keep the products of the sea from contaminating those of the land, and vice versa.

Persons used to a gentler world may flinch at some of the Eskimo's indelicacies, but one is likely to respect his cheerfulness, generosity, and ingenuity. Take a three-day trip, for example, with Okluk in the region northwest of Hudson Bay, where the winter weather is most extreme and where the scarcity of vital resources forces even an Eskimo to adopt special measures.

This is the region where a severe season is most likely to have disastrous results—even to the point where the living may have to feed on the dead or face death themselves. For Okluk times have not been bad lately, and it is almost time for the yearly festival, where the singing and dancing will make him feel young again.

But he has no sled, and there is not enough driftwood

to make one. So he soaks strips of walrus hide in water and rolls them up with salmon inside. Then he sets the bundle outside and allows it to freeze. Soon he has enough solid pieces to lash together to make a walrus-hide sledge. This will carry him and his baggage as long as the cold weather lasts.

He loads almost nothing on the sledge—food for his dogs, yes, but only a little meat for himself. He includes some seal oil to light and heat the overnight snow houses he will build, but that is about all. Yet as he urges his dogs forward, he knows that he will have a pleasant trip.

At night he builds a hut in short order and soon is snug. Lighting the lamp, he takes his clothing off so as not to perspire and rolls up in caribou fur.

Okluk brought no bow and arrow, but he would like to breakfast on one of the birds flying about in the early morning. So he enlarges the ventilating hole in the top of his snow hut, sprinkles some bits of meat around it on the outside, and sits beneath it, looking more like a philosopher than a hunter waiting for his prey. Presently a flutter of wings causes him to thrust his hand out the vent, and he pulls in a bird by the legs.

Okluk's trail crosses wolf tracks, and the next night he hears them howling. He doesn't like wolves. But how can he kill a wolf without gun or trap? He hasn't even brought along a piece of springy whalebone to tie in a bundle and freeze in a piece of meat. If he had, he knows the wolf would gulp it down, the warmth of his stomach and his digestive juices would loosen the sinew, and the sharp whalebone would pierce him internally.

Lacking that, Okluk smears his knife with blood and buries it in the snow with only the blade sticking out. From the door of his hut he sees the wolf come to the bait and lick the blade. Excited by taste and smell, the animal gourmandizes, literally whetting his own appetite, then drops, bleeding to death while gorged on his own lifeblood. Okluk has a fine pelt to take to the festival.

There is one thing that bothers Okluk as he tries to sleep.

His hut is warm and dry, and his belly is full of meat; but he is not alone in his furs. He has to keep scratching. So he unpacks a strip of bearskin with a string tied to each end. He threads this under his clothing and leaves it there for a short time. When he pulls it out, all his unwelcome guests have gone into the bearskin because of its thick fur. Since he may want to use it again, he puts it outdoors until all the lice are frozen and then shakes them out.

The next day the sun comes out warm, and the snow is so dazzling that he has to put on his shatterproof goggles —eyeshades of walrus ivory with fine slits in place of lenses.

Now Okluk keeps glancing at the sun. His frozen sledge is getting soft, so he urges his dogs on. He gets to the village just in time. The sledge is no longer usable, but no matter. After giving himself over to the joys of reunion with old friends, he feeds the walrus hide to his dogs and stuffs himself on the salmon that was inside.

In other parts of the world, the people of the Middle Stone Age graduated into the New Stone Age when they learned to plant and raise crops. Climate has prevented the Eskimos from doing this. However, their development of well-trained dogs for drawing sleds and for hunting has greatly strengthened their mastery over their environment in a way parallel to the domestication of utilitarian animals among agricultural people in Asia and elsewhere.

The Eskimos have never discovered how to domesticate reindeer as have the Lapps and other northern Asiatics. Nor have they benefited much from the opportunity to learn from imported Lapp herders.

The idea of keeping an animal alive (except for the dog) is foreign to the Eskimo. He believes that the supply of game will in no way be lessened, even if he kills it to his heart's content. Abundance, he thinks, depends upon the observance of rituals and taboos. The resources of nature belong to everyone, according to the Eskimo philosophy, and the hunter divides food among all who need it, not just his own family. It is hard for an Eskimo to understand that one man could own certain reindeer and another certain others.

In the months when the caribou are plentiful, the Eskimo hunts them intensively. When they scatter or migrate out of his territory, he gives them only incidental attention.

In two localities the Eskimos have been able to work metal. In North Greenland they have made knife blades from bits of meteoric iron, and around Coronation Gulf "nuggets" of pure copper found on the surface of the earth have provided the Copper Eskimos with material for hammering out arrow points and other useful things. But these developments affected only a small percentage of the Eskimos, and in all other ways their culture represents a modern hold-over from the Stone Age.

SEA-FOLK OF THE SUBARCTIC

The Aleuts

A mid-eighteenth-century navigator, scanning the stormy waters of the North Pacific through the crude spyglass of his day, might well have been brought up sharp by such a scene as the following:

A whale-hunter in his bidarka (the Aleut equivalent of an Eskimo kayak) is driving off a huge, enraged sea lion, but his boat is sinking in the foaming water, for the struggle has left it leaking. In the distance, the hunter's comrades are trying to put a harpoon into a thrity-foot whale and do not heed his calls. As the navigator watches, the whale disappears and minutes later suddenly arches its back out of water no more than eight boat lengths from the hunter.

Instantly the hunter lifts his spear, a heavy one with a poisoned tip, for no other weapon can succeed against an animal so large. With a sharp thrust of arm and wrist, he hurtles the shaft from the throwing board, an implement that fits over the butt of the spear and gives it added impetus. He sends the weapon arching high, for the whale is moving lazily and he wants the spear to gain added force from the descent so that it will penetrate the thick skin and blubber. The wind almost carries the weapon out of its course, but a solid *chunk* tells the hunter that the blade has driven deep.

His boat is now sinking fast, so he slips out of it and into the water, where an inflated sealskin attached to one of his other harpoons keeps him and his injured craft afloat. Since the waves are mountainous he cannot swim ashore, and the boat must therefore be repaired at sea. The cold is already numbing him.

Now his comrades, small, thick men clad like himself in rain parkas made of strips of seal intestine sewn together horizontally, are paddling toward him. The chase itself is over. Left in the whale, the poisoned spearhead, tipped with a fermented extract of the aconite root, will take effect, and in a matter of days the animal's carcass will be found, either floating lifeless on the water or stranded on shore. The conical hats of the approaching boatmen, fashioned out of thin sheets of wood bent around and sewn together down the back, can be seen bobbing up and down against the gray sky, and their double-bladed paddles flick in and out of the water, fighting the waves.

Two of the slender bidarkas come alongside. The paddlers lift the damaged boat across their decks and allow the man to crawl up behind them, teeth chattering. One of the boat's thin driftwood ribs has pierced the skin covering. They bind the split and patch the hole with a spare piece of sealskin. Sliding the boat back into the water, they hold it while the man crawls into it again. Amid their cheerful exhortations, he speeds toward a half-underground village on a distant island, where he can get a change of clothing.

The first description of a native of Alaska was written in 1741 by the German scientist Georg Wilhelm Steller, who was serving under the leadership of a Dane, Vitus Bering, on an expedition organized by Russia. The ensuing years witnessed many bloody scenes in the Aleutians. Extreme cruelty was used by the Europeans in the effort to subjugate the Aleuts, and many were killed through warfare or deceit. Their population in prehistoric times is estimated to have been as high as 16,000, which would make it one of the densest in aboriginal North America. But just fifty years after they were discovered it had fallen to only about 2500. In 1846 Father Veniaminof, a Russian priest who recorded valuable information about the Aleuts, counted only 2200 Aleut-speaking people. Since that time the figure has fluctuated, being more often below this level than above it.

Marriage regulations among the Aleuts were not strict. A man had as many wives as he could support by hunting, and a woman as many husbands as she could keep house for. Younger brothers of the husband were allowed to cohabit with his wives. So were parallel cousins (children of the father's brother or mother's sister), who were regarded as his "brothers." European guests were presented with a man's wives or slaves as a sign of hospitality, and white men frequently established transitory alliances. That is one reason why it would be difficult today to find an Aleut of unquestionably pure ancestry.

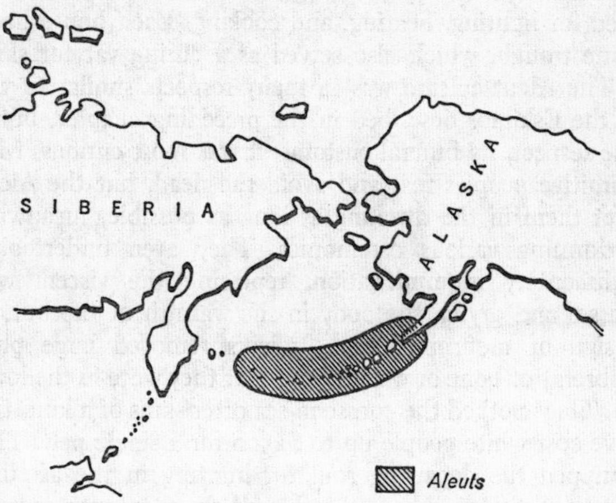

Explorers who have become well acquainted with the Aleuts have admired their hardihood and their resourcefulness in making a living in one of the most unpleasant climates on earth. Wind, fog, raw cold, and treacherous currents sweeping between the islands combine to form a homeland that is both uncomfortable and dangerous, as many an American serviceman who was stationed in the Aleutians will testify. Towering peaks, snow-capped and sometimes smoking with volcanic steam, add a certain grandeur to a landscape that is otherwise colorless, desolate, and austere. The territory of the Aleuts begins about where the 160-degree meridian crosses the Alaska Peninsula, from the end of which the seventy treeless islands of the chain extend for about eight hundred miles to the remote outpost of Attu.

These short, stocky, broad-headed aborigines differ in appearance from the Eskimos, though they also belong to the Mongoloid race. Whereas the Eskimo head shows an average cephalic index (ratio of width to length) of 78, the Aleut average is 84.

They originally built spacious but crowded lodges that were half underground, rectangular in shape, and covered with sod. Stone lamps burning the oil of sea mammals were used for lighting, heating, and cooking. Each house had a urine trough, which also served as a curing vat for skins.

The Aleut culture was in many respects similar to that of the Eskimos described in the preceding chapter, but in one respect, its funeral customs, it was most curious. Most primitive peoples fear and avoid the dead, but the Aleuts kept them in the dwelling as long as possible, meanwhile performing various ceremonies. They even undertook a rudimentary mummification, replacing the viscera with grasses and drying the body in the warmth of the hut. As a sign of mourning, the survivors removed large plugs (labrets) of bone or walrus ivory that they wore in the lower lip. They clothed the corpse in sea otter skins of a kind that have cost white people up to $2500 for a single pelt. They equipped the departing soul for hunting in the afterlife, and they may even have slaughtered slaves to serve as spirit attendants. When the time came to lay the body permanently away, the funeral procession was accompanied by the beating of drums and the wailing of the bereaved.

The bodies were laid in a cave or underground, and the writer was present at the discovery of one of the most impressive groups of mummies yet found in the Aleutians. Archeologists from the Stoll-McCracken expedition of the American Museum of Natural History, after fruitlessly searching in various other localities in the eastern Aleutians, had been led by rumors among the natives to visit a bleak, wave-cut table of rock jutting 125 feet above the sea. The island was located just north of Unalaska Island. It was strangely cleft at one end, leaving a pinnacle standing apart from the main mass, which was perfectly flat on top. The mummies were discovered on top of the main mass and very near the vertical cleft by Junius Bird, now one of America's foremost archeologists but then serving as engineer on the expedition schooner. The sarcophagus, eight by ten feet in size, and of heavy drift-logs, lay underground except for a wooden corner that projected from the slope.

Layers of skin and bundles of straw lay carefully arranged on slats of wood, which protected the interior from moisture. Beneath these and other layers were the bodies of four individuals. About half of the space was taken up by one of the bodies, presumably that of an important individual. All of the bodies were doubled up, knees to chest; and three of them lay in oval wooden hoops on animal skins attached like loose drumheads. They had been interred amid their mortuary finery, with lamps and spears for use in the afterlife. The face of one was decorated with a nose pendant of Korean amber.

The Aleuts were once famous for their weaving and basketry. So careful was their selection of dyed grasses and so fine was their workmanship that a basket no larger than a small cup has been known to bring $100 or $200 in the white man's market.

The Aleut language has a common origin with the Eskimo, from which it began to diverge, according to statistical computations, about 2900 years ago. Archeological evidence supports this computation, indicating that the first Aleuts, speaking a proto-Eskimo or pre-Eskimo language, moved out onto the islands from the Alaskan mainland about 3000 years ago. Thus, though there may have been scattered contacts with Asia directly, as when boats were drifted off their course, the main migration route from Asia to America seems to have followed a more northerly course, in the region of Bering Strait, where land is visible from both sides. In this connection, it is significant that no traces of aboriginal life have been found on the Commander Islands at the end of the Aleutian chain, between Attu and Kamchatka.

The Aleuts are stoical people, and, where not weakened by white man's diseases, they show great stamina. An Aleut in a bidarka has been known to paddle 132 miles in 27½ hours. The resources of the sea for a time kept these people in something like their original pattern of life, but they are now adopting many civilized practices, from wearing blue jeans and mackinaws in place of quaint fur, gut, and birdskin garments to listening to the music broadcast over short-wave radio.

AN AMERICAN INDIAN TRIBE

The Navahos

The image of the typical Navaho is probably more familiar than that of any other Indian seen outside picture books: A man with long hair knotted behind his head and a high-crowned felt hat or a colored cloth across his forehead. Next to him is his wife in voluminous skirts and velveteen blouse. Both are bedecked with silver jewelry, including bracelets set with turquoise, concha belts, and "squash blossom" necklaces. They and their progeny are most commonly seen along the desert roads of Arizona and New Mexico.

The domain to which they lay claim is vast, and the Navahos, aside from being personally and culturally interesting, are the largest Indian tribe in North America. In fact, they are something of a phenomenon among Indian peoples in that they have increased from about 4000 in 1743 to an estimated 82,000 today. How interesting they are to specialists is indicated by the fact that notes on them in the Human Relations Area Files of Yale University run to some 40,000 pages.

It is not easy for the casual traveler to become intimately acquainted with these extraordinary people or to inquire directly into their culture and history. Little English is spoken among them, and a visitor can scarcely expect to pick up a working knowledge of their language; in fact, it is so difficult that in World War II it proved to be one "code" that the Japanese could not break. Military information could be radioed from one Navaho to another and then put into

English, without fear that the enemy could interpret it.

Curiously, the Navahos are newcomers in the Southwest, having arrived no more than five hundred to a thousand years ago. Their language, like that of the Apaches, is not related to neighboring tongues but to the Athabaskan dialects spoken by tribes living just south of the Eskimos. The Navahos even call themselves Diné, "the people," just as do certain Athabaskans in the far north.

During their long trek from subarctic Canada, the culture of the Navahos necessarily underwent many changes in response to climate and biological requirements—an extraordinary departure from the usual slow course of aboriginal history. A notable evolution took place after they reached the Southwest, and with it a phenomenal growth in population. The explanation of their five- to tenfold increase in less than one hundred years lies in their cultural stamina in the face of strong environmental and social handicaps, in their ability to borrow advantageously from other cultures, and in their positive approach to life. Their tribal cohesion is strong, and they have the will and capacity to produce many children.

Though the appearance of the Navaho Indian is distinctive, it is entirely "modern." Before the Navahos met the white man, they wore only simple garments of skin and possessed no sheep, cattle, goats, or horses. They exhibited astonishing adaptability in their clothing and crafts; indeed, in their contacts with the Pueblo Indians, the Spanish, and the Americans, they have taken liberally from almost every cultural aspect except language. However, they have lent so much individuality to the blending that in outward appearance as well as thought they remain distinct.

It was probably somewhere between the years 1000 and 1300 that these woodland hunters of the far north came roving down the mountain chains and desert valleys into the land of the Pueblos. The social organization and religion of this newly arrived group were presumably not elaborate, for theirs was a simple hunting and gathering culture. However, they soon took to robbing the Pueblo people, and it may have been for this reason that many of the native Indians of the Southwest began building fortified towns on high mesas, such as Oraibi and Acoma, from which they have only recently begun to descend. By the time the Europeans began to encounter the Navahos, the culture of the tribe was already highly composite.

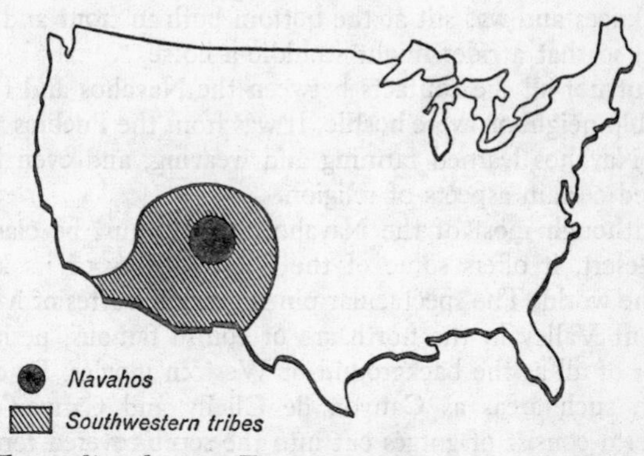

The earliest known European reference to the Navahos is in the report of a Franciscan missionary in 1626. No mention was made of their possessing livestock then, and their range was limited to about 3000 square miles, as compared with the 24,000 they occupy today. The European horse, which has had so vast an influence on Navaho history, was introduced at about that time. Earlier scholars believed that the Navahos got horses from Coronado in 1541. But John C. Ewers has shown that the two mares among the 558 horses Coronado brought with him apparently never got out of white men's hands and therefore could not have served as the beginning of horse-breeding among the Indians. It is thus likely that none of the tribes acquired horses until almost a century later. The animals seem to have spread north and east from Santa Fe shortly before 1640, and in very short order the majority of tribes west of the Mississippi acquired them. This brought peoples of many tongues into contact with one another, one result being the rapid development of the familiar sign language of the Indians. By 1954, the Navahos owned almost 30,000 horses, as well as 500,000 sheep and 100,000 goats.

Acquisition of the horse by the Navahos, coupled with the raiding habits they had developed, soon caused them to design a special suit made of several thicknesses of buckskin and capable of turning arrows. This "armor" reached to the knees and was slit at the bottom both in front and behind so that a rider might straddle a horse.

But not all the contacts between the Navahos and their Pueblo neighbors were hostile. It was from the Pueblos that the Navahos learned farming and weaving, and even borrowed certain aspects of religion.

Although most of the Navaho country must be classed as desert, it offers some of the finest scenery of its kind in the world. The spectacular pinnacles and buttes of Monument Valley in the north are of course famous, perhaps most of all as the background of Western movies. By contrast, such areas as Canyon de Chelly and Canyon del Muerto consist of gorges cut into the scrub-covered terrain by flood waters and the slow processes of weathering. A few feet above the flat, sandy bottoms of these canyons, the Navahos cultivate small fields of corn, beans, squash and other vegetables. Over these bottom lands tower vertical walls of orange-colored sandstone, on whose ledges can still be seen the crumbling cliff dwellings built by the predecessors of today's Pueblo people—"The Ancient Ones," as the Navahos call them.

Most of the Navaho country is about a mile above sea level and very dry, though there is somewhat more precipitation on the mountain slopes, which rise to a height of more than ten thousand feet. The average rainfall ranges from about seven inches to thirteen in the settled parts; and only about one-fourth of one per cent of the Reservation is cultivated. Only half of the farm lands are irrigated with an assured supply of water. In general, the Indians employ ancient, primitive methods of diverting the runoff onto tilled areas after each spasmodic shower. Corn is grown on more than half the acreage.

The fickle climate often visits the Navahos with alternations of poverty and plenty, and other factors have accentuated the extremes. The writer first had contact with these people in 1929 when, with a Navaho horse and surveying equipment, he mapped the wilderness of Canyon del Muerto. The Navahos were then poverty-stricken, living close to a parsimonious nature, their scattered hogans largely cut off from the rest of the world. By contrast, when in 1957 he visited the impressive Navaho tribal center at Window Rock, Arizona, he found the Tribal Council trying to decide how to spend $33,000,000 just received from mineral rights. It was anticipated that the royalties for the ensuing twelve-month period would amount to $100,000,000. The Navahos are today the richest Indian tribe in the world.

Despite their mobility and love of raiding, the Navahos were really no match for the more military tribes, such as the Utes and Comanches. Among these, war was the main purpose of living, whereas the Navahos developed raiding only as an auxiliary activity, using it for securing food, women, horses, and so forth. After about 1716, the Navahos were occupied in defending themselves against the Utes and Comanches, and so ceased molesting the Spanish settlements. An alliance with the missions resulted in an abatement of raiding around Santa Fe until about 1818.

During the Civil War, the Navahos took advantage of the fact that the attention of the United States government was fixed on other matters, and they began harassing the white man again. Then, in 1863, Colonel Kit Carson, as Indian Agent for the District of New Mexico, led an army to Canyon de Chelly and made prisoner between 9000 and 15,000 Navahos. The captives were marched three hundred miles eastward to a prison camp at Fort Sumner, a march that is known today to all Navahos as "The Long Walk."

They were interned there for four years and released in 1868. Confused and with hope shattered, but not markedly antagonistic toward their white oppressors, they promised to remain peaceful. Most of them returned to the regions they knew, and the government issued 15,000 sheep and goats and distributed food, seed, and implements to them.

Within a few years they were self-supporting and their flocks had increased phenomenally. Certain changes in their mode of life were now well established. The use of firearms had reduced the game reserves, but the horse had made it possible to transport food long distances to a central camp. The keeping of sheep had forced the people to spread into territories that had not been generally occupied. The pastoral life also obliged them to move seasonally in search of pasturage.

Meanwhile, they had also taken up and developed the weaving of blankets, for which they have become well known throughout the world. Their general mode of life had thus taken on the pattern familiar today.

Their reservation lands have been increased from time to time in response to population growth. At present, the Navaho Area, which includes within it the Hopi Reservation as well, covers about fifteen million acres—with one-fourth as much more in allotments and leased lands outside the reservation. The population density is twice that of neighboring areas occupied by whites.

That a primitive hunting people should have been able in a few centuries to migrate 1500 miles out of the subarctic wilderness and in less than a century to increase five- to tenfold shows how erroneous it is to consider primitive cultures static or incapable of surprising bursts of vitality.

Religion has been an important element in tribal solidarity, influencing almost every phase of Navaho life. Its central feature is the sand paintings, which are commonly made inside the six- or eight-sided lodge known as the hogan. The chief purpose of the paintings is to cure the sick or disturbed. The designs represent the concrete embodiment of sacred personifications and concepts, and have been likened in function to the stained-glass windows of medieval church art. Although some are only about a foot or two in diameter, others are more than twenty feet across and can be made only in specially constructed hogans. Fifteen men will work most of a day to produce one of these—only to have it ceremonially obliterated in less than half an hour.

The dry paintings, as they are more properly called, are actually not made with sand but with pollen, crushed flowers, charcoal, pulverized minerals, and meal. Everyone who has seen them has been impressed by the artistic balance and fineness of line achieved by the singer and his assistants, as those who create the paintings are called. The designs are integrated with an elaborate system of chants and rituals, and since there are more than five hundred paintings, all preserved by memory alone, the reader can appreciate how arduous is the apprenticeship of the medicine man.

The Navahos borrowed the idea of sand painting as well as their main religious concepts from their neighbors. However, they evolved their elaborate ritual and complex mythology along quite independent lines, all within twenty or thirty generations at the most. The paintings are strongly oriented in terms of direction, north, for example, being uniformly that of evil influences. One wonders whether the people may have acquired this belief at the time they began their historic migration out of their northern homeland.

The well-known American ethnologist Gladys A. Reichard, who pursued field studies among the Navahos for many years, connected the significance of the sand paintings with the mythology, art, and drama with which they are intricately interwoven. While the painting itself is static, it is deeply symbolic. Animation and drama are achieved by representations of birds that are made to fly and sing, and by snakes that pull their heads in and out of the sacred house and coil their tails. The evening performances of the last day of a big chant are especially theatrical, involving, according to Miss Reichard, clowns cavorting for the benefit of the audience, young men dancing with torches or with standing arcs ornamented with eagle plumes, priests making corn and yucca grow magically in half an hour, and feats of arrow-swallowing and other prestidigitation.

Physically, the Navahos exhibit a sturdy competency. They are attractive, the regular, pleasant features of both sexes sometimes attaining true beauty. J. H. Beadle, who visited them in 1872, proclaimed the Navaho girls the only Indians he had ever seen who approximated the ideal delineated by James Fenimore Cooper. "They are very shapely and graceful," he wrote, "and their strength is prodigious. How these mountaineers, on the thin food they have, manage to produce such specimens of perfect physical womanhood, is a mystery to me. One of the prettiest girls I saw . . . informs me that for months at a time she had nothing but goat's milk, boiled with a thin, watery root, which they used for food." Both sexes are tall, as Indians go, averaging more than five and a half feet for the men and five feet one or two inches for the women. They are broad-headed, but this is to some extent due to the flattening effect of the cradle board used in infancy.

Their health appears to have been excellent before the coming of the white man. So far as bone studies can tell us, the early Navahos did not suffer from rickets, syphilis, tuberculosis, or cancer. Even today, they are almost completely free from cancer and diabetes. Only 36 cases of malignant conditions were found in 30,000 admissions to the Ganado Mission Hospital–about one-fiftieth as many as would be expected among white persons. They also show a very low frequency of degenerative circulatory maladies, including coronary and cerebral accidents. Their worst afflictions are gall-bladder troubles, tuberculosis, and venereal diseases. Syphilis seems to have been first reported in 1872. Tuberculosis was found in one out of every eleven Navaho men examined by Selective Service physicians in 1943 and 1944, and their death rate from it is about four and a half times as high as among the general population in the United States. Diarrhea is a common killer among infants during the fly season (August–October), and there are recurring epidemics of the measles, chicken pox, whooping cough, mumps, and diphtheria. Strangely, scarlet fever has been absent. Trachoma, formerly serious, is coming under control.

There is very high infant mortality, and among adults the general life expectancy is definitely shorter than for whites. But the Navaho who survives beyond sixty-five is apt to possess great tenacity of life, so that the proportion of very old is unusually large.

That the Navahos have succeeded in multiplying so remarkably despite a high death rate and an impoverished environment serves to remind us that any population tends to increase unless there are rather strong deterrents.

In matters of sex, the Navahos show extreme reactions. They are frank about the subject but shy about exposing the body. A certain lustiness that gives way to ribaldry even in mixed company is counterbalanced by strict decorum in the matter of clothing. Boys are taught concealment at three or four, girls much younger. Men cover themselves carefully even in each other's company–as, for example, in the sweat bath. Anthropologists have reported one practice that may be a reaction to the general austerity. It is called "prowling." In this, an individual contrives in the dead of night to examine the body of a person of the opposite sex in the crowded quarters of the hogan. Men do this more often than women. If the sleeper wakes, there may be a bit of blackmail as a price of secrecy.

The Franciscan fathers noted that virginity was not prized and celibacy not practiced by the Navahos. Today, not more than one-fourth of the unmarried girls retain their virginity after twenty, and one count indicated that less than one per cent of the men entered marriage without previous experience. Normally, the Navahos are said not to feel guilty about a sexual act outside of marriage. Rape is scarcely thought of as such because women consider themselves able to protect themselves. Older women are known sometimes to take the initiative.

The taking of plural wives is approved by legends and is currently practiced in the remote areas. It appears more often in the western part of the reservation, and the birth rate appears to be appreciably higher there. Tradition has it that one rich man had twelve wives at once. In recorded genealogies the highest number mentioned is nine, and the man did not live with all at the same time. More than three at once would be very rare.

Marital fidelity is a less serious issue with the Navaho, and little disgrace is attached to having a child without being married. Divorce has, in general, been easy. Since the family is matriarchal, it is sometimes said that all a wife has to do is to put the husband's belongings outside their dwelling and the marriage is dissolved.

An important occasion in the life of a Navaho girl is the four-day puberty ceremony that takes place at the onset of first menstruation. The first three days are not public, and the girl refrains from washing, from drinking water except through a tube, and from sleeping except briefly on her back, and she must allow some of her hair to hang in front of her face. In addition, she must not scratch herself, and must observe various dietary taboos. These observances are intended to ensure diligence and a smooth complexion. On the evening when she has her hair ceremonially washed with yucca suds, the assembled relatives sing all night, and she must stay wide awake or bad luck will follow her. Another feature of the ceremony is the kneading of her body by a woman, or by a male relative other than her father, in order to shape her into womanhood.

During the ceremony the girl grinds corn for a cake, which is then baked in a wide pit, and the culmination comes with the sharing of the cake and the singing of songs appropriate to the transition to womanhood. When the girl cuts the cake, if she hands a piece to a particular young man, it indicates a predisposition toward him. At one point in the ceremony, she suddenly tears the curtain from the door of the hogan in which she has been waiting and runs southward. Half a dozen young men may pursue her; at one time there may have been more to this particular part of the ritual, but today the boys let her win the race against them and enjoy the good luck that her victory is believed to bring her.

In the old days, girls were often married almost as soon as they reached puberty; today the marriage age is fifteen to seventeen for a girl and nineteen to twenty-one for a boy. The suiter "buys" his wife from the girl's parents or clansmen. When Beadle visited the Navahos in 1872, he was offered an unusually beautiful young girl in exchange for the horse he was riding or for fifty dollars, and he adds that an average bride could have been had for less than half that. Today, the bride price may be as high as fifteen or twenty horses.

From the moment of engagement, the girl's mother may never again look upon or speak to her son-in-law. She cannot even see her daughter married. If by chance she does not know the bridegroom, she may be allowed a peek at him in the hogan so as to be able to avoid him from then on. This taboo is not easy for the two to observe, because for the first few years the married couple set up housekeeping near the mother-in-law's hogan. During this period the bridegroom is more or less on probation with his father-in-law and is required to perform a certain amount of work for him.

The Navaho woman enjoys a prestige and influence far greater than would be supposed by anyone who has seen one trudging along on foot behind her mounted husband. She owns property and has a continual source of income from her weaving. The mother has a voice in all family affairs and may control the purse strings. It is through her line that family descent is traced, and her importance is reinforced by mythology and folklore. Some of the most powerful deities are female. Though there are parts of the War Ceremony that women may not see, they have almost the same privileges in religious matters as have their men.

The Navahos show an intense antipathy to everything connected with the dead and prefer not even to talk about the subject. As parents, they are affectionate and will feed a child whenever it cries. They fondle their babies lavishly when the little ones are out of the confining cradle. Those who know the Navahos agree in general that they have a fine artistic sense, and in certain tests their youngsters have excelled white children in graphic skill. It has been a problem to evaluate their intelligence, owing to the difficulty of constructing fair and suitable psychological tests.

The Navahos learned their outstanding craft, weaving, from the Pueblo Indians, and have, indeed, surpassed them in it, excelling through artistic imagination rather than by improving the techniques. They have actually added only one variation to the Pueblo tapestry-weaving technique, namely the wedge weave.

Strange as it may seem, the Navahos do not use their own blankets. At first they wove mainly wearing apparel, and probably did not produce blankets until about 1780. In 1872, Beadle described the blankets as the wonder of all who saw them, asserting that the weaving was so close that a blanket would carry water for five hours before beginning to leak. The blankets enabled the Indians to build up credit at the trading post, and soon they stopped weaving anything for their own use except saddle blankets. They took, instead, to buying Pendleton blankets made in Oregon, and still do, using them for protection from the weather and, along with sheep and goat pelts, for bedding.

The weaving is done by the women, and a weaver who can produce five Navaho rugs a year is doing well. To facilitate the work, the woman frequently sings while weaving. Imperfections are purposely woven into the blanket, because the creation of a perfect piece would mean that the weaver's career had culminated.

Unfortunately, the artistic level of the rugs can scarcely be expected to remain above that of the purchaser's taste. Pathetic attempts to meet the more degraded standards of the outside world have led to the imitating of designs from soap wrappers and tobacco trade-marks. As far back as 1929, when the writer was living at L. H. McSparon's trading post at Chinle, a movement had been initiated to induce the Navaho women to get back to the old designs and to revert to natural vegetable dyes in place of cheap aniline dyes.

The resulting rugs, belonging to what is called the Revival Period, are an improvement, but many weavers in the western and northwestern parts of the Reservation did not alter their techniques. As of 1950, the quality of the western rugs was decidedly uneven, and only the best of them were comparable to the average Revival-style examples from Wide Ruins and Chinle.

Another craft for which the Navahos are known is the making of jewelry, especially of silver. The Navahos first worked silver about 1853 to 1858 but made little jewelry until they were interned in Fort Sumner in 1863. United States coins at first supplied the silver, but in 1890 their use was prohibited by the government and Mexican coins took their place. It was from the Mexicans that they learned to cast silver, cutting molds in stone or gypsum-like earths and pouring the molten metal into them. Cast bracelets date from about 1875, but the first ones had no settings. Later, one large stone in the middle became popular, with smaller stones sometimes added on the side.

The first Navaho to set silver with turquoise may have been Atsidi Chon, who set up a silver-working shop among the Zuñis in the 1870's. Navahos prefer "male" turquoise, which is a deep robin's-egg blue, whereas "female" turquoise is greenish, less rare, and more apt to become dull. Much cheap turquoise has been shipped to Germany to be dyed a deeper shade and sent back to the Southwest. Grease is sometimes also used to darken it, and this may cause the stone to turn oily when left in the sun.

Navaho jewelry designs possess no symbolism; they serve simply to beautify the silver. In recent decades, various new figures have been adopted, such as large birds, sun faces, and swastikas. The "Squash blossoms," made by adding three to five petal-like pieces to hollow silver beads, are believed to owe their origin to an old Spanish pomegranate motif. Necklaces of these beads probably did not come into favor among the Navahos until after 1880.

The well-known oval "conchas" for belts were not made extensively until after the 1920's. These four- to six-inch disks are said to be based on a design borrowed from the Plains Indians. Cheap, quantity-produced "identicals" are stamped out by presses. Fortunately these, like most other factory-made imitations of Navaho jewelry, are easy to detect. However, because tourists usually want inexpensive souvenirs, the genuine Navaho silverwork has been degraded. Traders sometimes encourage flimsy work, and imitation turquoise has come in. Zuñi jewelry, which places greater emphasis on the turquoise and less on the silverwork, is less easy to imitate by mass-production methods and may therefore survive longer as a native industry.

Unlike rug-weaving, silversmithing is done mostly by the men and is in the hands of a relatively small number of craftsmen. Navahos still make jewelry for their own use, trading it for livestock, blankets, or farm produce. They also wear it themselves, of course. The men formerly wore plain earrings of silver, but these were eventually melted down for their metal. Today, some of the men, particularly the older ones and those in less accessible areas, wear nuggets of turquoise strung through the pierced ear. Contrariwise, the women once wore loops of small turquoise but later took to using elaborate silver earrings.

Oil was discovered on the Navaho Reservation in 1923. This made it important for the Navahos to set up a representative council that would speak for the tribe as a whole in regard to earnings from mineral rights. This body was slow in forming, but in 1937 the present Navaho Tribal Council, providing for seventy-four representatives distributed according to population, was organized.

Today the Tribal Council sits in impressive desert surroundings at Window Rock, Arizona. The assembly chamber is shaped like a gigantic hogan and decorated inside with native-made murals depicting Navaho history. Subject to the approval of the United States government, the Council authorizes the expenditure of tribal funds, passes on mineral leases, etc. In addition, it regulates marriage, divorce, and inheritance, and it has a large share in the administration of justice except where major crimes are involved. Navaho policemen travel about the Reservation.

Even with the generous assistance that many have attempted to give the Navahos, it has not been easy for them to develop all the leaders they need in a day of rapid evolution in science, education, and government. Allocation of about $5,000,000 to encourage young Navahos in their education was made from the $33,000,000 accruing from mineral rights in 1957. But money alone will not solve the educational problem of the Navahos. Even when a young Indian graduates from high school and decides to go to college, he faces a very difficult adjustment. He is liable to find himself enough of a social oddity to want to give up fairly soon and "go back to the blanket." The transition from a wilderness existence to full participation in a civilized economy is far more difficult than most persons imagine, particularly when the people of the dominant culture consider their own way of life the only natural one.

Yet the Navahos with their conspicuous cultural vitality are, as Oliver La Farge has phrased it, the most promising Indians. In the face of "civilizing forces" that have brought about the decay of the spiritual and material culture of many other peoples, they have displayed biological vitality in spite of what is actually poor health. Living on a thin margin of subsistence, they nevertheless have thrived and—equally surprising—they have evolved many aspects of their distinctive culture almost while we have been watching them.

A CENTRAL AMERICAN TRIBE

The Lacandones

One of the most interesting of Central American tribes, especially in its relation to the great Maya civilization of old, is a remote one located in Mexico's southernmost state of Chiapas.

When explorers of the last century gazed on the crumbling temples of the Maya empire, overgrown by jungle, they wondered what had become of the race that built them. Myths and travelers' tales encouraged the hope that survivors of the great civilization might still be found, practicing their ancient rites, far back in the jungles of Central America. In the 1840's John Lloyd Stephens' two books on his explorations in the Maya area became best-sellers. In one of them, he told how an old priest had assured him that if he would travel ten days out of his way at Palenque, he would find a large stone city in which Maya-speaking people were living exactly as they had before the discovery of

America. But it was the young Harvard anthropologist Alfred M. Tozzer who, after five years of exploration between 1902 and 1907, made an exhaustive study of the Lacandones and pronounced them the present-day representatives of the ancient Mayas in customs, religion, and language.

The last refuge of the Lacandones is in jungle-clad mountains at elevations ranging up to about three thousand feet. Towering mahogany and chicle trees festooned with lianas screen the sky, and howler monkeys parade through the treetops. Tapirs and peccaries scour the forest floor amid orchids and giant ferns whose young fiddleheads are the size of base viols. Rushing torrents have to be forded, and the labyrinthian trails are steep and slippery.

The writer was able to visit this tribe in 1956 in the company of Frans Blom, the well-known Danish archeologist, and Mrs. Blom. We were trying to reach the largest settlement, at Lake Naja, but the trail forked three ways, and it was not till we tried the third that the path led out into bright sunlight at the edge of a thatched village on a shelf above a beautiful lake. There were eight huts large and small, half of them open on all sides, the others walled with vertical slats of wood. One hut was ranged with god-pots and other religious paraphernalia, and many sacred arrows stood in a bunch at the far end. Every Lacandon *caribal* has one of these sacred huts, often larger than any of the others, in which religious ceremonies are performed.

At first there was no one in sight, but as we moved forward, a Lacandon appeared in a doorway, advanced and began brandishing a machete in the air, apparently sparring with Mrs. Blom, who was in the lead. She dodged from side to side, meanwhile waving a large knife that she was carrying. The effect would have been most disquieting, not to say frightening, to anyone who did not know that these two were already acquainted and were merely greeting each other; presently each threw an arm about the other.

Among the tribesmen gathering about us we saw examples of the classic Maya profile so abundantly preserved in the ancient carvings. With their long, shaggy hair hanging close around their somber faces, the men seemed at first glance quite stern and almost forbidding. The Lacandones know that they owe their survival to their having avoided civilization, and even among people they trust, their manners show traces of their age-old tendency to resist intrusion. One immediate reason for this attitude is their fear of civilization's diseases. Thus the Bloms had warned me against coughing or blowing my nose. To the Lacandones, any such action is a reminder of the white man's epidemics, which have proved so damaging to them.

A hunter brought in a forest hog, and we all feasted on its rich meat around a campfire near the edge of one of the thatched roofs, which gave us shelter from the occasional drizzle. It would not have been surprising to hear harsh voices issue from people with such serious faces, but actually these Indians spoke in low tones, sometimes scarcely above a whisper, except in the urgency of a religious invocation. They are capable, nevertheless, of surprising bursts of jovial laughter, even at the slightest absurdity.

We communicated in rudimentary Spanish, which the men of the tribe have grown to understand through contact with Mexican chicle-gatherers and mahogany-cutters. Their ingenuity with the few available words enabled them to express themselves very well. For example, they indicated a preference for silver instead of paper money by saying, "Paper money dies," meaning that it deteriorates in the jungle.

As night fell, the men, squatting on their haunches, presented a shrunken and almost birdlike appearance. The look of austerity that had marked their faces earlier gave way to a haunting melancholy expression, their sad eyes seeming to swim listlessly beneath drooping lids. A light flickered in the darkness, and a melodious voice floated out of the distance—it was a young girl, carrying one of the resinous splints used for illumination, calling her dog back home. When she found it, she put it in a little dog hut behind the main dwelling.

The Lacandones themselves sleep on low wooden platforms that can be cut off from the rest of the house by curtains or light wooden screening. For lounging in the daytime, they use hammocks. It is possible that the idea of the hammock was introduced among them in recent centuries. They no longer weave their own cloth as they used to do, but they can still quickly make a piece of bark cloth by pounding with a grooved mallet the inner bark of a particular tree.

Until recently, the Lacandones made pilgrimages to worship at the ancient Maya temples, and they may still do so to some extent. They have stoutly resisted conversion, preferring their jungle gods—who, they believe, control the productivity of the forest—to what they call the white man's "tin-can gods." Traditional religious ceremonies take place in their villages almost daily. As incense, they burn the sacred resin of the Mayas, copal. They place great emphasis on the characteristic god-pots, on which grotesque faces of deities are molded and painted. These are stylistically reminiscent of ancient Maya carvings. Generally soot-blackened from the incense burned in them, the faces on these pots represent lesser personalities of the spirit world, who apparently serve chiefly as messengers to carry prayers and offerings to the many deities of the tribe. Morsels of corn paste (*posol*) and other foods are placed on the lips of the pots. It is even said that worshipers hold lighted cigars to the mouth of the image.

The women are not allowed to witness the four-week ceremonial process by which new god-pots are made each year. During this procedure, the men sleep in the ceremonial hut. Tozzer, whose treatise is our best source of information on this tribe, ascertained that the pots were baked in hot coals for a few hours and decorated afterward with soot and the red of the achiote pod (*Bixa orellana*). When the new pots are ready to replace the old ones, there is a ceremony that lasts seven days.

The fervor with which the modern Lacandon pursues his regular devotions is most impressive. We observed one who implored the deity for relief from a toothache, chanting in two or three different tones of voice, amidst god-pots, nodules of copal (exactly like those of the Mayas that have been excavated by archeologists) and a large platter on which the nodules were arranged in rows. The intensity with which he pursued his devotions was stirring to hear, and we wished we ourselves could do something to relieve his pain.

Later, at a neighboring settlement below the brow of the hill, we were able to record a ceremony in which a troubled Lacandon besought a spirit believed to live by a lake in their territory. He complained grievously of a sore shoulder, and far from being a carefree son of nature, he appeared to be ridden with anxieties. We saw no dancing in the Lacandon village, though a feeble sort is said to be practiced and to be pleasing to the gods.

The Lacandones all keep to the dense jungle and live by clearing patches in which they grow corn, sweet potatoes, cassava, beans, sugar cane, papayas, lemons, tomatoes, chayotes ("vegetable pears"), bananas, tobacco, cotton, and other plants. They hunt animals ranging from small birds to mountain lions. Two kinds of deer, as well as jaguar, tapir, peccary, and armadillo, are found in the surrounding forest.

Their cultivated fields are sometimes scarcely recognizable as such, so difficult is it to clear the ground by fire and machete. Because the soil is soon exhausted, new land must be broken about every three or four years. The work is done during the few weeks before the rainy season, which extends from May to January or February. At the time of the writer's visit, they were clearing a site across the lake and had to make the trip by dugout. Seven mahogany *cayucos* provided ferry service to the fields and back.

Their chief musical instrument, a kind of flute, is about fifteen inches long and is blown from the end. The men are willing to let visitors hear their shrill, piping tunes. To induce them to sing is more difficult, and when they do, they are apt to keep their voices so low that from a few feet away one cannot hear them at all.

It is remarkable that the Lacandones have changed so

little during the centuries of European influence in Middle America. They have a few guns of different sorts, for which they have difficulty in getting the proper ammunition, and they still rely on the bow and arrow. They are probably the surviving remnant of a culture that once extended over a much larger territory. While the Spanish Conquest brought one group after another under the complex influence of European civilization, they alone remained unconquered. Today they still try to conceal their whereabouts by pulling brush across the entrance of the trails leading to their *caribals*.

The first white men to meet Maya Indians were castaways who drifted west for fourteen days from a ship that sank near the island of Jamaica in 1511. Thereafter the Spaniards quickly penetrated many parts of the Maya area. By 1529 explorers seem already to have swung around the present Lacandon territory to its southernmost part and to have reached Lake Miramar. At that time a strong effort was made to conquer the Lacandones. Many of them were driven before the invaders, but in the end they successfully resisted all attempts to subjugate them. The last substantial effort to overcome them was launched in 1695 by forces that advanced from three directions. The Spaniards rounded up as many Lacandones as they could and tried to establish a Lacandon town near Lake Miramar. But family after family slipped away, and the settlement has long since disappeared and its site is marked only by a few mounds. The last attempt by Spanish missionaries to convert the Lacandones took place sometime during the 1700's.

Shortly before Tozzer's visit around the turn of the century, Spanish mahogany-cutters began entering the northern part of Lacandon country. The Lacandones were drawn into trade with them, chiefly for salt, and it has been from these people that they have sometimes taken Spanish names. But there does not appear to have been any extensive racial intermixture. The Lacandones never let the intruders see their sacred things, and Tozzer reported no perceptible effect on their culture.

The Lacandones of today live in three separate localities, among which there seems to be little or no contact. There are other Lacandones over the border in Guatemala, but they have been strongly influenced by civilization, and even wear overalls. The northern group, the one the writer visited, is known ethnographically as the Pelja group, and there is a plausible theory that they have been virtually out of touch with the other two groups since about the time of the invasion under Barrios, which broke up the original settlements in 1695. This theory is supported by the preliminary reports of language studies recently carried out among the so-called San Quintín group near Lake Miramar.

In the effort to survive in extreme isolation, this numerically small group has even abandoned rigorous ancient rules and resorted to brother-sister marriages, according to the ethnologist Donald John Leonard. A recent communication from Fredrick Peterson informed the writer that the San Quintín group had left this region and drifted toward Rancho El Real. Half the group was believed to have succumbed to dysentery and malaria. In 1950 they numbered twenty-four; by 1955 there were only twelve left.

The present Mexican government does not permit missionaries to try to convert the Indians. The Linguists, a missionary group specializing in the study of languages and in the translation of the Bible, have been in the Lacandon country for more than a decade, but they have made no converts.

Since the Lacandones preserve more of their original culture than any other people in the Maya area, it is interesting to note what in their daily life bears a relation to the customs or beliefs of the ancient Mayas.

Most important is the fact that the Lacandon language probably differs less from the ancient Maya than any other dialect of the area. Among the many minor links are the following: The nodules of copal that they burn in their ceremonies are identical with the ones excavated, and the pots in which they burn the incense are decorated in a style reminiscent of Mayan art. Bernal Díaz, who accompanied

Cortez and is one of our best sources of information on the early Spanish period, relates that at Campeche in 1517 Indian priests burned this copal in pottery braziers and fumigated the white men with the smoke.

In the early Spanish period, certain educated Mayas were taught by the Catholic missionaries to write their language, using the Spanish alphabet. The records they have left were probably copied directly from the surviving manuscripts in the Mayan hieroglyphic writing, and Tozzer points out that the religious rites thus recorded are identical with those still practiced in our time by the Lacandones.

A number of the names of Maya gods have apparently survived in the Lacandon religion, though their attributes may have undergone change. For example, the name of the culture hero of the pre-Spanish natives of Yucatan, Kukulkan, seems to persist among the Lacandones but is applied to a mythical snake with many heads that lives near the most important and powerful deity, Nohotsakyum. Tozzer also cites modern counterparts of the ancient custom of piercing the ear with a stone arrow point and letting the blood drip into a pot containing idols.

A sacred intoxicant used by the ancient Mayas is still brewed by the Lacandones today. They call it *baltché*, after the bark of the tree that provides its distinctive ingredient. The bark has a vile smell and taste which has to be overcome by adding honey or sugar-cane juice. The concoction is put in a large wooden trough and covered with sticks and leaves to protect it from sun and rain. The sour, milky drink that results is mildly intoxicating. It is supposed to have a beneficial effect on one's health and is more ceremonial than social in its significance.

Their relationship to the Mayas has thus won the Lacandones an unusual distinction: Many primitive tribes have, as far as we know, always been primitive; but the Lacandones offer a link with one of the great civilizations of the past. The imposing Maya pyramid at Palenque, where Maya art reached its zenith around 692 A.D., is only forty miles away from the village described here, and the ancestors of the present-day Lacandones may well have helped to build it.

Some accounts, to be sure, tend to exaggerate the extent to which Maya culture has been preserved among the Lacandones. The art of the latter, or what survives of it, does not persuade one that they could have created the sculptures for which the Maya artists are famous. Nor do they exhibit a trace of the remarkable mathematical and astronomical science that the Mayas developed. Nothing remains of the written language, or of the intellectual powers that found expression at Chichen Itza. The Lacandones know nothing of the system whereby the Mayas dated every event, using as a starting point an astronomical occurrence that they reckoned must have taken place more than 3400 years before their earliest recorded history. It is obvious that in the collapse of the Mayan Empire the higher aspects of civilization suffered most. The Spaniards were not the sole cause of the fall; it had begun to happen before they arrived, and they simply Europeanized the remnants.

When the last native stronghold of other tribes in the Maya area fell in 1697, only the Lacandones remained unsubjugated. And thus they have lived ever since, following their primitive patterns from birth to death, with the husband helping the wife to bring forth her baby on a bed of leaves in the forest, and with the widow burying her husband quite simply, head west, feet east, with a lock of hair in each hand and a bowl of corn paste between the thighs.

Whatever the explanation of the fall of Mayan civilization, in a time of adversity the leaders apparently lacked the will or the power to preserve their learning, and the shaggy Lacandones in the forest depths have saved almost nothing of that great culture. Leaf-cutting ants by the millions have taken over the mountains that were once tilled intensively; and if the soulful-looking Lacandones had not been so hard to reach, even they might long since have been "modernized."

A PANAMA TRIBE

The San Blas

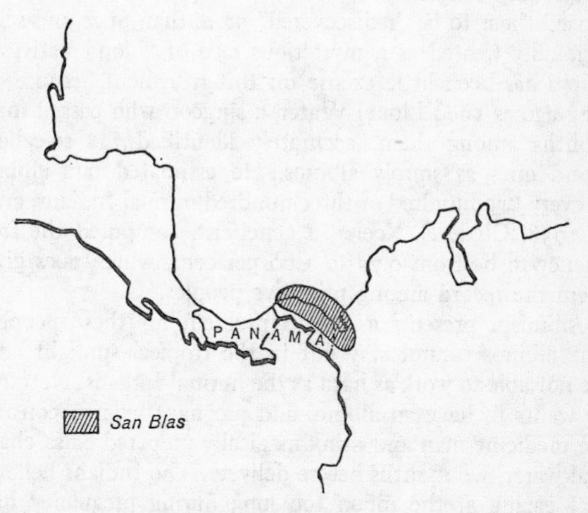

The first reference to the Indians of the coast of Darien occurs when Balboa, arriving as a stowaway on a Spanish vessel in 1511, talked his way into leading the Spaniards in an attack against them. His forces piously slaughtered many of the Indians and after the battle devised the unique insult of officially making some of the survivors the slaves of his ferocious dog Leoncico. Members of the tribe not only later guided Balboa across the Isthmus to the Pacific Ocean but their chief gave Balboa his daughter as a wife. Since then, however, the San Blas have permitted very few white men to marry into the tribe, and they remain almost entirely unmixed.

Fear of all Spaniards soon gripped the Cunas, or San Blas, and for two centuries efforts to convert them were marked by bloodshed. Gradually they moved northward, most of them settling on the Caribbean shore. Then, spurred by the prevalence of malaria there and perhaps because of a tidal wave in 1882, they moved out on the San Blas Islands as well.

The San Blas Indians are perhaps best known for the extraordinary frequency of albinism among them. This has caused them to be "rediscovered" more than once and sensationally treated as a mysterious race of "blond natives." There has been little excuse for this treatment because as long ago as 1680 Lionel Wafer, a surgeon who passed four months among them, accurately identified the so-called blond ones as simply albinos. He estimated one albino to every two hundred or three hundred normal Indians; and in 1956, Clyde E. Keeler, a geneticist, computed the frequency to be from 0.75 to 1.00 per cent, which does give them the record among primitive peoples.

Albinism presents a serious problem for these people. The albinos cannot stay out in the tropical sunlight and are not able to work as hard as the normal Indians. No family wants to have an albino, and pregnant women consult the medicine man and drink magically prepared balsa charcoal water two months before delivery. The Indians believe that gazing at the moon too long during pregnancy has something to do with albinism, and they therefore call albinos "moon children." The tragedy of being born an albino is increased by the difficulty of finding a mate. Parents are reluctant to have a son or daughter marry one, and there is a general aversion to two of them marrying.

The eyes of the albinos are sensitive to light and are often swollen. The iris is predominantly a rich blue, but there is some variation. The straight blond hair on their bodies sometimes reaches a length of one inch on forearms and lower legs. In the hot tropical sunlight they lack endurance, and they constantly have colds. They move slowly; they mature slowly. They are described as being characteristically stubborn and hot-tempered, and they rarely smile. Their intelligence is said to be as high as that of the normal Indians, but observers from Wafer's time on have reported that they have a shorter life expectancy. Formerly many were quietly killed by the mother at birth, and some may still be done away with.

Dr. Keeler believes the hereditary pattern has been complicated by the introduction of some normal blond European traits, a theory supported by tribal memories of two Englishmen and one Frenchman who were accepted into the tribe long ago.

Some compensations lighten the lot of the albino. He is believed to possess special spiritual powers, to be closer to God and freer of sin, and to have a better place awaiting him in heaven. Apparently the albinos come into their own once the sun has gone down. At night, Wafer says, "they are all life and activity, running abroad and into the woods, skipping about like wild bucks; and running as fast by moon-light, even in the gloom and shade of the woods, as the other Indians by day . . ." During an eclipse, they are believed to be able, by means of a small bow and arrow, to scare off the demon that is thought to be devouring the sun or moon.

Close inbreeding is not known to cause albinism, but once the mutation has appeared, there is no doubt that inbreeding fosters it. It is perhaps pertinent, therefore, to note that in earlier times incest seems to have been condoned or even required. According to Wafer, the father of the bride (or if he were not virile, her next nearest of male kin) was permitted to keep her privately in his quarters for seven nights prior to her marriage. Another reason for the continuing appearance of so many albinos among the San Blas may be their strong taboo against marriages outside the tribe. This exclusiveness is linked, as we shall see, with an unusually strong sense of sex modesty.

The writer ventures the hypothesis that the mutation occurred around the time of the coming of the white man or soon thereafter, and the Indians, observing that the children fathered by white men were lighter than their own, gradually concluded that the whites were in some way responsible for the blight of albinism. They may accordingly have developed a policy of tribal exclusiveness and prudishness to prevent further contact. There is no direct evidence for such a theory, but it would serve to explain the various alterations in and extremes of San Blas attitude toward the white man.

San Blas Indians, particularly the women, have a general aspect that is distinctive. The elaborate appliqué blouse (*mola*) and the gold nose ring, ear plates, and necklaces, together with the characteristic head scarf, are ample identification. They are, in addition, among the shortest of all people, the men averaging about five feet and the women about four feet eight inches, with the albinos even shorter. They have brown eyes, often "slanting," high cheekbones, and a somewhat sloping forehead. Like many Indians they pluck their facial hair.

Certain things stand out in the San Blas personality. They are strongly guided by group opinion, a fact that has helped to hold their culture intact in spite of disruptive influences since early in the seventeenth century. Their religious philosophy requires them to be friendly and compassionate. They encourage hospitality and strongly condemn lying, slander, and stealing. Gambling is unknown among them.

Their attitude toward sex would challenge that of the most puritanical of our ancestors. The children are shielded from the facts of life as strictly as parental surveillance can contrive. A boy who betrays knowledge of sex or childbirth is punished by a lashing with a fever-inducing nettle, *Jastropha urens,* which produces effects equivalent to a case of severe poison ivy. So anxious are parents to keep their children innocent of such matters that when a dog is about to have puppies, it is hustled out of sight and the adults tell the children that the dog "found" the puppies somewhere. Even brides believe that babies are brought in by outsiders in some fantastic way, and they generally go through their first pregnancy without understanding what is happening to them. Recently one young wife was found lifeless in the ocean after giving birth to her baby alone and presumably in terrified bewilderment. And a husband who had been married six months kept scolding his wife for not producing any children, when his own knowledge of her anatomy was so distorted that he could not have become a father.

The emotional effects of such biological obscurantism have still to be explored by psychologists and psychiatrists, but investigators will find it difficult to do so because the San Blas prohibitions on sexual laxity are directed most of all against the white man. No outsider is allowed to stay on the islands after sundown, unless the most urgent reasons justify official permission to do so. Fathers even frighten their daughters with crude tales of the way white men will attack them if permitted any liberties.

Curiously enough, if we go back to the time when the tribe was first encountered by Europeans, we find no such prudishness. The women went about with their breasts exposed, and the men wore only a small cone—a gold one when they could afford it—over the penis. Today both sexes go fully clothed and are most scrupulous about exposing their bodies before strangers. They even defecate under water, and clean themselves afterward with their heels.

The distinguished Swedish ethnologist, Erland Nordenskiold, took a San Blas Indian back to Sweden in 1927. After observing the Indian for a time, he expressed the opinion that the man lacked imagination. He copied much but showed little creative talent, and he seemed interested in objects only insofar as he could barter them, except when he once asked for a copy of a paper illustrating the development of a butterfly. The Indian was, however, greatly interested in the early history of the Panama area.

Nordenskiold admired the San Blas Indians chiefly for their ethical standards, which surpassed anything he had seen either among whites or natives in all his travels through Central and South America. The fact that they have been in contact with white men of many kinds over a period of four hundred years without decaying morally or politically is so exceptional as to merit the highest respect. Of course a major factor in this has been their rigid prohibition against social intercourse with outsiders.

The tribe today numbers about 20,000. They have settlements on about fifty of the three hundred or four hundred small islands that fringe the coast about one hundred miles east of the Panama Canal. These islands range in area up to a quarter of a square mile. They are free from malaria mosquitoes for the simple reason that they are without fresh water, an inconvenience of no small magnitude. The only one that has fresh water is the Isle of Pines, which rises to an elevation of two hundred to three hundred feet and is covered with large trees and jungle growth. The San Blas Islands lie only about a quarter of a mile from the coast, much of which is impenetrable mangrove swamp, abundantly populated by biting flies and scuffling crabs. The Indians visit the mainland frequently to get water and firewood and to farm in crude clearings. The women formerly took care of all the cultivation, but now the men do this work.

Their boats are seagoing dugouts, equipped since European times with two sails. A narrower dugout with platform ends, which probably represents the aboriginal type, is also used and is paddled and poled along. This type of boat is universal in the rivers that are inhabited by the mainland relatives of the San Blas Islanders, the so-called Cuna Indians.

The San Blas fish with nets, spears, weirs, and pronged arrows, and use decoys to lure sea turtles into stationary nets. They hunt peccaries, tapirs, agoutis, monkeys, deer, sloths, and many kinds of birds. They use guns for the peccaries and pitfalls for the tapirs, but their weapons also include bows and arrows, blowguns, and spears. Although once it was of primary importance, hunting has gradually become a secondary activity. Bees provide the natives with wax and honey and the surrounding waters abound in fish.

Most of the hundred inches of annual precipitation in this area is concentrated between June and September, but the humidity is high much of the time, and sand fleas, ticks, ants, and chiggers are a problem. In the sites they occupied on the mainland, the Indians were also troubled by vampire bats, and although these rarely visit the islands, the Indians, apparently out of habit, still keep a light burning at night.

The rectangular houses of the San Blas have thatched roofs and slat or cane walls. Some in the eastern section are raised on piles, and a notched-log ladder is used in those that have a storage loft. There is always a cookhouse, either standing by itself or connected with the dwelling. Members of the tribe on the mainland live in smaller villages along riverbanks. The San Blas sleep in hammocks and sit on low, one-piece wooden seats. In some houses a vertical loom in one corner testifies to the important part weaving once played in the work of women, but this is no longer a vital activity. When they do make cloth, they combine cotton with several bast fibers.

At the time they were discovered, this tribe recognized four social ranks: the head chief, who controlled several villages; the nobles, who had retainers or slaves; the commoners, who might marry nobles; and the slaves, who had been captured in war. The latter bore tattooed property marks, but tattooing is no longer practiced, and the social organization of the tribe has become much simpler.

Plural wives were once frequent among the leading men of the tribe, but today the San Blas are almost entirely monogamous. Married couples move in with the bride's parents. Each household thus contains one or more family units related by marriage to a lineage of women. The oldest male in each household is, however, its head, even his sons-in-law being subject to his authority.

The anthropologist Aleš Hrdlička has pointed out that the San Blas Indians are physically comparable to the Mayas of Yucatan, whereas their neighbors, the Chocó, are taller and have the head narrower. The Chocó are the only native tribe with which the San Blas have been in contact within historical times, but the relation has not always been friendly. The Chocó fear the San Blas people but seem to have had the edge over them in their clashes. At one point they even used the skulls of slain San Blas as drinking cups. Nevertheless, the Chocó are described today as a mild and friendly people. Marshes and other difficult terrain have prevented the two peoples from intermingling, and thus although they are both on the Isthmus—the Chocó on the Pacific slope and the San Blas on the Caribbean slope—they differ markedly in language, physical characteristics, and culture. It should be added that the Chocó long ago adopted Christianity and are much less intact culturally than the San Blas.

It is worth noting that although the San Blas do not have a true written language, they have developed a form of picture writing (but one that is not related to Maya hieroglyphics) as an aid to memory. The system is unfortunately not standardized, and so one man cannot read the "writing" of another. It is used in religious chants and serves in daily life as a means of recording such matter as jungle adventures.

The San Blas religion consists of a complex system of chants and other gestures of appeasement used by the medicine man and various groups to control evil spirits. The latter are thought to reside in storms, rocks, trees, and animals. Possession by these spirits must be overcome by rather expensive ministrations from the medicine man. There is also much reliance on innumerable small wooden fetishes in human form, especially in treating disease. Although their use probably far antedates the introduction of Christian concepts among these Indians, such concepts have to some extent influenced their design. The symbol of the cross, however, appears to have been original in their culture and refers to the four cardinal points of the compass. The religion of the San Blas has served to strengthen their cultural cohesion and has given them stability in a day when neighboring peoples have lost many of their traditions without developing a new cultural identity.

The funeral ceremonies of the San Blas include a chant by a special chanter to ensure a safe journey for the soul.

The body is wrapped in a hammock and taken to the mainland for burial, and while the grave is being dug the bereaved mourn over it. The hammock is then slung between two stakes in the grave. Personal belongings are placed beside it and on top of the mound. The various souls that occupy different parts of the body are believed to unite and form one soul, which may linger near the body for several days. It then gathers the spirits of the objects that were left at the grave and packs them into a votive canoe that is afloat in a nearby river. The soul paddles up the river and makes its way toward the rising sun, passing the summit of a sacred mountain and ascending into the sky. The soul has various adventures before reaching its destination and reuniting with its relatives.

Contact with civilization has brought its quota of diseases to the San Blas. In 1933 measles was introduced from a Colombian trading vessel, and even though doctors and drugs were rushed from the Canal, many persons of all ages died. Recently many San Blas men have gone to work in the Canal Zone and have brought venereal diseases back to the villages.

The San Blas are morbidly afraid of illness. One out of every three women is said to die in childbirth, so they naturally fear this event. However, the peculiar manner in which delivery is managed makes one wonder whether the offspring are not in greater danger than the parent. The expectant mother, screened off from all except the midwives, lies in a hammock in which a hole has been made, and when the baby comes, it drops through the hole into a canoe filled with sea water. Nor are the baby's troubles over after this rough introduction to life. If it develops a fever, it is drenched with cold water or exposed to cold winds on the theory that children die because "they get too hot." It is hardly surprising that many are lost at an early age.

For girls, the cold-water treatment reaches its peak in one of the most sacred observances in San Blas society, the puberty ceremony called the Flowering. This is held at the onset of menstruation and involves four days of almost continuous cold-water showers. There is nothing comparable for boys.

Despite their usual modesty in matters of sex, as soon as a girl has reached puberty, her father and mother make it known to the whole village. This is necessary, for many villagers, operating in teams, participate in the ensuing ritual. A large group of men gathers palm leaves for a house about ten feet wide, erected within the dwelling of the girl's family. Inside this, in a little wigwam barely large enough to accommodate her, the girl secludes herself during the incessant shower-bath. A large hole has to be dug under the floor and connected by a trench built to the sea to keep the house from being flooded during the baths.

As many as eight shifts cooperate in pouring water over the girl during the day, and four in the evening. By nightfall of the first day the girl, wearing only a loincloth, is shivering uncontrollably. Her only respite comes after dark, when she is allowed to add some clothing to the loincloth. Albino girls must also go through the ordeal, and with their sensitive skin it is even more grueling.

Another ritual at this time seeks to foretell the girl's future by means of a male and female crab found on the mainland. Two men go off in search of the crabs, and the depth at which they find the creatures is assumed to indicate the difficulty the girl will have in childbirth. The personalities of the two crabs are taken as representative of the girl and her future husband; if the crabs fight, it is supposed to mean that the two will not get along together. The order in which the crabs die presumably indicates which of the human pair will go first.

The most sacred part of the ceremony involves painting the girl black from head to foot to protect her from evil spirits who might be attracted by her beauty and subject her to a fatal disease. This occurs on the fourth day. Two men have been sent to the mainland to secure the dye from the genipa tree. As they approach the tree, they dance ceremoniously and place an offering beneath it; and the man who climbs the tree circles its trunk to gird it symbolically with a wall that will protect the girl from sickness. During the taking of the fruit, there is much chanting to the tree and to its "wives."

As they return to the village with the dye, the men announce their coming with a flute, for no one must lay eyes on them lest this cause birthmarks on the girl's future children. When the girl has been painted black, she presents an extraordinary spectacle even if she is a normal San Blas, and if she happens to be an albino, she is, as can be imagined, grotesque.

The painting signalizes the girl's attainment of young womanhood and gives her a status comparable to the one we accord a young girl when we begin to address her as "miss." After having her hair bobbed at sunrise the next day (it will be completely cut at a later ceremony), she is permitted to pull down the shelter in which she has been confined and to mingle with her friends. There is feasting and drinking, chants and songs interspersed with ceremonial tobacco-smoking, falsetto singing, and music provided by panpipes and by instruments resembling flageolets. In olden times, hollow logs, skin-headed drums, and bamboo drums joined in.

Important though the Flowering is as a ceremony, it is eclipsed in social and economic significance by the *inna* or "coming out" of a girl. This ceremony represents a severe crisis for the girl's father, for if he is not financially able to stage it, his daughter will not be able to marry. She will then become a liability and will possibly expose the family to moral shame, since almost the only sexual irregularities in the tribe occur among girls who have not been made "eligible" in this way.

For the ceremony the father must accumulate enough dried fish and dried meat to feed the whole village. The beer-making material—sugar cane juice, corn, bananas, or plantain—must be sufficient to keep as many as two hundred men busy in its preparation. In recent times, the celebrants have taken to substituting rum procured from trading stores or brought to the islands by young men working in nearby civilized communities. If the family can afford it, the father may be expected to import from ten to twelve cases of rum. Quantities of tobacco are also required.

A girl made marriageable by these rites becomes an economic asset to her father, because she will bring a man into the household. The result is that parents adopt a frantic attitude toward this obligation, and fathers sometimes give their daughters the debut ceremony even before the puberty ceremony for fear that there may not be enough money at the proper time.

It should be added that there is also fear that the ceremony may be outlawed by the authorities. The disorders after the introduction of rum were sometimes so great that in 1931 the Panamanian government imposed restrictions. In 1940 the administration instituted the practice of distributing free rum on ceremonial occasions on all the islands, though prohibiting its entry at other times.

The psychology of the religious drinking that is common in primitive communities in Central and South America may be difficult to understand if one is familiar only with alcoholism as manifested in civilized society. Tribal drinking is so rigidly determined by the religious calendar that we can scarcely call those who drink excessively under such circumstances drunkards in our sense of the word.

A somewhat similar distinction can be made concerning the use of tobacco. Among many Indian tribes tobacco is often purely an adjunct to religious observances and not a regular daily habit as among Europeans and Americans. An Indian may adopt the cigarette habit as we know it, but he is apt to reserve his traditional pipe, snuff tube, or cigar as a potent ceremonial instrument. The cigars of the San Blas Indians are loosely wrapped and are two or even three feet long. Instead of puffing them, one man puts the lighted end in his mouth and blows the smoke over the face and up the nose of a companion.

The "coming out" rites ordinarily occur from one to five years after the puberty ceremony. Up to that point, the albino girl has followed her normal sister along the ceremonial path to maturity. But since she has a poor chance of marriage, the "coming out" ceremony is denied her. If by some rare good fortune an albino does find a mate, there is not even the usual wedding ceremony.

In the "coming out" the girl enters a small hut built outside the family house and is seated facing east in a pit that may be as much as four feet deep and four feet long. The leader chosen to manage the rites may be assisted by as many as forty persons, including flute-players, tobacco smoke-makers, brazier-tenders, water-carriers, beer-servers, and others. The girl is within hearing of the music—a chant accompanied by flute-playing—which continues for four days and nights. The chant describes the progress of a woman's life from puberty to the grave. Parts might seem indecent by civilized standards. At least one of the chants is no longer understood by the tribe, and a person who aspires to the position of chanter must pay as much as $150 to acquire the art from one of its masters. The participants dance dramatically and imitate animals.

On the fourth day, the girl, still sitting in the hole, has the hair on her head cut short. There is much gaiety and drinking. Dried cocoa beans are burned as incense, and the large cigars are smoked ceremonially.

When San Blas parents face the real business of securing a husband for their daughter, they go straight to the point. Their negotiations may be most effective if they act when someone else's daughter is going through the "coming out" ceremony, for then they can take advantage of the general inebriation and confusion. The daughter will not be told of their intentions.

They go to the parents of a likely young man and after a little polite conversation speak of their daughter's eligibility. There may be some show of resistance, and a good deal of salesmanship may be required, but after a while the young man, who may be strolling about the village, quite possibly unaware of the negotiations or even opposed to getting married, will be taken into custody and rudely hustled off, willy-nilly, to the girl's house. There he is deposited in the "marriage hammock," and presently the girl is also captured and brought in, blindfolded by a cloth tied over her head. She is put in the hammock on top of the youth. A burning balsa log is placed under them, and they are rocked back and forth. When the cloth is taken from the girl's head, she and the boy are both expected to flee in embarrassment to opposite sides of the hut, where, for reasons not quite clear, they undress and bathe under upturned calabashes of water.

The boy may thereafter disappear for several days, during which time the father of the girl searches him out and tries to entice him back with promises of food and a place to sleep. Unless the boy has strong allies to support him in his objections, he comes—and is soon thrust back into the marriage hammock again. He and the girl must sleep there side by side—a rather awkward feat. The girl's mother, moreover, chaperones them carefully all night. Throughout this the boy can still try to resist the idea of marrying, but under the circumstances his resistance is likely to ebb. The girl's father watches for evidence of this, and the sign that the youth has succumbed comes when he accompanies the father-in-law into the forest to cut down a balsa tree. His fate is sealed when he lays the log in front of his mother-in-law's fire. The excitement is over, and the village can only look forward to another *inna* celebration.

A TRIBE OF THE EASTERN ANDES

The Head-shrinking Jivaros

Their practice of shrinking human heads to the size of an orange—and the extraordinary spiritual beliefs connected with this—make the Jivaro Indians (pronounced Hee′-var-o) one of the most interesting subjects in the field of ethnology. In addition, they are probably the largest tribe in northern South America, their domain on the eastern slopes of the Andes in Ecuador and Peru covers an area larger than Switzerland, and their culture is one of the most important.

Because they are the most warlike Indians in all of that continent, it has not been easy for anthropologists to study them intimately. Despite this, there is a substantial scientific literature dealing with them, including especially valuable works by Matthew W. Stirling (Director of the Bureau of American Ethnology), Rafael Karsten, Alfred Metraux, J. L. Hermessen, and Juan Vigna.

Geographically, the Jivaros are near neighbors of the so-called Aucas, who killed five American missionaries in 1956. Actually, the Aucas are more correctly termed the Zaparos, "Auca" being merely the word for any wild Indian who has not been Christianized. They are a small tribe with a relatively mild history, whereas the Jivaros' reputation for deadliness goes back to 1599. The early Spanish chronicles relate that in that year the Jivaros killed twelve thousand white people in one day. They first captured the Spanish colonial governor in a settlement called Logroño, poured molten gold down his throat "until his bowels burst within him," and then wiped out the settlement. A few nights later and twenty-five leagues away, they killed most of the male inhabitants of Sevilla del Oro, population 25,000. In these raids they took many white women alive, and to this day one can see traces of white admixture in the faces of some Jivaros.

If you should meet a Jivaro on the trail, he will be wearing a short skirt of brown material with narrow vertical stripes. Above this wrap-around his body will be bare except for painted designs and various ornaments. If "fully dressed," he will also have on a fur and feather crown. He likes delicately applied face paint in geometrical designs and never travels without a "vanity case," a little square bag containing feathers, face paint, and other toiletries. He adorns himself with necklaces and other ornaments, and is hypersensitive about his lustrous black hair. He cuts it straight across the forehead and lets it grow to about waist length in the back. He can be identified by his three pigtails–a long one behind and a short one at each ear. He believes that his hair possesses a sort of soul power, and the belt of human hair he wears is of more than ornamental or practical value to him.

He is rarely known to go abroad in the forest unarmed, and he will probably be carrying an eight- or ten-foot spear and a circular shield, or a blow gun of about the same length, together with a cylindrical quiver of poison darts. The wound scars on his face and body are the result of head-taking raids. If he is returning from a successful raid, you will have no doubt about it, for he will have forgotten his usual fastidiousness and will be carrying one or more heads strung on a cord around his neck. He will not wash off the blood with which his body is spattered until he has reached a place at which it can be removed with proper ceremony and without danger of a counterattack.

His skin is apt to be lighter than that of some of the other Indians in the region. If he shows some beard, and hair that is reddish brown instead of black, it can be attributed to the white women abducted by his ancestors, who did not lose their own heads but left their mark on those of succeeding Jivaro generations.

His height: about five feet three inches. His movements: light and quick. His manner and voice: solemn and incisive. He is suspicious by nature, particularly where his women are concerned. Anyone encountering a man of this description should assume him to be on the touchiest of terms with his neighbors and intent on the taking and shrinking of human heads. He is also likely to blame a stranger for any illness or other misfortune that coincides with the newcomer's visit.

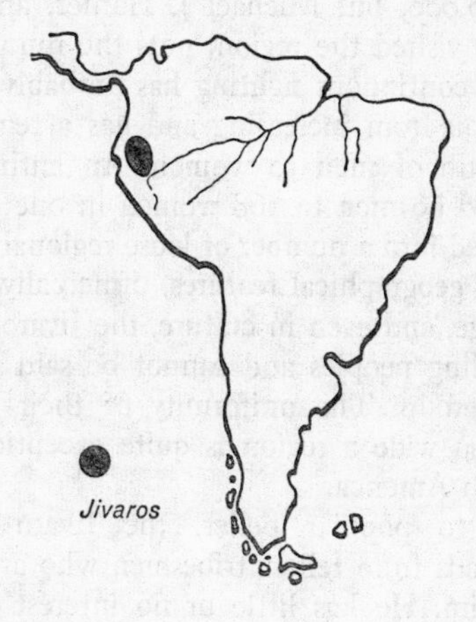

The Jivaro keeps his women close to home. They wear a simple rectangle of woven material, the upper edge of which goes under the left arm and over the right shoulder, where the two corners are held together by a wooden pin. Both arms and the left shoulder are thus bare, and the garment overlaps itself on the right side, being taken in at the waist by a simple belt and hanging down below the knees. Marriageable girls wear a small cane lip-plug in a hole in the lower lip. Men wear larger plugs in the lobes of their ears. Tattooing is practiced to a limited extent by pricking with a thorn and using a lighted piece of crude rubber to blacken the area. The teeth are often stained and are sometimes sharpened to a point in the front.

Each community of Jivaros lives independently in a single oval hut, or *jivaria*, which contains a family of thirty to forty persons. In earlier times the *jivaria* may have housed from eighty to three hundred individuals. Each hut is from one to five miles from its nearest neighbor. The people ordinarily live without tribal organization, but occasionally larger groups unite under one leader when they are preparing to attack in force. In 1580 there may have been about 30,000 Jivaros. Modern estimates have ranged from 10,000 to 20,000; but Michael J. Harner, an ethnologist who recently visited the region, puts the number at 4300. More or less continuous fighting has probably always kept the population from increasing and has a tendency to restrict the ratio of men to women. An anthropologist in 1929 reported 69 men to 168 women in one district. The tribe is divided into a number of loose regional subdivisions delimited by geographical features, principally rivers.

In language, and even in culture, the Jivaros differ from the surrounding peoples and cannot be said to be a part of a larger group. The uniformity of their own culture throughout so wide a region is quite exceptional for this part of South America.

Contrary to popular belief, the Jivaro secures his shrunken heads from fellow tribesmen who are not closely related to him. He has little or no interest in shrinking white men's heads, and during the first thirty years of contact with the Spanish, he seems for the most part to have been friendly. But animosity grew as a result of continued intrusion, the Jivaro resenting the effort of the Spanish to convert him and to deprive him of his freedom.

Though the Jivaros are among the most skillful hunters with the blowgun and curare-tipped dart, anthropologists have long held that they used this weapon only against birds and animals and not in warfare. However, Michael J. Harner talked with natives whose fathers had seen the blowgun employed against other members of the tribe. It should be noted that the attacking party would find the blowgun almost useless, because the board walls of the *jivaria* behind which the defenders hide are too sturdy to be pierced by the light darts. Spears and firebrands alone may avail. However, those inside the buildings can shoot the poison-tipped darts across the clearing while the attackers are still too far away to use spears.

One measure that can be taken by a man who is struck is to pull the curare-tipped dart from the wound and thus lessen its effect. But the Jivaro fighting men also carry their favorite antidote against curare, sugar. They believe that eating this in quantity, or taking chicken gruel with much salt in it will counteract the poison. The poison of course must enter the blood stream to be effective; therefore the meat of a bird or animal killed by it is perfectly edible. In fact, the witch doctor can taste the curare while he is making it to see whether it is satisfactory.

Hatred and fear, arising from the obligations of blood vengeance, dominate the Jivaro. As in many primitive societies, the Jivaro is required to take "an eye for an eye." Massacre leads to counter-massacre, and a tribesman does not even have to be killed by obvious means to keep alive the spirit of vengeance. Witchcraft is a common explanation for death from any natural cause among the Jivaros. The surviving relatives then blame the most likely suspect and pledge new revenge.

Equally important as a motive in head-taking is lust for a type of spiritual power that can be acquired in no other way. This concept is closely interlocked with the young man's puberty rites. According to Jivaro belief, it is necessary for every youth to acquire a soul, and toward that end he goes into the wilderness for meditation, preferably under a waterfall. There, under the supervision of an older man, he takes the powerful drug *maikoa*. This induces hallucinations; and he is expected to see a spirit, which is the soul of an unidentified ancestor. When he sees it, it becomes his. However, it will not remain in his body more than a few years, and if it leaves before he can get another, he will sicken. The only way he can replace it is to kill an enemy and get his soul. This is a basic purpose in the head-taking raids.

Shrunken heads are also, of course, a sign of bravery, a proof of responsible manhood. Since each settlement lives under constant threat of attack, the only man who is respected is the one who has proved his prowess by taking one or more heads. The emotional life of the village centers around these highly charged ideas.

According to the well-known French anthropologist Paul Rivet, the most important act for a Jivaro on arising each morning is to induce vomiting and recite his hatreds to his sons. Thus he first boils up a concoction of strong tobacco juice and repeatedly draws it up his nose. This is supposed to clear his head and protect him from disease. He then takes a magical mouthwash called *guayusa*, made from a plant of the holly family. He swallows some of this, and if, in combination with the tobacco juice, it does not cause him to vomit, he may thrust his finger down his throat. The object of the vomiting is to get rid of any evil substances that have remained within him all night.

Next comes his morning beer, which his wife has made by chewing large quantities of manioc, the tuberous root that is a relative of our tapioca plant, and spitting the pulp into a jar to ferment. Visitors, incidentally, are obliged to partake of the premasticated beer or give offense: one traveler describes having to sample six hundred gallons of it from individual containers at one gathering! It is the wife's first duty each morning to bring this drink to her husband, and his unmarried sons and sons-in-law may assemble at the fireplace to join him at the morning beer-drinking.

He believes strongly in dreams and visions, and if these substances do not enable him to see whether the day will be a good one for a head-taking expedition, he may partake of a more violent drug, *natema*, otherwise called *cayapi* and *ayahuasca*, which is used principally for this purpose. Whereas *guayusa* seems to be shared only among the

"Aucas" and the Quijo to the north of the Jivaros, *natema* is used widely throughout northern South America. Even stronger than either of these is the *maikoa* mentioned above, which is derived from the shrub *Datura arborea.* It has been likened in its effects to belladonna or opium and may be even more powerful. The usual dose, a small drinking glass full of the juice, is squeezed out of the light-green rind of the plant's stem. The hallucinations and even temporary madness that are induced are so extreme that when a youth drinks *maikoa,* older men keep watch over him and may even tie him down. He finally falls into a deep sleep. Before starting out on a head-hunting expedition, the warrior takes this drug to learn whether he will kill his enemies. It is also sometimes given to a young man as punishment for disobedience. Women are also allowed to drink it.

As has been said, the head of the house formally and energetically recites his hatreds each morning, particularly if he feels the *jivaria* may be threatened by attack. The outpourings of his rage always follow much the same pattern. He reminds the younger men—and even his six-year-old son is expected to listen—of the various crimes that have been committed against his people, and names the relatives who have been killed. Praise for himself and his friends is mingled with insults for the enemy. All are told to become worthy of their father and to cultivate valor. Unrelenting vengeance, he says, will be rewarded by blessings, good luck, long life, and the opportunity to kill enemies.

The *guayusa* may now be passed around again, and about eight o'clock comes breakfast, consisting of boiled manioc, boiled or roasted plantain, meat, or fish. Thereafter, the men go hunting or visiting (if it is not raining and if preparations are not being made for a raid), and the women, carrying their babies, go to the nearby fields to work.

On the trail, the hunter eats only fermented manioc substance, which he carries wrapped in banana leaves. The warrior is afraid of snakes and evil spirits and avoids the forest after dark. All the men are apt to return to the *jivaria* by three or four o'clock and have the second meal of the day about an hour later.

For a week before a head-taking raid, the men of the household assemble in the hut every night. The headman develops the plan of attack and exhorts the others to fight without fear and not to abandon their comrades. Great faith in the outcome of the raid is placed on the visions induced by the drug *natema.* Scientists familiar with its use testify that a person who takes it first displays violent behavior, then falls into a deep sleep and has vivid hallucinations in extravagant color. Finally he has a sense of losing his body and seeing distant things. Some partakers are said to awake with a severe headache, and a novice may vomit. *Natema* is made from the plant *Banisteriopsis caapi* or two related species.

Substantial beer-drinking may also precede the head-taking expedition. A man may take his seven-year-old son on the raid, not so much that the youngster may take part as to accustom him to the horrors and teach him to defend himself. The women, however, remain at home, singing and performing ceremonies to increase the chances of victory.

Approaching the enemy *jivaria,* the attackers have as their main purpose to slaughter as many of their opponents as they can before reinforcements can be summoned by a signal drum, which is made from a hollowed-out log. The invaders must approach cautiously, because the enemy will have fortified their *jivaria* by pitfalls cleverly covered over and containing sharp stakes to impale the invader. Spring-set weapons may also have been installed on the trail in such a way that a mere touch will release a multiple spear, driving as many as twelve foot-long wooden spikes through the intruder's body. Since the introduction of firearms, the Jivaros have taken to stretching a string across the trail and fixing it to the trigger. Furthermore, the hut sometimes has a strongly built watch-tower at one end, on top of which is a square room with walls three or four feet high. The hut itself has eight- to ten-foot walls made of upright wooden staves too solid for spears.

If a sudden onslaught is considered too dangerous, the attackers may lay siege, endeavoring to get close enough to hurl firebrands onto the palm-thatched roof and standing ready at any moment to drive their heavy spears at anyone who attempts to flee. The accuracy of their aim with these is attested by a missionary who saw a man hit a coin about an inch in diameter at a distance of sixty-five feet. Round shields of wood or tapir hide serve to protect them from the spears of the enemy. These are decorated with good-luck designs, and some are three feet in diameter, but the traveling warrior is usually content with a smaller one.

Ultimately the showdown comes. But before the defenders come out to fight or flee, they pause long enough to hold a dance ceremony in the doomed hut, using a special flute made from the leg bone of a jaguar. Extreme brutality follows. Each side tries to kill the opposing medicine man to free themselves of his evil magic. There is no rule against killing a relative, but everyone scrupulously avoids taking the head of one. Even during the fighting, if a man sees that a relative of his on the other side has been killed, he will shout to his comrades, "Do not take his head. He is my relative."

The heads of women are not generally sought, but Fritz W. Up de Graff describes the taking of a woman's head in a raid he witnessed in 1897. A group of Aguarunas, attacking some Huambizas, had been unable to annihilate ten or fifteen of the Huambizas, who took refuge in a hut, leaving their dead and dying strewn about. The Aguarunas then dashed forward to gather the heads, going from corpse to corpse with stone axes and split bamboo knives sharpened with clam shells. They also used chonta wood machetes. On this occasion, the warriors appeared eager to collect the head of one woman who had been stricken down by several spear thrusts. Though she was still alive, one man held her down while another hacked at her neck with a stone ax and a third wrenched at her head. The writer, unable to control the attackers in any way, finally felt obliged to lend his machete to hasten the inevitable. The head was strung through the neck and out the mouth along with another, but Up de Graff saw other heads tied together in pairs by the hair. In removing the head, the skin is usually cut low on the chest in a V just above the nipples.

Women are always subject to capture, especially young ones. But it is known that mature women, imbued with hatred for the hostile group, are likely to make poor wives.

The victorious warriors hurry away from the scene, dripping with blood and with the heads dangling at their backs. How quickly they move off depends upon how much signaling with the drum the enemy has been able to do. At a safe distance from the slaughter, they halt and devote about twelve hours to cleaning and shrinking the trophies and about eight hours more to smoking them. Or they may keep going until they reach home.

Hatred, fear, and blood lust now give way to a mood of triumph, made more gratifying by the opportunity to perform indignities upon the enemy head. The sense of achievement is marred only by the knowledge that the enemy's spirit can work evil magic on the slayer until proper ceremonies have enslaved it. The head-takers now seat themselves naked on their trophies and each is approached from behind by the medicine man. The latter bends the man's head back, takes his nostrils in his mouth, and forces a quantity of tobacco juice up his nose, presumably to protect him from the spirit of the slain enemy. The rituals that follow are directed toward acquiring mastery over the soul during the relatively brief time that it can remain theirs.

The actual process of shrinking the head begins with the victor cutting the scalp up the back of the head far enough to peel it off the skull. Special care is exercised in trimming the inside of the face away from the bones and from the cartilage of the nose. When removed, the scalp and face hang limp. The skull is disposed of with little ceremony. But the flesh is cooked in hot water to which has been added the astringent juice of a parasitic vine called *chinchipi*. After two hours, the skin is thick, rubbery, and pale yellow. It is cooled on a stick, and a ring of a vine is made to fit the final size of the shrunken neck opening. The scalp is then sewed up.

Further to shrink the skin and to remove fatty tissue, three stones are heated and rolled around separately in the head. Following this, the head is filled more than half full of hot sand many times and rotated. Between treatments, the face is carefully molded. Some of the hair is plucked, particularly to keep the eyebrows in proportion to the size of the head, which is finally about one-quarter natural size, or about as large as a small orange. A loop is passed through a hole in the top and tied to a stick on the inside so that the shrunken head can be suspended. Three two-inch splints of chonta wood are skewered through the lips and tied with red string, perhaps in order to confine the powerful spirit in the head. Lastly the head is dyed black with charcoal, and smoked and polished, much as any piece of leather, until it is quite hard. The ears, with lobes pierced, are perfect miniatures of the original. Sometimes fifteen-inch strings decorated with feathers or the iridescent wing covers of beetles are suspended from the lips.

Too much has been made of the recognizability of shrunken heads. However, the late Harvey Bassler, one of the writer's colleagues at the American Museum of Natural History did have the dreadful experience of finding himself in possession of the head of a former friend. He had purchased it quite innocently, only to find that it had on one nostril a telltale scar which identified it as that of an Indian companion of earlier journeys.

After completion of the shrinking process, there is dancing and feasting. The slayer, as well as his wife and daughters, begins a period of strict dieting. For two or three months the man wears only a loincloth, lets his hair hang loose, uses no face paint or ornaments, and abstains from sexual intercourse. Then there is an intermediate ceremony whose primary feature is to purify him further of the evil influences that adhere as a result of taking and handling the head.

The taboos are now to some extent temporarily relaxed, but the slayer works even more seriously toward the great Victory Feast—the culmination of his acquisition of a head trophy. This ceremony may not be held for one and a half to two years after the slaying, or even longer.

Just as we are indebted to Up de Graff for the best first-hand description of a head-taking raid, so must we thank Rafael Karsten, of the University of Helsinki, for the best account of the Victory Feast, contained in his valuable studies of the Jivaros. Between 1917 and 1928, he spent three years in their general territory and learned the native language, and for one period of two weeks he ate and slept in the center of a hut in which this ceremony was being enacted.

The loud and horrifying activities that went on around him day and night kept him from getting any sleep. The first night, he testifies, the dance was so ghastly and the noise so frightful that he got no rest at all. The second night was as bad as the first. But the third night he put cotton wool in his ears and succeeded in sleeping for a few hours. At one point, when the participants were deranged by intoxicants and narcotics, an ominous situation developed. While at the fire, one of the men dropped a pot of hot liquid and fell in convulsions. The Jivaros attribute misfortunes of this sort to witchcraft, and the visiting anthropologist was an object of suspicion. The Indian lay unconscious for some time, and Karsten admits that it took all his strength of will to take note of the rest of the ceremony.

For three days the slayer remained outside the hut, constantly attended by the medicine man, who ritually supervised the preparation of the manioc beer and a special manioc wine. The day before the slayer was to make his entry for the main part of the Victory Feast, the head was placed on a shield and set on a staff beside a smaller hut that the slayer had been using. The priest gave the slayer a tobacco-juice treatment in the nose to protect him from the attacks of the spirit of his victim. Then, taking him by the wrist, he made him touch the hair of the trophy, saying: "Have courage. Do not fear the Great Serpent." This had reference to the boa, which the Jivaros hold in great reverence as the father of witchcraft. After this, the head was taken back to the main house and kept under a cloth and hung over the smoke of a fire. Occasionally the Indians danced toward it and chanted to it.

Many guests may arrive the next day, and in the afternoon the slayer and the warriors proceed slowly and ceremoniously to the house. En route, repeated doses of tobacco juice are given the slayer. Feasting follows, and a dance is enacted, the name of which means literally "the killing of the enemy's soul." During all this, the victor carries the head trophy hanging on his back. Karsten describes the song that is sung at this time as having a "dismal, almost disagreeable, howling effect," and the dancers appeared to approach a state of ecstasy.

All this night the victor is not allowed to sleep. Girls of eight or ten take part, while outside the boys are required to engage in savage wrestling matches, the significance of which is unknown.

The following day is given over to the drinking of *natema,* often mixed with tobacco juice to increase the dreams. Even half-grown children—indeed, all who want to have visions—take part. The hope is that they will have a revelation showing the manioc fields fertile and abundant. On an empty stomach, each swallows about a pint of the fluid, immediately goes out and throws it up, and repeats the process twice more. When the visions come, the person must then tell the older Indians whether the future looks good for the slayer.

That night the "ghost-laying" dance continues, and in a prolonged ceremony the shrunken head has its lip skewers and strings renewed. The killer and his womenfolk are given repeated doses of tobacco juice until they grow pale and shake all over, and the head is put in a soapy foam formed by soaking the root of a liana called *sikimuro*. The hair is later combed with a special comb, and beer-drinking follows. The last ceremony takes place when the priest, dressed in festive attire, causes the slayer to break his fast, cuts off the end of his long pigtail, removes the side pigtails entirely, and blackens him with a coat of genipa dye. The enemy's soul presumably does not remain in the head much after this, though enough of it may linger there to cause a Jivaro, when selling a head trophy to a white man, to "release it" by telling it to go away and stay away.

The Victory Feast is sometimes called "The Eating of the Trophy Head" (*Tsantsa yuoma*). Formerly the medicine man cut a piece of flesh from the neck of the trophy and had the slayer eat it. This symbolized his acquisition of the soul and denoted final mastery over the spirit of the slain enemy. But latterly the morsel of flesh has simply been thrown away, and the slayer is then freed from his long observance of taboos.

There is scarcely any limit to the number of *tsantsas* a Jivaro may hope to acquire. Matthew Stirling tells of two men in the region of the Ganga River and the upper Yaupe who had each taken more than fifty heads during the preceding ten or fifteen years. These two had always been close friends and leaders in their respective territories, but, in time, both groups lost many warriors and many women. One of the two leaders died in 1929, and his son, who was sickly and unable to go to war, went to his father's old friend and suggested that the two groups unite under him. This was done, but there was not enough strength to uphold the old record for head-taking. When the remaining leader next led an attack, he found the enemy well entrenched and lost all his fighters except two. This brief history can probably be taken as typical of the ebb and flow of rival groups among the Jivaro head-shrinkers.

If a man kills an enemy but cannot take the head, he is allowed instead to shrink a sloth's head and go through the ceremonies with it. In fact, *tsantsa* rites have been held with sloths' heads even when there have been no human killings.

Archeological evidence indicates that head-shrinking is very old and that it may have had considerably wider distribution than at present. The first shrunken head reached Europe in 1862 and created quite a stir. Others followed and brought substantial prices. Laws were finally passed in Ecuador, Peru, and Brazil in an effort to stop the traffic, but without success. Stirling tells how as early as 1872 a white man living on the borders of the Jivaro country learned how to shrink heads. A traffic in fake heads soon arose, and many have been sold to tourists all along the coast to Panama. Not a few have found their way into museums, but such counterfeits are not difficult to detect. Most of them are made from unclaimed dead in city morgues or pauper asylums, and their short hair betrays their falsity. A genuine *tsantsa* will have long hair, with the lips sewn or pinned, the forehead compressed laterally, the nostrils dilated, and all facial hair removed except the eyebrows. The skin should be smoke-blackened and polished, and there should be little ornamentation besides the lip threads.

As the French anthropologist Paul Rivet put it, "The state of war is the normal state of the Jivaro . . . he never knows the restful, beneficient calm of peace . . . there is nothing but assaults, surprises, blood scenes, and never-satisfied hates. . . ." So tense is the atmosphere of distrust that whenever one Jivaro meets another in the forest or goes visiting, he must go through elaborate formalities in order to justify his presence. At the same time, he must not lose face. He explains himself in an explosively artificial voice and with strange gestures. Before approaching the *jivaria,* he makes a loud noise to give notice that he is coming and to give the host time to paint and decorate himself, an operation that the visitor himself has performed at a nearby river. Then, stepping up to the men's door of the hut (there is a women's door at the other end, which the visitor must not use), the newcomer says "Winyaheil" ("I have arrived!")

The host then coolly asks the visitor why he has come. He also instructs the women to prepare manioc beer. The visitor throws his whole body into his answer. He speaks loudly and in a syncopated rhythm, while holding his clenched fist up to his mouth, palm in, with his lips pressed against the knuckles. He frequently punctuates what he is saying by spitting vigorously and accurately between his fingers. He never looks at the other man, but his eyes flash. He gestures with his arms; his chest heaves. There are smackings of the lips and clickings of the tongue.

This may go on for ten minutes, even fifteen. The host only grunts occasionally or utters some such phrase as, "You say it was that way?" Finally the two men relax and resume their normal voices, but if there are others in the party, each must make his own formal speech, with the same outlandish gestures and emphasis. The simple handshake is unknown.

Having established his good intentions, the visitor can expect to be received hospitably. The hut is oval and from forty to sixty or even eighty feet long. Around the wall are low cane beds, on which the people sleep with their feet on a rack over a fire of converging logs. Though the altitude does not exceed a few thousand feet, and in the heat of the afternoon the thermometer may read above 80 degrees Fahrenheit, the nights are cool. It is very damp, the rainfall averaging from one hundred to two hundred inches or more annually. The Jivaros generally use no covers at night, but the beds slope up toward the head, which helps the heat to reach the upper part of the body as well as the feet. They make fire by twirling a stick.

The men, at least those who are unmarried or are guests, occupy one end of the house, the women and dogs the other. The women have privacy behind split bamboo walls but lack the foot rack.

The earth floor is kept clean by sweeping, and the interior is neat and orderly. The largest pot in the house contains the manioc beer substance, which the hostess is ever ready to mix with water and serve.

The visitor, in addition to the premasticated beer (variously called *nijimanche* or *chicha*), will be offered a fair variety of foods. Corn, sweet potatoes, squash, peanuts, plantains, beans, bananas, and papaya may be available. Also there are various fish that the Indians have hooked, trapped, harpooned, netted, or poisoned. For poisoning fish, they use chiefly a plant which, according to Karsten, is *Cracca toxicaria*. They pound the roots, dip the juice in baskets in a pool in a stream, and capture the fish as they surface for air. The poison in no case impairs the food value of the flesh. It is also one ingredient used in the poison for blowguns. The Jivaros also catch fish alive with their bare hands.

Though they depend on crops more than on game, the Jivaros are excellent hunters and bring in a variety of animals, from wild hogs and peccaries to various birds, including partridge, toucans, and "wild turkeys." They catch crocodiles, tortoises, lizards, and frogs; and they eat the fat larvae of certain ants found in the tops of a species of palm tree. They also esteem the contents of a monkey's stomach, which, mixed with water, is said to resemble a good fruit drink. They preserve meat by smoking it. The food that is most often stored is the manioc beer substance. Properly mixed with saliva and buried in crocks in the ground, it is said to remain palatable for six months. Most of the cooking is done by boiling or roasting.

Saline springs and salt rocks do not provide enough salt, and occasionally earth-eating (geophagy) is indulged in, possibly as a reaction to the salt shortage. They grow enough peppers, however, to suit the most jaded palate; one kind is so strong that it is used only in the making of dart poison. All in all, the Jivaros live plentifully, and hunger is certainly not as instrumental in holding down their population as is warfare.

Anteaters and tapirs are fairly abundant in this area, and the jaguar and puma may be encountered. The electric eel is treated with respect. When Up de Graff tried to chop the head off one with his large jungle knife, the implement flew out of his hand as if he had tried to cut a charged wire with uninsulated pliers. Another fish that is disliked is the tiny *carnero*, which is said to enter the urinary tract. Its backward-pointing fins make it very painful and difficult to remove, which may explain why a Jivaro ties a string around his penis when he has to enter a river. They claim, however, that this practice is followed to avoid loss of sexual vigor. The mosquitoes in this area are bad, and the Jivaros sometimes carry smoldering material from a termite nest to repel them.

A "camphor tree" grows in the Jivaro country, and so do rubber and ivory nuts. Orchids are seen in abundance. Vanilla plants have pods a foot long and surpass the commercially grown ones in flavor.

Malaria occurs among the Jivaros, but their health otherwise seems originally to have been good except for a few afflictions such as a licheniform affection that has a tendency to darken the skin, and a "worm" that they say invades the lower intestine. Unless treated promptly, this "worm" is said to cause the patient to "rot away" in a few days. The Indians treat it, apparently effectively, by making a syringe from the bladder of a hen and the stem of a hollow plant and injecting a powerful infusion into the rectum. They set broken bones and put them in casts made of the chicle of the chewing-gum tree, reinforced with splints.

Serious medical problems have been introduced by the advent of the white man, including measles, smallpox, and tuberculosis. The latter is spread rapidly by the common beer pot.

The Jivaros are usually described as mentally alert and industrious. Opinions differ widely, however, concerning their temperament. Karsten says that they are arrogant; Dyott labels them as extremely proud; however, Herbert Spencer Dickie, who knew them over a period of nearly nineteen years, calls them humble. Fritz Up de Graff sums them up as "a compendium of all that is cunning, knavish, and diabolical," and Günter Tessmann refers to their "overwhelming bloodthirstiness, trickiness, and deceitfulness." Karsten concedes that they always kept their word; if illness prevented them from carrying his baggage, they would always return the payment. These widely differing statements show, if nothing else, the weakness of generalizations and make clear the complexity of the situation that arises when civilized men come into contact with a people of nature. Obviously, as Karsten points out, much depends on whether the Jivaros are dealing with someone they trust or someone whom it is their duty to hate. This sharp demarcation between their hatred of members of the outgroup and their affection for those of the ingroup is a bit difficult to comprehend for those who are used to broader concepts of nationalism. That a people who practice such frightful customs as the Jivaros could hospitably entertain a guest may at first seem contradictory. But it would be well to remember that the kind of antagonism civilized people develop in time of war is cultivated almost constantly by the Jivaros against their neighbors.

Authorities are in general agreement regarding the Jivaros' jealousy concerning their women, a trait not conspicuous among some of the other tribes of the region. The preponderance of women, resulting from the loss of men through warfare, is harmoniously adjusted through the practice of polygyny. One man is known to have had eleven wives, but from three to five is more common. The co-wives are said to show no signs of jealousy among themselves.

A man's second wife may well be the younger sister of the first one. Girls of six to twelve sometimes enter into token marriage, waiting till maturity to assume a wife's full duties. Marriages outside the peace-group are frowned upon, and if a woman becomes pregnant by a man of a hostile group, she is compelled to kill the child at birth if it is a boy. No premium is put on virginity. In arranging a marriage, the suitor must secure approval from the girl's father and from others in her family. The girl herself has less to say in the matter than the women in many other parts of the world. Yet the Jivaro is said to be satisfied only with a wife who reciprocates his affection.

The primary requisites in a husband are courage in warfare (as evidenced by the shrunken head) and skill in hunting. Participation in many hunting expeditions is advertised by possession of a long ornament worn down the back. It is made from as many as 140 pairs of leg bones from the oil bird or guacharo (*Steatornis caripensis*), a bird that is somewhat dangerous to take because it lives in caves that may be occupied by jaguars.

The young man wants his wife to have gardening ability and other domestic talents. If she can keep from vomiting the strong drugs that are administered in the important Tobacco Feast, it is a sign she will be an able wife. She prepares for the Tobacco Feast from puberty, just as the young boy prepares for the great Victory Feast. Though not exactly a wedding ceremony, the Tobacco Feast has analogous characteristics and is performed only for women who are about to be married. It prepares them spiritually for successful wifehood, equipping them with proper supernatural aids, particularly through the power of the tobacco spirit. The "initiate" is attended during the ceremonies, which last several days, by a sister and another young female relative. But an older priestess is the chief functionary.

Two or three years may be consumed in the preparations for this important feast, for the gardens and the domestic animals must be in a flourishing state. For two years the girl observes certain dietary taboos; otherwise she would be vulnerable to evil influences.

Each evening for eight days, the young men perform the dance called the *Wuimchi*. In this, the names of the animals the men hunt are mentioned repeatedly, as well as details in the crafts proper to men. Three days before the feast proper, the women chew manioc roots ceremonially for the making of manioc beer. But the significant part of the ceremony occurs when the girl who is to be married takes a potion called *chiki*. This acts as a vomitory and prepares her for the all-important ministrations of tobacco medicine, called *savinya*—a thick syrup which the priestess makes by chewing tobacco leaves and spitting the juice into a clay pot. The priestess administers this medicine to the three young women on an empty stomach, and it never fails to produce the dreams so important in Jivaro life. The three women sleep in separate little shelters. The Earth Mother (Nungüi) should appear to the girls, promising abundance.

During the third day, the girls receive only doses of the tobacco medicine, and songs are sung to the Earth Mother. The husband-to-be ties the bride's hair with a band and wets her head and shoulders because "she has been vomiting." That night, at about three in the morning, the important slaughter of the swine occurs, and the next day the final doses of tobacco medicine are administered, incantations are sung on behalf of the hunting dogs, and there is ceremonial hair-cutting and painting with *genipa. On the* fourth day the bride washes out her mouth with *guayusa* and breaks her fasting. Also on this day the manioc wine, a dark brown essence that collects at the bottom of a specially prepared pot, is drunk by the men. The women do not partake.

The central purpose of the Tobacco Feast is to give the young woman the supernatural capacity for good fortune that is possible only when W*akáni,* the spirit of the tobacco, is administered to her with proper ceremony.

After marriage, the bridegroom takes up residence in the household of his wife's parents. He performs certain work there, which is comparable to the bride-price paid to the father-in-law in many primitive tribes. After one or two children have been born, his duties to his father-in-law cease.

Children appear to be numerous, although the women are said to possess a knowledge of vegetable abortives. Some writers have described the status of the wife as low, but Karsten mentions instances of tender consideration on the part of the husband. The wrath of the head of the family is terrible, nevertheless, if he suspects infidelity. He will cut his wife's head or legs repeatedly with a machete, and stop just short of killing her. A mistreated wife, in turn, may try secretly to poison or bewitch her spouse, or she may hang herself.

Upon the death of a man, his wife is passed on to his

brother unless the latter is willing to let her marry someone else—a custom paralleling the levirate in old Hebraic tradition.

The strict division between men's and women's work is religiously emphasized in the belief that certain plants and animals have male souls, others female. This concept imposes on the Jivaro numerous taboos and observances. They form a pattern of religious behavior that is linked to the food-gaining pursuits and are intended to avoid contamination or discord in the spirit world. They are comparable, in a sense, to the Eskimo system of taboos designed to prevent mixing the animals of the land with those of the sea. The manioc plant has a female soul; therefore, the planting and growing of it, as well as the chewing of the tuberous roots in making the beer, must be performed solely by women. Corn and plantain, on the other hand, have male souls and are planted by the men. The women may, however, later tend a plantain tree and sing incantations to promote its growth. The two narcotic plants, *natema* and *maikoa*, are on the man's side spiritually, and for some days before planting them the men must abstain from sleeping with their wives. Women must not come near the place where the arrow poison, curare, is being made, and since cotton has a man's soul, the men do all the spinning and weaving.

Overlying these taboos is the belief in two main deities, the Earth Mother (Nungüi) and the Great Serpent. Nungüi is probably the primary spirit and is identified with ideas of procreation and growth. The women in particular are required to address her with songs and prayers on many occasions connected with planting and cultivation. Information on the Great Serpent, or Anaconda God, is less detailed. This deity may, in fact, be no more important than the Rain God, who inhabits mountain peaks. All these spirits possess a supernatural essence called *tsarutama*, as do the innumerable nature spirits in animals, places, and things. There is also evidence of a belief in sympathetic magic—the idea that like affects like: for example, eating a swift animal to become swift. Taboos too various to enumerate are connected with the making of canoes, spears, blowguns, and other implements.

Most primitive people have some sort of a growing-up ceremony for men and women, but the Jivaros also have such a ceremony for dogs. In fact, it is one of the five important Jivaro ceremonies—a three-day affair signalizing the completion of the dog's training as a hunter. The principal feature is the repeated dosing of the dog with a special drink made from a plant called *kunguna,* which the Jivaros cultivate solely for this purpose. *Guayusa* is also put into the concoction. The medicine man, after blowing tobacco smoke on the dog, puts the potion into its mouth, presumably imbuing the dog with powers that will make it skillful in the pursuit of game. The dog is also painted with *genipa,* and there are various other observances that resemble the rites for people.

The Jivaros are convinced that amulets and taboos must be employed in connection with practically every action of life. Stimulants and narcotics are believed to have strong spirit forces in them. Even the painting of the body has magical import. The red coloring derived from the pod of the plant *Bixa orellana* and widely used from Central America through the Amazon country is to the Jivaros a potent magical aid, at least when applied in the proper designs. A man would not go to war or on a hunting expedition without applying these. In facilitating the application, the Jivaros use a miniature "printing press." A roller of clay or wood, which is incised with the pattern, is plastered with the coloring matter and then applied to the skin by rolling. This is one of the few useful purposes to which anything resembling a wheel has been put by native peoples in the Western Hemisphere.

Religious motives appear to have worked an unnecessary hardship on the Jivaro in some instances—or so the outsider is apt to think. Thus, two of the largest animals the Jivaro hunter might bring home—the deer and the tapir—are taboo. The Jivaro believes that these are tenanted by evil spirits. They are not exactly sacred; he will kill one for his white companion, but he will not risk absorbing the evil spirit by eating the meat himself.

The medicine man, or *wishinu,* officiates at important group ceremonies. He also receives pay for performing private services of a spiritual nature, such as curing sickness, bringing trouble upon an enemy by magical means, or concocting love potions. The potions are made from various herbs, including the leaves of one called *simaika.* Contact with this plant is believed to arouse an irresistible longing in a person. The medicine man may or may not be the head of the household. He learns his practices from an older man, and his training includes dieting and the taking of tobacco juice, *natema,* and other drugs.

Strangely enough, the weapon for which the Jivaros and many other Indians across northern South America are most famous, the blowgun, seems not to have reached them until the seventeenth century. Natives of southeastern Asia, perhaps from the Philippines, traveling in Spanish galleons, may have brought the blowgun to South America. Dr. Stirling has suggested this in explanation of the parallels frequently noted in the production of blowgun equipment on both sides of the Pacific. Sixteenth-century writers never mentioned the blowgun among the Jivaros but described them as using lances with spear-throwers, and bows and arrows. The first mention of the blowgun in South America occurs in 1620, among the Mainas, a more accessible tribe immediately to the east of the Jivaros. Among the modern Jivaros, the blowgun has completely replaced the bow and arrow for hunting small game.

The Jivaros are said to surpass all Indians in their vicinity in the use of the blowgun. The weapon is from seven to ten feet long and is made of two pieces of chonta neatly grooved and bound together with pitch and fiber. The whole process of manufacture requires two months. The poison "arrows" are somewhat like knitting needles and have a tuft of silk cotton on one end, against which the breath operates. There is a fairly deep groove around the end just back of the poison tip, so that it breaks off in the wound. The Jivaros are accurate with the blowgun up to about forty-five yards.

The poison, curare, is apparently an American invention. Its main ingredient is derived from various species of the genus *Strychnos*, but many other plant juices are added to the brew. The making of the poison is restricted to certain "wizards" in the art. The Jivaros get some of their best curare from outside their own tribe. Birds struck with curare darts fall to the ground almost instantly; monkeys may linger for from five to thirty minutes, and larger animals several hours.

The Jivaros have had abundant opportunity to accept Christianity ever since the Jesuits established missions about 1638 in the country to the west of them. In 1656 about one hundred soldiers and one hundred Indians from the Mainas mission under Father Raimundo Santa Cruz penetrated along the entire length of the Marañon River. Near its confluence with the Pastaza they founded the city of Santiago de Santander. But the Jivaros killed a number of the Spaniards from ambush and fled. In 1692, another determined effort was made to convert the Jivaros, but the results were once more meager.

Then, in 1767, Father Andrès Camacho traveled extensively in the territory and gained the confidence of the people sufficiently to baptize two hundred children. Mission work was interrupted by decrees from Spain, but was resumed by the Franciscan fathers from 1790 to 1803.

The Jivaros have shown an inclination to make a game of conversion, returning for another baptism simply to get another length of trade cloth. And there have been many attacks on white settlements, with much loss of life. The expedient of establishing military posts in the region has failed repeatedly. This unique and difficult tribe has thus remained in much the same condition as when the white men found it, with the addition of rifles to increase its capacity for carnage.

Most of the tribes that are loosely called "savages" scarcely merit the name, for they are normally as gentle, friendly, and hospitable as "civilized" people, if not more so. It could perhaps be argued that the Jivaros make up for this. But even the Jivaro warrior has his mild side. When he is not on a head-taking expedition, he is the picture of domestic tranquility—a little man dressed in a skirt and decked out in feathers, content with his weaving and other fancy work. The women never touch those tasks—they are the farmers. They live in more or less constant fear of an attack and are expected to remain calm when the fighting starts. When the men are off on a raid they keep the home fires burning and sing the proper songs, not knowing whether they will ever see their husbands again—unless perhaps in miniature.

A TRIBE OF CENTRAL BRAZIL

The Camayurás

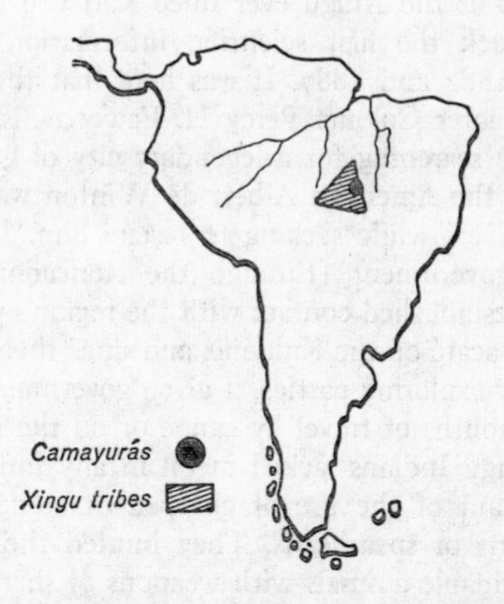

In the Brazilian state of Mato Grosso, almost two thousand miles southeast of the Jivaros, lies a vast wilderness that is the home of some of the purest aboriginal cultures left on earth.

Exploration was long impeded by the remoteness and inaccessibility of the area. Dense forests and swamplands make the approach difficult except by canoe, and even the rivers are broken by rapids. Some of the inhabitants, moreover, are of uncertain disposition. In most other parts of tropical South America, slavers, traders, prospectors, and missionaries have left their imprint in varying degrees, but here near the center of the continent are regions where civilized influences are only now beginning to be felt.

Some of the peoples of the upper Xingu (pronounced Shing-*goó*) exhibit great simplicity and natural beauty; indeed, they have a touch of the idyllic charm that writers of the last century were wont to ascribe to South Sea islanders. Although the "noble savage" of romantic literature never really existed, some of these Xinguanas, as they are called, do approach the popular conception of the "unspoiled child of nature."

An aura of mystery and adventure has surrounded the headwaters of the Xingu ever since Karl von den Steinen brought back the first scientific information about this region in 1884 and 1887. It was here that the celebrated British explorer Colonel Percy H. Fawcett disappeared in 1926 while searching for a legendary city of great wealth, and where the American Albert de Winton was murdered by the Indians while seeking to rescue him. In 1947 the Brazilian government (through the Roncador-Xingu Expedition) established contact with the region by cutting an airstrip at Jacaré on the Kuluéne, and since then it has been possible for exploring parties, if given government sanction, to avoid months of travel by canoe or on the trail.

The Xingu Indians lacked metal in any form and were even ignorant of the use of chipped or stone blades for arrow points or spearheads. They hunted the jaguar and other formidable animals with weapons of sharpened bamboo or those tipped with monkey ribs or the spines of sting rays. All were expert at shooting fish with the bow and arrow.

Some of the tribes of northern Mato Grosso remain unknown and hostile. Others have so recently acquired metal knives and other tools that their economy is still virtually unchanged. They are living the jungle life of old—true relics of the aboriginal past. Their ceremonies are impressive, their dances beautiful; and their religious beliefs give rich insight into the efforts of primitive people to understand and control the unknown. That people so innocent of the modern world can be studied in an era when civilized man is planning to make the moon his first stop in outer space is a startling thought.

It is still a uniquely exciting experience for a white man, accompanied only by a few natives, to make his way, as the writer did in 1953, to the chief settlements of the Camayurá tribe. In approaching one of their villages, we had slogged barefoot through swamps to our knees and tramped for miles over a blazing hot grassland north of the marshy end of the lake the Indians called Ipavú. There my native companions found a dugout they had hidden in the flooded forest, and soon we were paddling along the palm-fringed shore of the lake, pausing now and again to shoot fish from the canoe with bow and arrow.

These Camayurás were all quite naked except for a single strand of shell beads around the waist, an occasional necklace of jaguar teeth, or bright red and yellow feather ornaments stuck through the ears. They wore their straight black hair in a "sugar bowl" bob, with bangs hanging well down toward the eyes and curving evenly around the back of the head so as to cover the top of the ears. Though their average stature of around five and a half feet was not tall by Caucasian standards, their straight and muscular bodies gave them a statuesque appearance. They were handsome men, equally at home on the trail and in the canoe, and they showed great stamina.

We were in the region between the three western tributaries of the Xingu (the von den Steinen, the Ronuro, and the Batoví) and the two eastern ones (the Kuliséu and the Kuluéne). About a dozen small tribes live in the eastern part of the rough triangle formed by these five rivers. Little is known about the groups that inhabit the three western streams. These five main tributaries of the Xingu join like the fingers of a hand at a point about 12 degrees south of the equator, to flow northward to the Amazon, 750 airline miles away.

The solitary white man traveling among these people senses a strange excitement on approaching one of their villages. No settlements are usually visible from the water. The Indians build on higher ground to escape the mosquitoes and the floods that cover wide areas in the rainy season. Also they seek the concealment of the forest for safety from hostile neighbors. To the east live the warlike Chavantes, whom white men consider the most dangerous tribe in Brazil. To the north are the Suyas, from whom these Camayurás had stolen a wife for their chief. To the west, on the Rio Batoví, are the Tumurí, who had recently massacred one of the other Xinguana settlements. And there are others.

Out on the broader Kuluéne, mutual suspicion had prevented us from fraternizing with passing canoes. Back here in the lesser and even lonelier waterways, the endless hours of paddling grew monotonous; but though the heat lay heavy on us, there was a mood of vague expectancy. Then all of a sudden we heard cheerful voices, and paddling around a point of land, we came upon a group of Indians enjoying an afternoon swim.

Glistening bodies glided past us up the path to a clearing a hundred yards from the shore. A number of large oval huts ringed this space, and from the doorways streamed Indians, the men with bows and arrows, the women holding back with babies on their hips, and the youngsters inquisitive but waiting for a signal. In the babble of voices that followed, the chief's son was obviously trying to explain the presence of the white man.

Young women took the visitor by the arms, fingered his clothing and the blond hair on his forearms, and beckoned their sisters to examine him more closely. A loose shoelace required his attention, and after he had bent over to tie it, the press of bodies made it almost impossible to rise again. When he was unable to suppress laughter at such an intimate reception, his open mouth gave opportunity for one of the warriors to reach in and feel the gold in a few of his teeth.

These were clean, healthy, and evidently happy natives. The women wore their hair low across their foreheads and loose down their backs. Their skin was a rich, lustrous tan, and their bodies were plucked completely free of hair, giving them the appearance of living statues. Some were altogether naked, but most of them wore only a "fig leaf" about the size of a triangular postage stamp. This *uluri*, as it is called, is so characteristic of the upper Xingu that the area is sometimes called "the uluri region."

The women were not embarrassed by their nudity, except that when seated on the ground they drew one heel close in against the other thigh. When they arose, it was with perfect poise, and their physical coordination was particularly evident when they lifted one of the pottery bowls, about two feet in diameter and weighing close to fifty pounds, onto the head.

There were no fat people in the village and no thin ones; no baldness and no gray hair. Their manner was open and self-reliant, for their culture was intact and they were masters of their world. The only puzzling fact was the almost total absence of elderly persons. The Camayurás do not abandon or kill the aged as do some primitive peoples, nor does the malaria from which they suffer seem an adequate explanation. Perhaps intertribal warfare had taken a heavy toll or some civilized epidemic had killed a large percentage in one generation. White man's diseases, which can be communicated from tribe to tribe, are generally far more severe among people who are not used to them and have no way of caring for the ill. The people of this region are known to have experienced an epidemic of grippe in 1948; and measles had an even more serious effect in 1954.

This being the dry season, the village had a number of temporary sun shelters decked out with leaves, and under these the women worked almost constantly, grating and squeezing the bitter manioc, their staple plant food. Manioc is the poisonous relative of our tapioca, and it has to be processed rather elaborately to remove the prussic acid in it. It may seem surprising that primitive people should have hit upon a method for converting a poisonous plant into their main food. But this discovery was made sufficiently long ago for the secret to have spread throughout much of tropical South America and to have led to the development of various types of equipment for making the plant edible.

The tuberous roots of the manioc grow up to two feet

in length. One woman scrapes off the tough outer covering with a fresh-water shell; another grates them on a board set with hundreds of nail-like thorns from the trunk of a certain palm tree. The white pulp falls into a pottery bowl as much as three feet in diameter. Still another woman then mixes it with water and has the all-important task of squeezing the poison out. For this she uses a rolled-up piece of matting about two feet square. After squeezing the pulp, she forms it into a brick that looks much like cottage cheese. These bricks are piled on the flat roofs of the sun shelters, where they take on an orange hue brought about by a harmless mold. Eventually they are stored in yard-long baskets lined with green leaves. From these, quantities are taken as needed, crumbled in water, and made into pancakes.

In accordance with the dictates of tribal hospitality, the chief's son took the writer's hammock into the central hut and after hanging it invited him to partake of the special food that must be served a visitor. This is a delicate pancake made of a very fine manioc flour reserved for such occasions. With the pancake, the visitor is given tasty tidbits, such as roast fish and delicious small white sweet potatoes.

The ordinary pancakes, made from the coarser manioc, are prepared on a two-foot pottery griddle set on three-inch stones over a low fire. They have a sour flavor and a tripelike elasticity, tasting, in short, like a partly vulcanized rubber sponge. However, they are exceedingly sustaining, and one can cultivate a taste for them.

The typical hut in this tribe is a forty- or fifty-foot oval, dome-shaped structure thickly thatched with long grass. It has two entrances, one facing the clearing, the other the forest. Inside the hut, two main posts about fifteen feet tall support the ridgepole, and from these posts ten or more hammocks radiate outward, like the spokes of a wheel, to points around the curving wall. There are often two or three levels of hammocks. The women occupy the lower ones and are expected to tend the fires, which must burn all night if the naked inhabitants are to be warm enough for sleeping. Although it is swelteringly hot during the afternoon, the temperature at night falls to 55 degrees Fahrenheit and lower. The central third of the house between the two poles is kept fairly clear for cooking and other household work.

In this tribe first cousins are expected to marry each other, and thus the several families occupying one hut are apt to be made up of brothers and sisters and their husbands and wives. The members of the household are not only likely to be closely interrelated but of about the same age. There is such profound respect for the older generation that it is perhaps just as well that the young married couples have quarters separate from those of their parents. The writer never saw the chief enter the hut where his sons and daughters lived. For a year or so after marriage, a young husband goes to live with the parents of his bride to demonstrate his capacity to support a wife, but after this trial period, especially if a child is on the way, the couple moves into separate quarters.

Husband and wife must be first cousins through the mother's brother or through the father's sister. This is the relationship called "cross-cousin" in anthropological terminology. Cousins who are related through the father's brother or the mother's sister must never marry among the Camayurás; in fact, they call each other brother and sister. It is allowable for a man to marry his sister's daughter but not his mother's sister's daughter. The community shows no adverse genetic results from this close intermarriage. Geneticists believe that inbreeding only accentuates the existing traits, good or bad, and that it is not harmful in itself. But not everyone marries a close relative in the Camayurá tribe. There are marriages outside the village and even outside the tribe, either by friendly arrangement or by capture.

At puberty, both boys and girls go through a fairly rigorous training, which in the case of a girl may last three or four months. Both remain in seclusion, at least during daylight hours. They undergo scratch scarification, which is supposed to prove fortitude. The boy learns tribal lore and practices sacred music on the flute. The girl is instructed in the duties of a wife and mother and is told how to make and use an abortion medicine, *pirai'i*, which is extracted from the bark of a tree.

Most important in the religious sense is the fact that both the boy and the girl receive at the time of puberty a new name, which is the name of an ancestor. This serves to unite the individual with the tribal past. It is significant that the puberty rites are generally arranged to end at the time of important yearly ancestor ceremonies. Ancestor observances, creation myths, and rites stressing the perpetuation of the tribe form a strong central theme in the religion of this people, and they reach a peak every year at the beginning of the rainy season.

At the core of these concepts is a system of beliefs and ceremonies having to do with the Creator, Mavutsine, whose wife Noitu, a "jaguar woman," gave birth to the Sun and the Moon. The Creator made the ancestors of the Camayurás from the wood of the camiuva tree. Each year in the important ancestor ceremony called *kwarup*, crude, stylized effigies are made out of this wood to represent the four original ancestors and all members of the tribe who have died during the year. These are set up in the center of the clearing. Four men sing a certain song that the Creator is said to have sung when he created the Camayurá, and all the boys and girls who have gone through puberty training dance around these central figures. This dance ends their puberty rites, and the girls are thereafter allowed to wear the uluri. Boys and girls who choose this time to enter marriage signalize their relationship by publicly cutting and caring for each other's hair.

The Camayurás believe that if they fail to perform this ceremony, the tribe will die out. Thus the uniting of young people in marriage in the presence of their ancestral spirits and under the solemn eyes of their living relatives evinces strong concern over the spiritual continuity of the tribe as well as its physical perpetuation. It should be said that we owe such insights into the spiritual concepts of this tribe as well as into other features of the culture of northern Mato Grosso to the work of the distinguished ethnologist Kalervo Oberg.

The Camayurás are not as innocent of the facts of life as certain other primitive peoples. That they have long been aware of the father's role in paternity would seem to be indicated by the fact that the word for "son" has the same stem as the word for "sperm." Babies, moreover, are born in full view of their young brothers and sisters, and the young grow up knowing quite well what goes on in the family. There is almost no privacy. Women urinate in the open but go away from the village to defecate.

Another ceremony, which normally follows the ancestor observances, is designed to bring rain and make the fruits of the forest flourish. The men who participated in this dance wore gorgeous feather crowns and decked their arms and shoulders with leaves in imitation of trees. Carrying their heads low, they waddled about, waving their outstretched arms gently to the music provided by two musicians. One of these shook a rattle, and the other beat the ground with a large gourd in imitation of thunder. They have great confidence in this ceremony, but when the spirits appear obstinate, they add a "bull-roarer" to the other effects. The bull-roarer of the Camayurás is an eighteen-inch wooden slat in the shape of a fish, decorated with zigzag or diamond-shaped designs in red. Tribes scattered over a large part of the world whirl instruments of this sort on a string to produce a whirring noise. Great religious significance is attached to the bull-roarer, and among the Camayurás, as among the natives of faraway central Australia, a woman must never lay eyes on the implement. One wonders whether this is coincidence or whether the bull-roarer is so ancient and powerful in primitive belief that it has circled the globe and survived down to the present in regions utterly different in every respect.

The most sacred object of the Camayurás is a flute about a yard long. The spirit that inhabits this is so terrible that if a woman were to lay eyes on the instrument, even by accident, all the men of the village would rape her and leave her to perish. They also have seven-foot double flutes that are less revered but are used in perhaps more spectacular ways.

Just when the heat of the afternoon has reduced the visitor to a condition of lassitude, he may be startled to hear these enormous flutes. The furniture in all of the huts will have been moved back against the walls to make room for the *urua* dance, and two men holding the heavy instruments to their mouths with one hand as lightly as if they were piccolos dance from hut to hut to their own music. Inside each hut they perform a rhythmic maneuver, ducking, sidling, and sashaying as though to have first chance to leave through the small door. But each time, after an exchange of courteous advances, one partner slips through the doorway ahead of the other and the dance proceeds without interruption. The dancers always mark time more heavily with the right foot, as hour after hour, heedless of the heat of the sun, they continue their strenuous performance.

Then two young woman join them, each with a hand on the shoulder of the man in front. One is Koo-yah-yoo, the chief's daughter, the other her friend. Whereas the men wear gorgeous headdresses of yellow and blue macaw feathers and other adornment, the girls modify their nudity only by putting on an eighteen-inch "broom straw" of a tail, a single strand curving up behind. Round and round the village in counterclockwise direction the dance goes on, in and out of each hut in turn. The timing is as perfect as in a well-trained ballet. If there are any religious implications to this dance, the writer was unable to determine them. Perhaps it is purely an aesthetic display.

Almost every object in Camayurá tribal life has its spirit, or *mamá'e*. Some plants have three of them. Headdresses, masks, and even body paint have their own mama'e, and there are objects fashioned of wood that represent the mama'e of important food crops.

The mama'e of tobacco is particularly strong and is used in puberty rites. At certain times the men smoke tobacco until they fall into a trance, and it is in this way that one gets in touch with one's own mama'e or reaches a state where it is possible to impersonate other mama'e. In treating a sick person, the witch doctor, who may be either a man or a woman, grunts, blows smoke on the afflicted part, and pretends to suck out an object representing the evil spirit. The medicine man possesses an especially effective mama'e, and when he dies and is being buried, a young man may be able to see the sorcerer's guardian spirit and hear its song. This is a sign that the youth has inherited the other's spirit, which entitles him to high respect in the community.

The Camayurás bury their dead in the center of the village. A mature man is wrapped in his hammock, bound to a post, and buried in a standing position with a pot over his head. A chief has a little cave dug underground and is interred lying in his hammock in this space, supported between two posts. The mourners demonstrate their grief by trying to jump into the grave but are prevented from doing so by others. The soul journeys to the abode of the ancestral spirits never to return, and the mourners observe taboos until the next annual ancestor ceremonies.

Indians not of pure Camayurá descent are buried in a horizontal position. Less ceremonious treatment is accorded total outsiders. Albert de Winton, for instance, the white man who was murdered by this tribe because they mistakenly thought he had come to avenge Fawcett's death, was buried under leaves on a riverbank, and when his bones had turned white they were brought back to Lake Ipavú and dropped in.

Though the formalized head-hunting so often pursued in various parts of the Amazon was not practised in this region, savage fighting has frequently occurred. Kalervo Oberg reports that when hostile Indians came within hearing distance of the Camayurás at Jacare in 1948, the fear shown in the faces of the women and children was clear evidence of the reality of war among these people.

Raiding parties generally attack during the night or at

dawn, attempting to set fire to the huts by shooting flaming arrows onto the roofs. If the Camayurás have sufficient warning of attack, they may disperse into the forest, each person carrying his own hammock, and try to survive the assault. But if caught unawares in their burning huts, they are forced to flee, and it is then easy for the raiders to rain arrows or spears on them from the cover of the forest. Even so, neither side can easily score a victory without some fierce infighting. The raiding parties of some Amazon tribes traveled weeks or months on their war trips. The Mundurucú on the lower Tapajos are known to have made a round trip of a thousand miles in order to attack other tribes, and they sometimes remained in enemy territory over the rainy season.

Till one has flown at moderate height over northern Mato Grosso, one is apt to underestimate the extent of open grassland between the rivers. Foot trails among scrubby trees and termite hills crisscross these areas. It is easy for the foot traveler to go astray, but tribes accustomed to raiding learn their way about over large sections.

The several tribes of Xinguana who are friendly toward one another come together to trade and hold intertribal contests. Wrestling is popular. Each contestant keeps grunting "*Hooka, hooka, hooka*" as he grapples for a hold that will enable him to throw his opponent on his back and thus win a victory. The champion is held in great honor.

There is also a rough contest with blunt spears or arrows, which are hurled by means of a throwing stick. Each contestant stands behind a ten-inch bundle of sticks resting on the ground and tries to avoid being hit. Injuries are frequent. Singing and dancing accompany this "duel," giving it a ceremonial flavor. When the outcome has been decided, instead of cheering the victor, the chief of the winning side kneels in front of the loser and weeps, while his womenfolk engage in loud wailing. These contests may serve as a safety valve for possible antagonisms between tribes that to some extent compete but know that it is to their advantage to preserve a united front against other possible enemies.

The Camayurás and one other tribe, the Aueti, speak dialects of Tupi. The other tribes in the upper Xingu speak variants of Arawak, Carib, and Trumai. But intermarriage provides interpreters. In physical appearance the Xinguanas resemble one another closely, and their way of life is similar enough for them all to be considered a cultural unit. They have many traditions in common. All are familiar with the large oval hut, the rolled-up sieve for processing manioc, openwork hammocks made of string, small pottery vessels in the form of animals, necklaces and waist strands of thin shell disks, sacred flutes, and canoes made out of the thick bark of the jatoba tree, removed in one piece and shaped while still pliable.

Intertribal contacts are facilitated by 1000 miles of large rivers within a triangle scarcely 150 miles on a side, as well as a complex network of small streams, lagoons, and swamps. Fishing is more important than hunting among these tribes, and the lesser streams, with their clear water, provide good fishing for people who use the bow and arrow. For reaching fish in deeper water the Camayurás use a thin spear that has a total length of twenty feet or more and can be carried in two sections. Poison is also used, being introduced into the water by bruising and dousing the bark and stems of several vines called *timbó*. This causes the fish to come to the surface gasping for air, where they are easily captured in baskets or shot with arrows before they can recover. The poison is more effective in still water. Much less fishing occurs in the main streams, which are often half a mile wide. They are too large for the use of poison or traps and too muddy for the bow and arrow.

Village sites are chosen for their accessibility to good fishing places, and scarcely a day passes without fish being brought in. Several members of the household may be resting in their hammocks after the heat of the afternoon when voices indicate that the fishermen are coming up the path. The latter enter the hut and dump a basketful of fish on the bare ground. The women may clean them and boil them in pots, but the men are apt to roast them on a platform tied part way up a tripod of sticks a foot and a half high, or even lay them right in the embers.

Nightfall blots out the world of reality and gives play to more imaginative moods. As the sun drops over the far shore, a little boy with a long pole coaxes a pet macaw out of a tree and brings it into the hut for the night. The sunset colors grow somber, and almost in a matter of minutes the forest roundabout is so black that no one would think of venturing away from the village. The people cluster in family or household groups; outside, the men kindle a fire in the center of the village. Here they range themselves on raised log seats to enjoy their evening cigars—which they are never seen to smoke during the day. This is their time for sociability. They tell stories and plan for the morrow. The smoking gives the scene a ritualistic atmosphere, and some partake so vigorously that their speech seems to be affected. It is the moment for chants and divination.

Except close around the fire, there is not enough light to work on a bow and arrow or a manioc basket. A bright moon will bring the women out under their leafy shelters to continue processing their manioc, but on dark nights the practical arts are discontinued and the people are drawn closer to the supernatural. Stranger and friend now look alike as one gropes one's way with difficulty about the village. The sound of flute music comes from the darkness where a young man approaching his initiation is practising the sacred music. From another quarter, where a medicine man is performing a curative ceremony, grunts and sucking sounds issue. A chill creeps into the air, and the visitor seeks the warmth of the hut, whose entrances have been closed by matting to keep out the cold.

Within, one experiences the full flavor of aboriginal life. The young women have lighted the fires between the hammocks, and shadows from moving figures dance against the pattern of spears and arrows tucked into the wicker of the walls. Now and again a parrot or macaw in the darkness among the rafters overhead lets out a chuckle. Several Indians are sitting on low stools or bamboo mats. The others are in hammocks, mothers nursing their babies, young men casually chatting in hammocks higher up, girls swinging themselves at the ground level with one foot on the floor. Gourd containers, baskets, and ears of corn preserved for the next planting season hang from the walls and from crossbeams overhead.

Some are still picking pieces of fish out of the embers and eating them, ashes and all. The odors of cooking mingle with wood smoke and the spicy smell of *urucu*, the vegetable coloring matter with which some have painted designs on their bodies. This is the persistent aroma of the Amazon village. It is the main pigment of adornment, and objects are also decorated with it. Moreover, it has been eaten and is perhaps exuded through the pores. With it are blended the mustiness of basketry, the straw smell of grass thatching. This composite aroma localizes one and establishes the mood more strongly than sounds or sights ever could. Some have called the scent faintly nauseating, but to one who has experienced only a pleasant excitement in these surroundings it is a welcome smell.

Outside, the parrots and jabirus have long since circled to their roosts and the far-off calls of monkeys have ceased, but the men on the log bench are still chanting. Inside, a continual babble rises and falls: laughter, complaint, cajolery. Someone scolds the macaw back up to its perch.

Suddenly a masked figure, led by a small boy, bursts into the hut, speaking in a falsetto voice. The young women scream and crowd back against the wall. But the intruding spirit quickly departs and the excitement passes.

The hut is growing chilly with the approach of midnight. Babies lying against their mothers in the hammocks awaken and whimper, and the mothers begin to blow their warm breath over them with a low hissing sound. They add sticks to the fire. The crying stops. So does the chattering of the men in their hammocks.

Now and again someone talks in his sleep. Outside, the

last fire has died under a three-foot manioc bowl. A forest hog or a jaguar utters a gruff sound at the edge of the forest, and the village dogs break into loud baying. On and on they bark, but the snoring continues. The village is asleep, and there will be no signs of life again until dawn sends the young people down to light a fire at the water's edge and plunge into the lake for their first swim of the new day.

A TRIBE OF ARCTIC EURASIA

The Reindeer-herding Lapps

Viewed from a height, the V-shaped mass of mingling antlers shifting against the snowy land seems more like a natural phenomenon than something organized by man. Only at the head of the herd, where a thin line probes forward like an antenna, are there signs of conscious direction. As the mass surges forward, it gives off a cloud-stuff, for at minus 50 degrees Fahrenheit the animals are not only exhaling vapor but their bodies are giving off a steam known as biofog. Where the hindmost fringe fans out into a wake of trampled snow, red-trimmed furry figures dart here and there in a swirl of mist and loose snowflakes. This is the rear guard coaxing strays and stragglers back into place with the aid of their dogs.

The men wear loose conical hats with huge red pompons, and their boots turn up at the toes. The almost two thousand reindeer in the herd represent sustenance and security to six families of Arctic herders. It is a dynamic spectacle, yet in relation to the vast landscape of icy peaks it is minuscule.

On closer view we see in the forefront more definite signs of human agency. Some fifteen reindeer, moving in single file, are carrying packs. On each of two others, in place of saddle boxes, is a tiny infant, huddled in a welter of furs. Other red-trimmed men scuffle along beside these. Farther forward, the line is made up of six curious boat-shaped sleds drawn by reindeer, all tied nose to stern. Out of the back of one sled a large bundle of tent poles drags in the snow. In some, women are riding with their babes. Still other "snow boats" crunch and sidle along under the weight of family belongings stowed beneath decklike covers.

At the sensitive tip of the spearhead are two figures plainly acting as the nerve center of the whole organism. One is dressed gaily like the rest, but he carries an ornamental staff representing authority in the clan. He moves along on skis.

The other figure beside him is a reindeer, but it is different from the common herd. The difference represents a discovery that turned the early course of cultural evolution almost at right angles. It was man's first experiment in endocrinology, for this deer, the smartest and best-trained in the herd, is a male castrated in calfhood and taught to lead. The draft deer have also been altered; otherwise they would be intractable.

Without the chief herder's wisdom or the disciplined behavior of the lead deer, this vital and intricate microcosm, which alone can keep the clan within reach of its seasonal sources of sustenance—all, indeed, that makes survival possible—would disintegrate.

Their foes are the wolf and the blizzard. Fuel shortage, famine, and winter gloom haunt them and weld their religious philosophy into a shield against the unpredictable factors of nature. Their ally is their heritage of experience, expressed in tools and methods developed ages ago out of the struggle with the Arctic wilderness.

That the end product of this ancient culture can be observed not many miles from great cities and universities is an anachronism that is surprising to all when they first learn of it. This remnant race, reminiscent of the Paleolithic era, is the only European group that allows us a glimpse of the time when the continent was largely covered by the Great Glacier and the only inhabitants were people of nature. Those Lapps who still push across the tundra in response to the changing seasons, in an environment resembling that of the Ice Age, are actually one of the most successful modern-day primitive groups insofar as they have been able to thrive adjacent to civilization. Of course, civilization is changing the traditional pattern of their lives, and the time is approaching when they may no longer retain much of what they originally were. Even today there are many who have abandoned the herder's way of life.

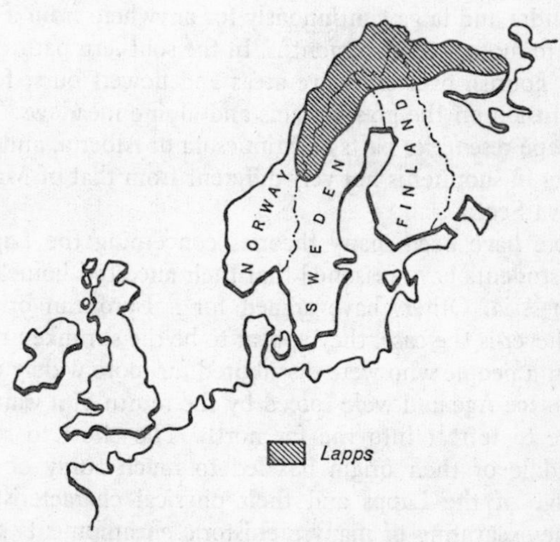

The Lapps can be seen by anyone who visits the region of North Cape, Norway, or travels a hundred miles north of the Arctic Circle in Sweden, as the writer did in 1956. They can also be found in northern Finland and the Kola Peninsula in Soviet territory.

Almost all of the typical Lapps live north of the Arctic Circle. Near the center of their domain (at Karesuando, Sweden) the temperature drops below minus 50 degrees Fahrenheit, and the extremes farther north are even more severe.

The reduction or lack of sunlight in these latitudes in winter adds to the hardship of life. Midway between the northern and southern extremes of their territory, the Lapps endure about a month without any sunlight, but there is good twilight during the greater part of each day. In the extreme north of Lapland, however, the sun is absent for about two months, and twilight bright enough to be of use in hunting and traveling is limited to a few hours each day.

In summer, prolonged sunlight makes up for the winter deficiency. In most of the Lapp territory, the sun circles the tundra and taiga continuously for anywhere from a few weeks to more than two months. In the southern part, evergreens flourish over extensive areas and flowers burst forth in profusion on the grassy plains and alpine meadows. The landscape resembles parts of Minnesota or Alberta, and the weather in summer is not very different from that of Maine or Nova Scotia.

There have been many theories concerning the Lapps. Some students have reasoned that their ancestral homeland was in Asia. Others have argued for a European origin. Whichever is the case, they appear to be the shrunken remnant of a people who were distributed far more widely during the Ice Age and were forced by the return of a warmer climate to retreat into the far north. The effort to solve this riddle of their origin has led to much study of the language of the Lapps and their physical characteristics, and the excavating of many prehistoric encampments scattered over Scandinavia and neighboring lands.

The Lapp tongue is classed with the Finno-Ugric, a family of languages spoken in northern Europe and northwestern Asia. Lappish, like Finnish, is even related to Hungarian, but the connection is actually no closer than that between, say, French and Greek. There are three separate dialects of Lappish–Eastern, Western, and Southern–as well as several subdialects, and the differences are so great that one Lapp sometimes cannot understand another.

Lappish has borrowed words from Norwegian, even from pre-Icelandic, and from Finnish and Russian. Racially, however, the Lapps do not resemble any of these people. Nor can we class them either with the Indo-European or Mongoloid divisions. They are the shortest people in Europe (the men average only about five feet three inches and the women some five inches less), whereas their European neighbors are among the tallest of peoples. The Lapps are also sharply distinguished from other inhabitants of Scandinavia by their broad heads. Their cephalic index (that is, the ratio between width and length of head) is extremely high, being 83.4, whereas that of the Swedes is a moderate 78.

We cannot link the Lapps to the always dark-eyed Mongoloid peoples of Asia because between 8 and 31 per cent of them have blue or gray eyes. They also lack the Mongoloid epicanthic fold, which gives the Oriental eye its slanted look; and about one-fourth of the Lapps have blond hair. Since we also cannot affiliate them elsewhere, it is perhaps best to regard them as a vestige of an ancient Arctic race of their own.

Some of the leading authorities believe that ancestors of the Lapps came from the region of the Ural Mountains. How they could have retained such a distinct racial character through long periods of contact with the Scandinavian peoples to the south and with the Finns, Russians, and others to the east, has not been easy to explain. But it seems probable that they invaded northern Europe at a time when the mountainous interior of Scandinavia was still covered by the Great Glacier. There is evidence that an ice-free corridor existed actually *north* of the main icecap, and the ancestors of the Lapps are supposed to have passed through this during the latter part of the Ice Age.

Herds of wild reindeer would have used this ice-free area, and the primitive hunters would therefore have found it to their liking. Some of the oldest Stone Age relics that archeologists have found in Scandinavia, representing what is called the Komsa culture, may have been left by these early Lapps. In this remote pocket, they could have remained isolated from the rest of mankind.

During the earliest stages of their cultural evolution, the Lapps were hunters and fishers, pursuing the herds of wild reindeer and killing them with lances or bows and arrows but not domesticating them. Just how long ago the herding of reindeer was developed, archeological evidence is not able to tell us. Animals closely related to the modern reindeer are known to have lived in various parts of Europe down to about two thousand years ago, although today they are found only on the northern fringe of the continent. The earliest references to the Lapps as engaged in the herding of reindeer comes from European travelers of the ninth century. We may therefore assume that at least by that time the Lapps had acquired the inventions on which the northern Eurasian reindeer culture is based.

Evidence that they have had their culture for a very long time can be found in their highly specialized vocabulary relating to reindeer-herding. About 300,000 reindeer are tended by the Lapps of Sweden alone today, yet they have a terminology that permits each of the 2800 herders to distinguish his own reindeer from all others in the land. Distinctions of age, sex, color, and form of antlers form the basis of identification. A reindeer in the general sense is called *potsoi*, a male is *sarves*, a castrated domesticated male is *hierke*, a male castrated but not trained is *svaljes*. A female is *vatjau*, a female that does not produce calves is *stainak*, and if she calves only rarely she is *rotno*. From birth to seven years of age, the reindeer changes its name every year. There are, furthermore, at least fifty terms to designate coloration, and another fifty for the formation of the antlers. In addition to knowing his deer by appearance, the Lapp protects them against theft by notching each animal's ears. Since both ears may be marked differently, the number of combinations is vast.

The earliest accounts extol the Lapps for their ability to pursue and kill animals. The northern Europeans who saw them were impressed by their hardihood in the wilderness and by their meat diet. "As soon as a woman gives birth," wrote Prokopios in 550 A.D., "she wraps the baby in fur and hangs it in a tree, puts a piece of marrow in its mouth, and goes hunting with her husband." To this day one can see a mother hang her cradle (*komse*) on a low branch as described.

There is evidence that the Lapps may have been familiar

with the use of skis from early times, for a specimen that may represent the original Lapp form has been dated by pollen analysis at from 1200 to 1500 B.C. First mention of the use of skis among them was made by the monk Paulus Dioconus in 780 A.D. He explains that the Nordic name by which the Lapps had apparently been known since 550 or earlier meant literally "the Skiing Finns." Their own name for themselves is Samer, and they have accepted the name Lapp (which is apparently of Finnish derivation and may mean something like "Land's-end Folk") only because it has been thrust upon them.

The 32,600 living Lapps include 8500 in Sweden, 20,000 in Norway, 2300 in Finland, and 1800 in the Soviet Union. They are estimated to have a total of 440,000 reindeer. The classic example of the Lapp reindeer culture is the so-called Mountain Lapps of Sweden, a somewhat misleading name in view of the fact that they migrate in winter to the lower lands near the Gulf of Bothnia. Their traditional dwelling is a portable tent of reindeer skin, and they have a more permanent hut of similar design covered with sod to keep out the cold. The tent is conical, with seven to twelve poles to support the skin covering. At the top is a rectangular smoke hole, which measures two or three feet on a side and is sometimes closed to conserve the heat. Compared with an Eskimo snow hut, this arrangement is exceedingly inefficient. At night the temperature in the Lapp hut approaches that of the outside, which is sometimes minus 60 degrees Fahrenheit; and even with robes of reindeer skin, conditions can hardly be called comfortable. If the smoke hole is closed, the tent fills with smoke; and even when it is open, the people sit on the floor where the air is more bearable. The floor is covered with birch twigs to make it warmer and drier for sleeping purposes. In many districts, plank or log cabins of a Scandinavian type have been adopted.

To preserve mobility, utensils are kept to a minimum. There is no furniture except the "travel box" and the cradle, which hangs from the ceiling. On the march and during the prolonged periods devoted to tending the reindeer, it is customary for the people to eat only cold food. Their principal meal is in the evening and consists mainly of a soup of meat or fish, cooked over a wood fire. The winter camps are chosen in terms of the availability of wood fuel. In the warmer season, some berries and other vegetable foods are eaten. Bone marrow is considered a special delicacy. The diet, like that of Eskimos, contains the vitamins necessary to prevent scurvy and other deficiency diseases. Their simplest method of storing meat out of reach of animals is to hang it from a tripod of forked poles. In permanent camps it is stored on wooden racks and in chests raised on platforms.

The nomadic clan is composed of from two to six families and is called a *sita* or *sijda*. It is under the leadership of the father who has the largest herd; and, as indicated earlier, the discipline of the entire mass of animals depends upon the behavior of the lead deer. When attacked by wolves, the Lapps pursue them on skis; in the old days they used to stab them, but now they use guns. A moderate-sized family will need three hundred deer, of which forty or fifty will be slaughtered each year.

After passing the winter in the lowland areas, the clan leaves the fringe of the forests and climbs to low mountain pastures in the interior. This migration occurs toward the end of April and constitutes one of the eight seasonal phases that mark the life of the true nomadic Lapps. These phases correspond to the four seasons and the four periods of movement between them. Only children up to five or six years of age are permitted to ride on the reindeer. The draft deer are hitched to the boat-shaped sleds by a trace that passes between the animal's hind legs. These sleds are unique among primitive peoples and are probably of ancient origin. One theory is that they were originally used as boats or were made by cutting a boat in two, and their shape certainly supports this theory. In the Northern Museum in Stockholm are specimens showing that in early times the Lapps made boats by lashing boards together with roots or sinew. In camp at night, the Spitz-like dogs, which have exhausted themselves keeping the deer in a herd, are given every consideration, even being allowed to crowd the people in the sleeping area.

In the spring camping place the cows have their calves. Then at the end of June, the nomads, leaving their winter equipment below, climb out of range of the heat and mosquitoes and make their way to mountainous districts near the Norwegian border, sometimes traveling as much as 150 miles from their wintering areas.

When August comes, the herders lead their reindeer back down to autumn camps, which are the same as or close to the ones occupied in spring. A famous one is at Vaisaluokta, which can be reached by a road and lake boat from Jokkmokk and Porjus. It is here that the reindeer pass the rutting season. When the snows of November make sledge travel possible, the caravan begins its journey down to the wintering grounds in the evergreen forests of the lowlands. The slaughter occurs from late autumn through the winter, because the temperature then permits preservation of the meat and the hides are in good condition.

In looking into the origin and development of reindeer-herding, we must remember that the trained male deer that forms the rallying point for the herd is the key to the whole reindeer culture. It is virtually impossible to manage the large herd during its elaborate seasonal maneuvers without the training that can be given only to altered males. The traditional Lapp method of altering the animals—crushing the testicles with the teeth—is widely used throughout Arctic Asia and is doubtless older than the knowledge of metal knives. We cannot assume that the Lapps originated the reindeer culture, for too many other large tribes in Siberia exhibit well-developed versions of it.

In its early stages, reindeer-herding must have been a loosely managed pursuit in which the people exercised little control over the animals. Perhaps they followed them with spears or bows and picked off animals, as needed, from the edge of the herd. The first "domestic" reindeer were probably fawns captured very young and raised more or less as pets, or wounded animals held in reserve against famine. In early times, the herds of the Lapps were probably much smaller than those we see today, for the current trend is toward larger and larger herds under the control of fewer herdsmen.

The lasso, which the reindeer Lapps use with great skill, could have developed naturally out of the effort to get a loop over the antlers of a wounded animal or of a mother deer that had come up close in order to protect her fawn. Today it is used principally in the corral, where animals have to be separated for breeding purposes and for marking. A good deal of trouble results from the intermingling of the herds during the year.

Certain features of Lapp reindeer-herding are perhaps of fairly recent development. The marking of the ears and the use of the corral may be modern; so may the milking of the deer and the making of reindeer cheese. Some or all such features of the Lapp reindeer-herding may have been borrowed from the cattle-herding peoples of Europe.

The weather is extremely important to the men who tend the reindeer, and with the aim of predicting and controlling the elements, the Lapps developed elaborate rites. So great has been their reputation in these arts that as early as 922, a man named Asur Tote sent his daughter Gunhild to live with the Lapps in order to learn witchcraft. A comet that appeared in the sixteenth century caused Ivan the Terrible of Russia to send for Lapp magicians to explain it. Even in fairly recent times, students of the Lapps have sometimes hesitated to express outright skepticism concerning the shaman's powers. The stories that are told of medicine men—for example, how they stop a flow of blood from a distance by throwing a stone into a lake—will probably receive support from the credulous for some time.

For predicting the future, the Lapp sorcerer (called a *naid* or *noide*) used a magic drum, oval in shape and divided into three or more areas representing the spirits of the sky, the earth, and man himself. These areas contained symbols that enabled the sorcerer to make predictions concerning almost every human problem. The designs were painted with saliva reddened with alder bark. The magician placed either a divining stick (*arpa*) or, more recently, a few links of copper chain on the drum. He then chanted as he beat the drum, and fell into a trance. Meanwhile, the "indicator" took a position on the symbols on the drum, and this was supposed to enable the magician to foretell the future.

Each social unit, or *sijda,* originally had its own place of worship. The chief objects with religious significance were stone idols shaped by nature and called *seite* or *seide.* The places where these objects were located were kept sacred down through the generations. There the medicine men would sacrifice animals or make offerings to ensure good hunting and fishing. If the ceremony failed, the sorcerers might whip the spirit-stone. More than one hundred sacred places of this sort have been located in Swedish Lapland alone, according to a map prepared by the small but distinguished museum in the town of Luleo in northern Sweden. The belief in *seides* still persists in secluded mountain districts. In the old days, many reindeer antlers were found around these primitive "altars." Some of the *seides* may originally have been strangely shaped pieces of wood, but there is little indication that the people actually carved them.

In addition to these sacred places, at which was concentrated the spiritual power of a given district, the Lapps believed in a host of nature spirits in the sun, wind, water, and similar phenomena. The chief deity seems to have been the "Thunder God." The Mountain Lapps, moreover, accepted the existence of personal guardian spirits that protected the individual from calamity. If mistreated, however, they might also lead him to destruction. In the Kola Peninsula we find the belief that each side of the family had its familiar spirits and that the son inherited his from his father, the daughter hers from her mother. These spirits resembled animals, and when one of them was seen in a dream, it was supposed to be an ill omen. Rival medicine men were said to send their spirits to fight against one another.

One of the other important deities was the Earth Mother, *Madar-ahkku*, who presided over the birth of every child and had important curative powers. Spirits, fairies, gnomes, giants, and goblins were also believed to haunt the home and the out-of-doors. One ogre that figured most prominently in the myths was the *stalo*, a tall, powerful being, part human and part devil. A *stalo* would, it was asserted, sometimes capture a Lapp girl for a wife or rouse a man from sleep and challenge him to fight for his life.

The Lapps believed that at death the spirit and the body were permanently separated; and a hut was often abandoned when a person had died in it. The Russian Lapps sometimes sacrificed a reindeer at the funeral so that it could accompany the soul of the deceased. They believed that the person's spirit flew to the afterworld for three days and then returned to visit with its reindeer all the places known in life.

They accounted for illnesses in three ways: those sent by the gods, which could not be cured; those sent by an individual, usually a sorcerer, which could sometimes be cured; and ordinary sicknesses, which were not fatal. Various vegetable potions, as well as amulets, were used against illness. Among the amulets were bear's teeth, the penal bones of the bear, a bracelet made of a tendon from the hind leg of a reindeer, and a rattle-like staff.

As among many other northern peoples, even as far to the east as Alaska, the bear was one of the most important ceremonial animals, and many beliefs and taboos were connected with it. According to the tales, men were believed to change into bears, wolves, reindeer, dogs, or other creatures. However, nothing survives in Lapp religion comparable to the bear ceremony of the Ainus.

The majority of the Lapps, whether they herd deer or not, make fishing an important pursuit. Even the herding

Lapps choose their summer encampments for their fishing opportunities. Other groups depend to such an extent on fishing that they are known as Fishing or Fisher Lapps. A well-to-do Lapp may own forty to fifty fishing nets of different sizes and purposes. Most Lapps also hunt small animals and birds as an incidental occupation. Ptarmigan and the large European grouse known as the capercaillie are among the important birds.

About one-fourth of the Swedish Lapps belong to the purely nomadic Mountain type. Another 8 per cent are Forest Lapps, who herd reindeer to some extent but are less nomadic. The rest are either Fishing Lapps or have adjusted themselves more or less to Scandinavian ways. Somewhat similar divisions exist in other parts of the Lapp country.

The original sinew-sewn clothing of fur has been strongly influenced by the fashions of medieval Europe through contact with Scandinavian peoples of that period. The Lapps weave artistic ribbons and belts by methods seemingly borrowed from the Norse people, but in aboriginal times they had no textile arts. During the historical epoch, they have also become skillful in working metal for ornamental purposes. They have even mastered a primitive way of making flat tin wire almost as fine as a horsehair, and embroidery with this thread is one of their specialties. The wire thread is made by drawing the tin through a hole in a piece of bone.

The position of women among the Lapps has always been relatively good. Girls marry at about the age of twenty, keeping their unmarried name and retaining possession of their reindeer and other property. The suitor is expected to give presents, and the newly married couple may live with the bride's parents for a year so that the young man can "earn" his bride. Infant mortality is high, and childless couples commonly adopt children.

Since the time when Europeans first glimpsed these remarkable little people, their fortunes have changed many times owing to political, economic, and perhaps even climatic factors. The earliest centuries of contact are obscure, but as we enter the era of written records, the relationship of the Lapps to the outside world becomes uniquely interesting. At times they have lent their energies to causes that must have seemed alien and puzzling to them. For example, armed with bows and arrows, they fought in the regiments of Gustav Adolphus in Germany during the Thirty Years' War in the seventeenth century. A little-known episode in their history occurred when they adapted their trained reindeer to commercial porterage. This took place when iron was discovered above the Arctic Circle near Gallivare in the early 1700's and no other practical method of transportation was available. One of the truly picturesque sights of history must have been the spectacle of Lapp herders leading their long trains of pack animals or reindeer sleds laden with iron ore into the cities of northern Scandinavia.

Generally considered to be a practical, friendly, and parsimonious people, the Lapps have seldom given their neighbors trouble. Many of them were at one time virtually enslaved to perform farm work, but through it all they showed great cultural vitality and resilience. Even as early as the seventeenth century, some of them were finding their way to the University of Upsala, and a number have attained higher degrees and distinguished themselves among educated men.

They were exposed quite early to Christianity, and although the pagan beliefs and practices lingered for a while in secret, these have now practically been eradicated. It is a loss to ethnographic science that their music was destroyed by the missionaries so early that we know almost nothing about it. A later wave of missionization, which changed the lives of the Lapps more radically, came around the middle of the last century and was led by a Lutheran, Lars Levi Laestadius. Boisterous expressions of religious ecstasy became characteristic of the Lapp services, and even today in some localities a church service that does not evoke public avowals is hardly regarded as a success. In an atmosphere of pious pandemonium, the people openly confess to adultery and reindeer thieving, and no one is embarrassed. A few moments later, all will be chatting quietly over a cup of coffee in their tents. The Lapps of the Kola Peninsula have been converted to the Russian Orthodox faith, and their regular services and marriage ceremonies are consequently quite different from those of other Lapps.

The Norwegian Lappish language was adapted to European characters two centuries ago, and despite dialectic differences, it is said now to be comprehensible to five-sixths of all Lapps. The Norwegian Lapps have written and printed their own newspaper for fifty years.

The Lapps enjoy reasonably good health and long life. Here and there across Arctic Sweden one encounters government-supported homes for aged Lapps. And in any of the northern towns, one may be treated to the sight of a gaily dressed reindeer-herder from the primitive past entering a hotel dining room.

He is lean and hungry, this little man out of the ancient wilderness. His face is lined and darkened by wind and cold. Reindeer curds and lean meat have kept his sinewy frame functioning under rigors most of mankind can hardly conceive of.

He is a man of two worlds—the primitive one of the timeless tundra, and that of Europe's northernmost villages where there is a market for meat and hides. He represents the successful amalgamation of two quite different cultures. He has, however, lost a great deal that was uniquely his.

But perhaps it is chiefly the visiting anthropologist, equipped to record primitive music on a high-fidelity machine, who regrets that it is too late to hear some of the tunes that Europe's last people of the Ice Age may have sung around their campfires.

art and culture. [illegible] to enter a cultured [illegible] women [illegible] sitting quietly over cups of coffee in their tents. The Lapps of the Kola [illegible] have been converted to the Russian Orthodox faith and their icons, candles and religious [illegible] quite different from that of other Lapps.

The Norwegian Lappish language was [illegible] to [illegible] several times, and despite [illegible] the [illegible] it is said now to be comprehensible to Swedish [illegible] Lapps. The Norwegian Lapps have written and printed their own [illegible] for [illegible].

The Lapps enjoy [illegible] good health and a long life [illegible] Arctic Sweden [illegible] homes for aged Lapps and [illegible] many of [illegible] The [illegible] to [illegible] [illegible] than [illegible] children [illegible]

[illegible] little [illegible] of the ancestral [illegible] and [illegible] by [illegible] and [illegible] have kept [illegible] from most of mankind [illegible]

[illegible] worlds—the primitive [illegible] the [illegible] where there is a [illegible] and [illegible] successful [illegible] of two quite different cultures. [illegible] however, [illegible] this [illegible] [illegible] perhaps [illegible] the [illegible] [illegible] that it is too late [illegible] [illegible] of the [illegible] [illegible] their [illegible]

SLAVE TRADERS OF AFRICA

The Ovimbundu

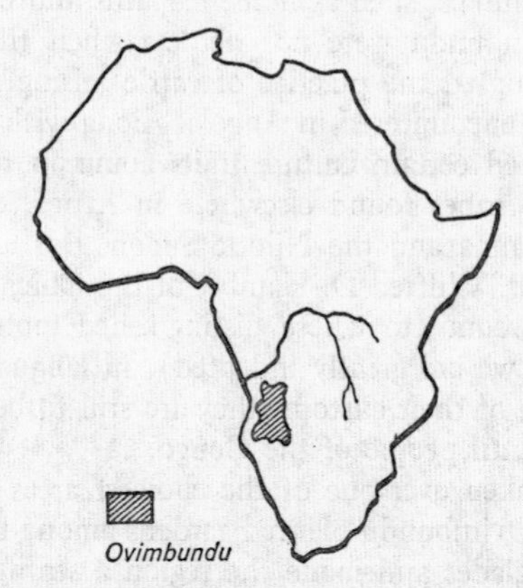

At the heart of the Negro slave trade in southwestern Africa was a tribe called the Ovimbundu. This tribe is estimated to have captured and traded more than three million slaves destined for the New World. A warlike, roving people, they left the Congo Basin shortly before the Portuguese discovered Angola in 1560, crossed several hundred miles of tropical wilderness and established a powerful federation of kings and chiefs in the Benguela Highlands of central Angola. They became the most celebrated caravan travelers in southern Africa. Today they number about a million and a quarter.

Their tribal name means "People of the Fog" and may refer to the mist-shrouded heights of their adopted homeland, so different from the tropical lowlands they had occupied. They are also called the Mbundu, though this word more properly refers to their language.

Since they restricted themselves almost entirely to lands about 5000 feet in elevation, their domain is like an island in the sky, surrounded by hot, arid grasslands and savannas.

The Ovimbundu were skillful hunters, and they found in the highlands and surrounding lands giant sable, kudu, and other kinds of antelope, as well as zebras, giraffes, ostriches, elephants, rhinoceros, and hippos. There were also predatory animals, such as lions, leopards and cheetahs.

The Ovimbundu were not herders when they arrived, but they adopted the practice of cattle raising from other people they encountered in Angola. Along with the cattle, they borrowed certain culture traits common to many of the pastoral tribes found elsewhere in Africa, even as far away as Uganda and the Nilotic Sudan. But as has been shown by Dr. Wilfred D. Hambly of the Chicago Natural History Museum (to whose distinguished monograph on this culture we are greatly indebted), in language and art and in most of their customs they are still to be identified with the Bantu people of the Congo.

Having taken over one of the choicest areas in western Africa, the Ovimbundu planted gardens among the wooded knolls and glades and made the region a stronghold from which to conduct raiding and trading expeditions into Northern Rhodesia and beyond. This pattern was probably well established in their culture more than three centuries ago. In time, the caravans of the Ovimbundu may have extended their operations as far as Lakes Tanganyika and Nyassa, 1500 miles to the east. They made use of a trading center that grew up midway across the continent, near Katanga in the southern Congo. Here traders congregated from as far away as Uganda, the basin of the Zambesi, and Zanzibar, and rich copper deposits were worked by the Swahili from East Africa.

Before every Ovimbundu caravan departed, a special ceremony was performed. The head of a former chief was taken from its sacred box and sprinkled with the blood of a sacrificed animal, while the living ruler asked the head of his predecessor for good luck on the journey. Then there was an appalling clamor as the porters raised their loads to their heads, each man uttering a deep grunt and his companions replying with equally deep groans. The men would carry sixty pounds on an average day's march of twenty-five miles, the women half as much. To enable the carrier to rest without lowering his load, it was tied in the fork formed by lashing two five-foot poles together along part of their length; when tired, the porter would bend forward and rest the butt end of the poles on the ground. The Ovimbundu carriers also developed a peculiar limping gait, believing that it prevented fatigue by momentarily allowing all the leg muscles to relax at once.

It was of course impossible to carry all the food that was necessary on these great journeys. The Ovimbundu therefore established truces with tribes along the way so that they would have opportunity to trade for provisions and be assured of safe passage. Nevertheless, warfare was common, and there was the added danger of becoming lost if they sought a new trail. In that event, the medicine man who accompanied each caravan would bring out a figurine of a woman wearing feathers on her back, kneel before it, and ask the way. The packers believed that the reply came from the figurine, but what they actually heard was the falsetto voice of the medicine man, who had plugged his nostrils to produce the effect.

It is said that the Ovimbundu made their tremendous journeys as much for the sheer excitement of it as for the hope of economic gain.

The first white men with whom they came in contact—Portuguese traders—were also motivated by a spirit of adventure. The Portuguese had entered the Congo as early as 1482, but a century passed before they met the Ovimbundu. In 1576 they founded the seacoast settlement of Luanda, opposite the northern edge of the Ovimbundu territory, and eleven years later built a fort at Benguela, 250 miles farther south along the coast. They then moved inland and by 1590 were making war in the interior. Ruined stone fortifications found at practically every strategic point in the Ovimbundu country were certainly used during the succeeding centuries in the wars between the

Portuguese and the natives, but they may have been built even earlier for intertribal fighting. By 1645, the Portuguese had penetrated to the very center of the Ovimbundu territory and had made commercial agreements with local chiefdoms. Their strategy included the forming of alliances with groups willing to assist in the subjugation of less amenable tribes.

Out of this grew a class of solitary traders who became the great adventurers of their day. Their name, *pombeiros descalcos* (combining the Angola word *pombe*, meaning "wilderness," with the Portuguese word for "barefoot"), signified a kind of advance guard that made contact with the natives. To reach the foot of the mountains from the coast, they had to cross a particularly arid desert and climb one of the most imposing escarpments in Africa. Once within the highland stronghold, the *pombeiros* would establish a trading relationship and exchange guns and liquor for slaves and ivory.

Any *pombiero* who happened to be in the capital of one of the dozen or so federated kingdoms of the Ovimbundu at the time of a king's death had a grisly tale to tell his comrades back at the coast. There was a chance, however, that he might not return, for any stranger might be suspected of having caused the death by witchcraft. So firmly did the people believe that one person could murder another by sorcery that it was customary to make a test for foul play whenever anyone died. One method was to suspend the corpse on a pole between two men and ask it questions. The manner in which the body swung was supposed to reveal the cause of death. When a king died, however, the people would not announce his passing at once, but would say that he was suffering from a cold. Everyone was aware that the situation was more serious, because the king's body was suspended from the neck in a hut. Each day, a specially chosen tribesman would twist a rope more tightly around the neck, so that the head was gradually severed from the body. In about a week, the body would fall into a basket beneath it and the tribe would then announce "The king is dead."

The body and the head were buried in separate places. Approximately a year later the people would dig up the head and place it in a box, where they could consult it, or, having reverently poured beer over it, ask it for favors. In order to learn what sacrifice the head wanted, they might sling it on a pole between two boys and ask it questions.

A medicine man was also entitled to special funeral rites. As he was being buried, other medicine men would dance about while tearing a live chicken apart and eating it.

In one part of the country, when a pregnant woman died, fear of the soul of the unborn child would cause the tribe to bury her with the point of a stake resting on her abdomen; when the grave had been filled with earth, the stake was driven through her body. Another method of allaying such a fear was to remove the foetus before burial.

A widow had to confront the corpse of her husband and say good-bye. Then she had to sleep for three nights with only a stick between her and it, presumably to permit the ghost to avenge any witchcraft she may have employed. It may have been some comfort to her that the corpse's thumbs and big toes had been tied together in order to restrict its influence. Great hunters were interred in tombs made of granite slabs, above which were placed the skulls or horns of animals.

The solitary trader learned to approach a native by clapping his hands and saying "*Kalunga* (greeting)," and, when receiving a gift, to hold out both hands, because otherwise a slur would be implied. He noticed that when a commoner approached a king, he bowed his head low and extended his hands, while clapping them and saying "*Chosi akuku*," which means "Lion grandfather." And he learned to bargain by means of a sign language invented by the Ovimbundu. A man could signify the absence of any object or the completion of an operation by rubbing his hands quickly together or drawing a finger across his mouth. He could indicate numbers by a system of finger signs quite different from anything familiar to Europeans. Those traders who acquired the spoken language could make themselves understood far and wide, for Mbundu became a lingua franca throughout the other 94 per cent of Angola.

The trader would be given lodging in the village community house. This consisted of a cone-shaped roof set on poles, without the usual walls of mud and wattle. It served also as a clubhouse where all the males over four years of age gathered for meals, the food being brought by the women from their kitchens. Here village affairs were discussed and criminals were brought to justice, and here the young learned everything from tribal history to etiquette.

The community house was usually near the king's compound, or, in a lesser settlement, the chief's. For each of his wives, the king had a separate house and kitchen. He also had a "spirit house," where he kept his insignia of office and prayed to the ancestral spirits. A favored guest might be lodged in this spirit house.

Only the hearty and reckless were likely to leave the comfort and security of Portugal to follow the career of *pombeiro*. Many of the barefoot traders died of malaria or other tropical diseases, or by violence. Some married into the native culture, but usually on its fringes. Native marital customs included an interesting procedure somewhat like the early American practice of bundling. The young man would send a friend to ask the girl's mother whether he could sleep with the girl each night in his hut. He would not be permitted to do this unless he had accumulated enough to be able to give gifts to the girl and make the betrothal payment.

The parents might give their daughter permission, but they would warn her not to let the boy become too intimate. If his advances became too ardent, she must run away from him, even in the dark. A couple enjoying such a relationship called each other *ombaisi*. And because the young man gave the girl a present, they would be looked upon as engaged. It is said that the purpose of this practice was to enable the couple to get to know each other better before marriage. As to how long the "bundling" might continue, we have little information.

If a girl had a child out of wedlock, it cost her a lack of status, and she would have to be satisfied with a second-rate wedding. The man concerned would be fined. To induce abortion the Ovimbundu used a certain root boiled in water, and they also sometimes resorted to mechanical means.

When courtship had been completed and the marriage was to take place, the youth prepared for his bride a hut in which both families feasted for three days. Each night the couple separated and went to their own quarters. Strangely enough, six unmarried girls and a married woman chosen by the bride passed these three nights in the new house provided by the husband. On the fourth day, the bride moved in bringing her own utensils, but for the first month she had to cook in the house of her husband's parents. If the husband found that he was not the first with his wife, he would burn a hole in her dress and send her back to her parents to collect a fine for him.

After a month of married life, a man's mother customarily invited three old women who had been happily married to lay the hearthstones in the new home. A chicken was then killed and its blood was sprinkled on the hearth. Sometimes a husband and wife would "exchange blood" in secret as a strengthening of the marital bond. They then believed that they would both die at the same time.

Whenever a man wanted to speak to his mother-in-law, he had to stand back-to-back with her; and if he met either of his wife's parents on the trail, he had to step aside and face the other way.

Married people were not supposed to call each other by name, and after the birth of their first child they would be referred to as "the father of so-and-so" or "the mother of so-and-so." A woman slow to become pregnant would sometimes allow herself to be covered with mud on a special mound near a river, while the medicine man sang songs and administered potions. Babies were named for close relatives, living or dead. The name was supposed to have spiritual power and was the property of the family, but if a person had continual bad luck or illness, he might change his name.

After a quarrel, a wife could give her husband an opportunity to patch things up by going into the bush and returning with many burs sticking to her clothes; if her husband removed them, peace would be restored. Adultery was punished by a fine of two oxen, a pig and a slave; and if the offended man were a king, the rival might be castrated.

Even talking too much might be considered grounds for divorce among the Ovimbundu. Then, in the presence of the village headman, the wife's father would give the husband a roll of tobacco and a pig as compensation. The husband would place leaves and palm oil on his wife's back, slap her from behind, and say, "It is finished."

Wealthy men, as well as chiefs, might have more than one wife. In that case, the husband is said to have slept regularly with each wife for either four or seven consecutive nights. Some kings are known to have had as many as twelve wives, with apparently little conflict among the women. But the great majority of the men had only one wife. Instances of homosexuality were known, and some men insisted on dressing as women.

A king's first duty was to hold a great feast, at which the flesh of a specially fattened slave was served. He would then undertake a military campaign, since profitable warfare was necessary to provide his court with tribute and his warriors with plunder. It was also the king's duty to make agreements with other kings and promote trade. A young king might accompany his fighters to war, but there was also a permanent war leader, called a *Kesongo*, who might come from the slave class and thus be an outsider. The *Kesongo* could not meet the king face to face except on certain state occasions, and he had to follow the strategy laid down by a council of village chiefs.

The kings of the Ovimbundu sometimes fought each

other. The defeated group would be made to pay taxes, and their women and cattle would be taken. Beyond their borders to the east, the greatest enemy of the Ovimbundu were the Vachokue, a warlike hunting people who did little farming and kept no cattle at all. These people made a practice of plundering the caravans of the Ovimbundu as the latter returned with slaves from Rhodesia.

Before the Portuguese introduced guns in about 1680, the Ovimbundu fought with spears made of iron. They seem to have brought the knowledge of ironworking with them to the Benguela Highlands. They drew upon surface deposits, as do a number of other ironworking tribes of Africa, and heated the metal in a forge. They used a bellows made of a pair of loose leather "drumheads" which were pumped up and down with sticks to produce the draft. They would then hammer the red-hot iron into spears, arrowheads, hoes, and other implements.

A young man who wanted to become a blacksmith had to serve under an experienced smith for two years. Then, at about the age of twenty, he would be inducted ceremonially into the craft, and his teacher would make his tools for him. The hammer was the most important, and while it was being made, the young man stood on the anvil. Various animals were sacrificed and their blood poured over the new implements. The youth was then given a new name, and the assembled people clapped their hands as he stepped down from the anvil, an authorized blacksmith.

Unless a village was located on a steep slope, its form would be circular, and near the center there would be a specially prepared dancing ground where ceremonies were performed. The Ovimbundu won recognition for their music and dancing; and the magnitude of some of their ceremonies can be imagined when it is realized that their villages in the old days numbered as many as 5000 inhabitants. Three-fourths of the dancing was connected with religious ceremonies, such as rain-making, funeral rites, and harvest observances. At times, the people danced the greater part of the night for several nights, the mood varying from pathos to ribaldry. A long tubular drum, held between the knees and beaten in compound rhythm, was the most important instrument. The dancers wore rattles of seed pods and used other kinds of rattles and friction instruments to produce rasping or buzzing sounds. They also played a stringed instrument in the form of an ordinary bow, the string of which was plucked or tapped. Resonance was imparted by holding one end of the bow in the mouth and placing a hollow gourd near the string. The pitch was modified by pressure on the string.

Horrifying as some of their ceremonies were, the Ovimbundu made a high art of conversation; and the early traders had to admire their powers of expression. They had a rich fund of proverbs and a varied folklore; and the discussions that took place nightly in the community house after the evening meal revealed a culture with strong social and intellectual roots.

Their art also has commanded respect. Distinctively engraved gourds, incised with geometric designs and with realistic or semirealistic human scenes are a favorite form of artistic expression among the Ovimbundu. Especially noteworthy are their wood carvings of figurines with elongated torsos and partly bent knees. Mission influence has suppressed much Ovimbundu art because of its relation to their original religion. And as elsewhere in Africa the style has been Europeanized in other ways.

For almost two centuries, the culture of the Ovimbundu was influenced more by South America than by Europe. From 1677 to 1845, in fact, the Catholic Church included Angola in the archdiocese of Bahia, Brazil. Contact with Portugal dwindled, and a lively trade grew up across the narrow part of the Atlantic. Soon many of the chief crops of the Ovimbundu were no longer African, or even European, but American: maize (Indian corn), manioc (including the "bitter" or poisonous variety), squash, tomatoes, sweet potatoes, peanuts, papayas, and guavas. The rum with which the slaves were purchased was largely distilled in Brazil, and the Portuguese word for it, *cachaça*, was borrowed by the Ovimbundu, in the form *ochasa,* for the beer they make with honey.

Thus the federated kingdoms of the Benguela Highlands grew strong and rich, funneling slaves from the interior to the seaports of Luanda, Lobito, and Benguela. The Ovimbundu had probably practised slavery for a long time before the arrival of Europeans. It was quite common for a man in debt to clear his obligations by submitting to slavery, or as more often happened, requiring his sister's children to serve in his place. Some of the slaves taken in war were trained to serve in the king's household, and were able to reach high positions there; in fact, certain of the king's ministers always came from this class.

In 1799, one of the kings dominated 2056 villages, another 900. Members of a king's family might rule subdivisions (called *atambu*) comprising from 3 to 300 villages. Each king collected taxes through his chiefs. A king was regarded as a divine representative, an incarnation. The more powerful of them had elaborate, though primitive, establishments. There was a council, however, that could dispose of an unpopular king, and it was the duty of the councils to elect chiefs of villages or groups of villages.

The king's duties included the performance of ceremonies, such as those connected with rain-making and with sacrifices. The queen's special duty was to treat ceremonially the sacred seeds distributed and mixed with each granary to ensure abundance. In former times, her kitchen was sanctified by human sacrifice to guarantee the food supply. The children of a king were able to trace their ancestry for many generations through both the father's and mother's line.

The peak of Ovimbundu prosperity probably culminated, as did the "Golden Era" of the Slave Trade, about 1825. The Portuguese had by no means been the sole participants: ninety ships of Liverpool registry are known to have left the port of Luanda alone. In earlier eras, even the Church participated in the slave trade. According to the missionary Gladwyn Murray Childs, the Jesuits employed three of their own ships continuously during a period when slaves constituted four-fifths of the value of all exports. Amid the widespread brutality of those days, it required courageous work on the part of many individuals to bring about the abolition of the slave trade in Angola. But the law that forbade it was passed twenty-seven years before the Emancipation Proclamation.

Trading in slaves continued illegally for some time. But gradually the caravans began to specialize in ivory, rubber, beeswax, and other products. A new era was dawning for the Ovimbundu, as for the rest of Africa.

The Protestant missions began their work in the Benguela Highlands in 1881 and in the following decades extended their influence energetically. In regions where they had stations they abolished polygamy, cannibalism, and various religious rites. Modern medical practices began to challenge the ancient arts of the witch doctor. The traditional Ovimbundu version of bundling, chaste though it may have been, was misinterpreted as "trial marriage" and condemned; and the young people, becoming more sophisticated through travel, entered a period of relaxed premarital relations.

The main railway line, which now connects the seacoast with Katanga in the Congo, cuts through the very heart of the Ovimbundu kingdom. Along this line and its feeder highways, mission influence has extended to almost all corners of the Ovimbundu domain. The caravan trains have become a thing of the past. Regions that only a short time ago were primitive wilderness, now echo day and night to the roar of trains that carry in a single load as much freight as could 13,000 of Africa's best porters. Yet beliefs that have been the warp and woof of tribal life die hard, and a people's pattern of thought has deep roots in their cultural past. The proverbs and legends of the Ovimbundu are still part of their philosophy, and the old men like to tell stories of the gory and glorious past. In out-of-the-way places, many superstitions linger on. As late as 1930 cannibalism was reported among the Vasele living just to the northwest of the Ovimbundu. The last authority on many ills and omens is still the witch doctor. And who knows when his "medicine kit" may not contain, along with some goat's fat and charcoal, a piece of human leg bone, ceremoniously exhumed as of old.

A PEOPLE OF THE SOUTH AFRICAN DESERTS

The Bushmen

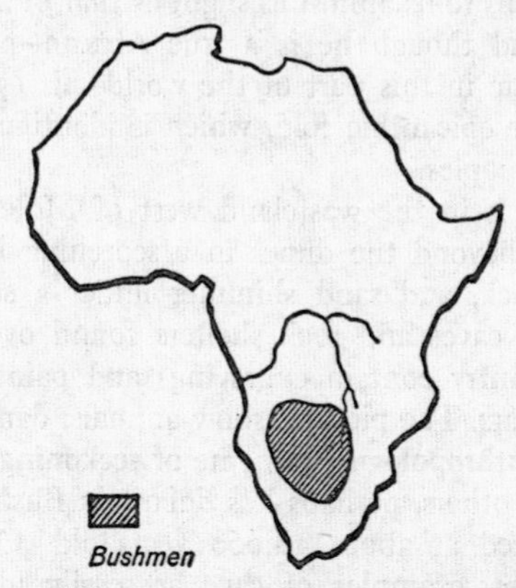

The wrinkled little man one meets at a waystop between Mafeking and Bulawayo is straight in from the desert, and if he has kept away from outside influences, he lives much as did his ancestors ten thousand years ago. He does not know how to plant a seed, and he cannot tend a herd. His people are among the few on earth who live wholly by hunting and gathering wild foods. They are almost constantly on the move and possess no more than they can carry. They depend for their survival on tools and implements that originated in the Stone Age.

At one time the Bushmen extended over a large area, but they are now confined to certain parts of the Kalahari Desert and adjacent regions. They number between 10,000 and 30,000, and four divisions of them are recognized: the Northern, the Central, the Southern, and outlying groups.

The Bushman's dingy, yellow-brown body is gritty with the ashes of the campfires beside which he has slept. His blackish eyes are deep-set beneath prominent brows in a puckered triangle of a face. His frizzy hair is tight-drawn in "peppercorns," and his parchment skin, shriveled by sun and drought, shields his bones like a lizard's.

Some of his womenfolk show the protuberant fatty development of the buttocks known as steatopygia. His own physique seems to us almost as slight as that of a preadolescent girl. And though he is a true African—perhaps the basic aborigine in this part of the world—his eyelids show a trace of the epicanthic fold, which is identified with the Mongoloid peoples.

His home is in the wasteland west of Molepolole and Serowe, out beyond the dunes in a scorching land where red earth, rock, and sand shimmer under a searing sky. Hundreds of caves and rock shelters found over the surrounding country contain engravings and paintings made by his forebears. The pictures show animals, dancers, hunters. In the anthropologist's scheme of reckoning, many are fairly recent; others, perhaps less definitely Bushman, have been estimated at about 12,000 years old. Outside the Bushman area, examples of cave art easily identified as sharing a common origin with those of the Bushmen have been found as far away as Tanganyika and even North Africa and Europe.

A distinctive and prominent figure in some of the Bushman cave frescoes is a grotesque, spindly creature, part human and part insect, known as a mantis man. Modern Bushmen regard the mantis spirit, Kang or Kaggan, as a gifted and mischievous deity, and he is the favorite hero of their folklore. Thus we have an instance wherein the mute testimony of archeology yields knowledge concerning an abstract concept in prehistoric thought. If the pictographs of the mantis man prove to be very old, this evidence of a prehistoric spiritual concept continuing into the living present will be among the most remarkable in the whole of archeology.

Another interesting aspect of Bushman cave art is that it indicates that the ancient hunters had better perception of how an animal runs than many latter-day artists. The Bushmen depicted the galloping animal with all four of its legs in the proper position, whereas civilized artists persisted in portraying the "flying gallop" (all four hoofs off the ground and in a relationship not true to nature) until photography revealed their error.

On the basis of his skull and other features, the Bushman has been described as a combination of at least two human strains. He seems to derive some features from the prehistoric Boskop man (whose head was larger but otherwise somewhat similar to the Bushman's) and the Negrito, that small dark stock, apparently very ancient, that today survives in scattered localities as far east as the Malay Peninsula and the Philippines.

No one enjoys a greater reputation than the Bushman for skill in tracking animals with such a simple hunting kit. With only a skin *kaross* thrown over his shoulder, a bow, and a row of poisoned arrow points stuck under his leather headband, he can survive under well-nigh unbearable conditions of dearth and drought. He roams unchallenged in the most inhospitable regions away from the rail line skirting the eastern fringe of the Kalahari and beyond the Ngami Road, where his people have long led thirsty white travelers to the scattered water holes. A few of his more conservative clansmen still have little contact with outside life today.

We shall call our typical Bushman !Kun, for that is his word for "man." The exclamation point at the beginning is the symbol for one of the several clicking sounds in his speech. We sometimes approximate such sounds when we urge a horse forward or try to clear a foreign object from the throat or when expressing shocked surprise or disapproval. Other sounds that he uses in recounting his legends have never been given symbols. These clicks impart to his speaking voice a staccato quality. !Kun repeats his nouns in order to form plurals, and he gives the same word three different pitches to convey three totally different meanings; for example, *ka* when high-pitched means "to eat," when moderately pitched means "to deprive," and when low-pitched means "to gush like a fountain." He uses the same word for "he," "she," and "it," but uses completely different words for the male and female of every animal he knows.

He is restless to go his way. Offer him some tobacco and perhaps he will tarry until an interpreter can be found. Note how he mixes the tobacco with some of his native narcotic *dagga,* the hemp known botanically as *Leonotis leonurus*. Now he makes a little hole in the ground and puts the mixture into it. From around his neck he takes a bone pipe tube and puts it into a little tunnel that leads to his "pipe bowl." He twirls his fire stick in a socket of wood with dry bits of fuzz from a bird's nest, and soon he has fire. He puts his mouth to the ground and draws the smoke into his lungs and coughs. When a native who knows his tongue and ours asks him a question, he strains his memory in silence; then the words flow from his mouth in an explosive chatter.

Through many such interviews, particularly with elderly Bushmen who know more of the old life, anthropologists have amassed enough facts to enable us to recreate the life of these curious people.

Vivid among our typical Bushman's early memories are the anxious moments before his puberty initiation—the threat of mysteries too awesome for women and children, and the dread of the pain of circumcision. Even before he has reached this crisis, the elders have let !Kun know that intercourse with the opposite sex before his operation—or before a somewhat comparable one for the girls—would be equivalent to allying himself with the lower animals. So, as the urges of adolescence come over him, the tension grows.

Some have died under the rigors of the initiation, but if he survives it, !Kun will be free to court the girls. After their initiation, the girls will suffer few restrictions on their conduct until they are married. After that their comportment will be strictly governed, and no woman other than !Kun's wife will sit beside him in camp. His people speak openly about the intimacies of marriage, and young men and women are not left in the dark concerning such matters.

!Kun knows no bed from birth to death. He sleeps on the hard ground at the fireside or on a little grass just inside the tiny circular or semicircular shelter that is his only home.

In advance of his initiation, he receives arduous training in hunting from the older men, all of whom are sinewy from long inurement to the chase, and they do not spare the adolescent. When an animal is struck with a poisoned arrow, they may have to pursue it for two days or more before the poison takes effect. During this time they snatch brief sleep, are hungry and often chilled to the bone.

On these forays !Kun learns not to trust rock shelters, much as his ancestors may have liked them, for caves are likely to invite attack by lions or leopards. Once, even with a fire burning at night, he saw a lion carry off his younger brother in the moonlight. His father taught him how to cut the center of a thick thornbush and bend the branches together to make a safe sleeping place, or to pick a spot near a tree into which he could climb in case of danger. He learned always to make sure there were no snakes in the tree, for some of his clansmen had been killed in that way. When danger was especially great, he and his father often slept the whole night in a tree, wedged among the branches.

Once when they were with two other families away from the main body of the clan, !Kun learned a lesson on the cost of carelessness and the value of knowing how to make poison. The lightweight, three-foot arrows were of no use without the poison, but because !Kun's father was one of their best makers of poison, no one foresaw the need. They had found a place where springbok were abundant, and they were looking forward to an interlude of ease and plenty. !Kun's father had two of the half-dozen or so plants that were used in different combinations in the preparation of the poison, but he wanted the poison bag of a cobra. Seeing a cobra disappear into a hole, he fixed a hook on the end of four reeds that he had tied together and pulled the serpent out. Then in the approved manner he began dragging it about rapidly, while the women and children tried to strike it with their knobkerries and spears. But he became careless and dragged the snake into the grass, and it escaped. The next moment he let out a cry of pain; he had been struck. !Kun's people had been using the poison for countless generations, but they had no way to counteract it, and his father, his face twisted in pain, died before the sun had moved more than a little.

They tied him knees to chest and pushed him into a hollow dug in a termite nest, laying him on his left side, facing east. They put his wallet and other things beside him and leaned his long spear against a bush nearby. !Kun's people had no problems of property inheritance, because what they carried they needed in the next life and there were no other belongings. In this emergency they could not leave the dead man any food or water. Hunger and thirst kept them from pausing to paint red and white stripes on his body. So they said "*Tabete*" (good-bye) and hurried away from the unpleasant spot, never to visit it again.

The bereavement gave !Kun a deep respect both for the potency and danger of poison and for its importance to survival. For now there were gazelles in abundance but no way to capture them. The women and small children were sent out to scour the land for roots, bulbs, and other plant bits, while !Kun went with the two older men, tracking the animals on the off chance of finding a weak or injured straggler.

The search failed, but just as all appeared lost, !Kun's sharp eyesight turned their fortunes. In the middle of the second day he detected the tiny clue that saved them, a mark in the clay at the entrance to an abandoned den of an ant bear. He crouched for hours motionless in the hot sun, with his arms ready to seize the steinbok that he knew must eventually emerge. Finally it did, and with one blow of his knobkerrie he crushed its skull.

They ate and were able to rejoin their clan. The elders praised him for having saved the group and told him that he needed only a few moons more of hunting training before he would be initiated.

After that experience, !Kun never let himself be caught without poison. Scorpions, spiders, and puff adders were good for the making of it, but most desirable of all was the pupating insect they called *nga* (known scientifically as *Diamphidia simplex*). Weak poison would be used for small animals; strong, fresh-smelling poison, double dipped, for an ostrich or giraffe or to make a lion tear up the ground and grow weak to the point where it could be knifed or speared. It had been a hard year, but soon a few spasmodic rainstorms might be expected, and they could then dig up the valuable insects on the ground under the branch ends of the marurie-papierie bush (*Commiphora dinteri engl.*); it was on the leaves of this bush that the caterpillars grew fat before dropping down and burrowing to arm's length into the ground.

At the right moment all hands were busy digging them out, and basketfuls of the poisonous pupae were gathered. Some would be used fresh by squeezing the entrails directly onto an arrow point. Others would be dried and rolled up in a skin, later to be ground to a powder in the hollow part of the neckbone of a giraffe, then mixed with the roasted-out juice of the mozana tree. !Kun learned to put the gummy poison into a special grooved stone and then roll the arrow point in the stuff, always making sure not to get any on his hands, under his nails, or especially in his eyes. Once, when some white men molested the women and were driven off, one of his clan sent an arrow into a white man's neck. Their scouts hid near the white man's camp and saw the wounded man die in great pain scarcely a day later.

Because !Kun had saved his group by capturing the steinbok, he had only to kill one more animal before being initiated. It was the beginning of the season of occasional rains. The women were therefore catching basketfuls of winged termites. Close to the projecting nest they would dig a hole in the ground, using their digging sticks, made by thrusting a length of wood through a hole in a four-inch disk of stone. The stone gave the necessary weight for jabbing the stick into the earth. Then, just as the termites were ready to emerge, they would cut away the nest and catch them when they fell into the hole below. They also dug edible roots with the digging stick, and it was the season for gathering wild *tsama* melons to cook in hot ashes under sand in a hole in the ground. A few thunderstorms in the higher country had put some water in the "pans," attracting thirsty antelope. The men would never make camp near one of these water holes for fear of frightening the animals away. But each day they would crawl upwind toward the water, concealing themselves behind camouflage made of the branches of bushes. It required much patience, and !Kun was soon rewarded with success. When he carried his animal back to camp, the women stopped their work to praise him.

And so the dreaded day arrived when !Kun and several other twelve-year-olds from related clans were marched into a secret camp, where for one whole moon they were kept secluded for the puberty ordeals.

They subsisted on roots and berries, and they danced much of the night. The older men taught them about the tribal deities and the mysteries of reproduction. On their ankles some wore rattles made of the husks of wild beans or dried moth cocoons. In one dance they decked themselves out in ostrich plumes; in another they wore the head and beak of a white stork as a head ornament. The boys learned to join in the dances, grunting "honk-a-honk," and the music of the reed flutes was much slower and more solemn than they had ever heard; nor did anyone fall into fits as sometimes happened in the dance games around camp.

!Kun had heard of another group of his people where the men made an incision straight up between the eyebrows of the boys at such a time and kept it open by rubbing powdered roots in it while it healed. Instead, like most other Bushmen boys, he and his partners faced the more frightening operation of circumcision. The elders of the tribe believed it to be a very ancient rite. A new knife had to be made for the operation, and then buried. !Kun sat with his legs apart, and the older men held him so that he could not move. Some of the boys fainted, though the single stroke of the knife was swift. But !Kun did not flinch or cry out.

When at last the puberty ceremonies were concluded, and they rejoined the women, he felt as though he had grown a great deal.

!Kun was not told what the girls were going through at this time—a less severe operation also performed with a stone knife—nor did he know until much later. But there were whisperings about the Eland Bull Dance, which was held for each girl at the time of her first period. From among the men of the clan two grandfathers were selected to don eland's horns and hide in the grass. Then, when the dance reached a certain stage and the performance had become a suggestive one, the men came out and joined in the movements, jogging along in a humped-over position. Each night during this time the girl would witness this dance, and during the day she would be kept in a special hut attended only by women. No man was allowed near her.

!Kun could not marry a girl bearing his own totem name, but there was a girl in a neighboring band whom he wanted. When he heard that she was going through these ceremonies, he had a feeling of emotional urgency. He knew that soon she would be permitted to do as she pleased, and he might then lose her to another boy.

Before his initiation !Kun had enjoyed the moonlight dances and drama-games, and he even took part in some. Many of them enacted episodes from tribal myths. The dancers impersonated snakes, four-footed animals, and other creatures. A frequent theme was the shortage of water and the struggle to gain possession of a pool. Most of these story-dances were of interest to young and old, but one dance took on a special meaning for !Kun after he had undergone his initiation and become a man. On a clear bright night, the girls would begin clapping their hands and singing. Some of the men would then begin dancing in front of them as though courting them. The men would dance closer and closer, holding out their arms but never touching the girls. Sometimes one of the girls would leave her line and dance around beside one of the men. When !Kun was thus chosen, he would dance as he had seen the others do, paying attention to the girl and showing his desire by gesture. When he did this, holding his hands out as though to take her in his arms, he thought of the girl of his choice. His desire was stronger when she appeared at his camp with a trading party, wearing around her eyes the red paint that showed she had completed her growing-up rituals and was looking for a mate.

That night the girls played formally at getting captured as wives. Other girls pretended to be the bridegrooms, but this scarcely lessened the excitement or made it less clearly a reminder that a "real" marriage involved some violence, either from the mother-in-law or from the girl's menfolk. Between friendly clans the struggle might be largely symbolic, but when a man captured a wife from a group so distant that they genuinely sought to prevent abduction, it was a more serious matter. Some of !Kun's tribesmen, on the other hand, had simply eloped with a girl and moved elsewhere, but this was not the conventional way.

So !Kun sought the opportunity to kill one of the larger animals singlehanded in order to be able to lay it at the feet of the girl's father as a bride-price and proof of his ability to feed and clothe her. He trekked off with the older men day after day, helping them dig pitfalls at the shrinking water holes, V-shaped trenches large enough to hold any animal smaller than an elephant and covered over with branches and grass. But the rains had been poor this season, and the traps remained useful for only a short time.

For ostriches they made slip nooses baited with a small *tsama* melon, so that when the bird swallowed the food, the noose would go tight around its neck and quickly choke it. In seeking honey, !Kun learned to tell by the weight of a bee in flight whether it was flying to the nest or away from it. He learned how to approach an ostrich nest upwind and use a long stick to take out one egg at a time so the bird would not stop laying; and when he found a nest with a stick planted beside it, he learned to respect it as the property of another group. He could now tell from the tracks of a herd if one animal had been only slightly wounded, so that if they scattered he could pursue the faltering one until it fell. He learned how to attract the mother animal by imitating the cry that would be made by her wounded young. And sometimes, out on the veld, he would use a stick in the shape of an ostrich neck to work his way within arrow range of a flock. But once the cock attacked him as if he were a rival bird, and !Kun was able to escape only by fleeing as fast as he could.

His impatience to be off hunting by himself made this a year of friction for !Kun. He was sure he knew the trails through the dried marshes, but his elders insisted that he stay with them. They skirted the muddy fringe of a shriveled lake, avoiding the sticky blue-black muck, and reached a pock-marked flat where the hoofs of animals had dimpled the mud around a dried-out pan. Some seasons there had been enough water here for them to put euphorbia branches into the pond and weight them down with stones so that the scum from their juice would poison the zebras that came to drink. Now only the deeper hoofprints held a little muddy water, and the men took out their drinking tubes made of hollow reeds and sucked up every bit of it. !Kun had heard of other Bushmen over in Namaqualand who had sometimes found herds as numerous as a large swarm of insects and had driven the animals over a cliff and killed them all. There were also rumors that up north at Okavango the kudu, gemsbok, blesbok, wildebeeste, buffalo, and zebra were abundant. But men dared not venture out of their own territory for fear of risking war.

Now they were in the worst part of the year, the season of dry, spasmodic winds. The air would remain motionless until mirages appeared around the sky line, frightening the people, and the heat was suffocating. Then there would be a distant roaring sound, and a whirling dust storm would sweep across the desert, blotting out the sky line, the sun itself and finally one's own feet. Their legs burned with the wind-driven sand and dust. Torrid daytime heat was followed at night by piercing cold, for the temperature sometimes fell almost to freezing on this three-thousand-foot desert plateau. For ten months they might not see a drop of rain. Fuel was hard to find, and they had to sleep so close to the tiny fire that a shift of wind often burned them badly.

Everyone dreamed of the first flash of lightning that would break this monotony of stifling heat, dust, and thirst. Then the bulbs and the berries and orchid roots would grow, and the water holes would fill. Now there was only a thin trickle at the most dependable seepages, and they dared not hunt more than a few days away from them. The old man who was a witch doctor repeatedly threw down the divining bones—four pieces made from the hoofs of animals and decorated with dots and lines. But the bones only gave the same wrong answers, again and again, until the witch doctor feared for his reputation.

!Kun never stopped hoping he might make a kill and take his bride. Finally he sighted a full-grown male kudu. The others said it was too far from water, but he gained permission to follow it, and he tracked it till dark. After a sleepless night beside a fire of a few crackling twigs, he picked up its track at dawn and within a few hours was within belly-crawl or quick dash. He paused, reversed the point of his arrow, which had been turned into the socket to protects its poison. He sniffed the death-dealing varnish on it to make sure it was still fresh enough, and fitted the featherless shaft to the bowstring. A quick, crouching dash took him to within fifty paces. With lightning speed he took aim, and the fragile shaft flew through the air. The animal gave a start; the shaft broke and fell to the ground. The kudu's flesh twitched high on its neck, and !Kun knew that the blade had penetrated where neither tail nor hoof was likely to dislodge it. The animal wandered on in the direction it had been going. Hours might pass before it felt the pain or showed the paralysis that would surely overcome it.

!Kun did not now want the kudu to die quickly. He had the problem of getting it back to camp. Still crouching, he let a fine stream of dust fall in the almost breathless air to confirm earlier readings of the wind. His camp and that of his girl's people lay almost downwind, a difficult direction in which to urge the animal, but while it still remained vigorous he must not risk putting it to flight. He chose his course, a rather circuitous one for the sake of safety, and began the long, slow pursuit. He might have to travel thirty or forty miles, urging it forward on its dying legs. And he knew that all the while his hunger and thirst would tempt him to make a quick kill. He was too far from the others to use a smoke signal to show them where he was.

Through the heat of the day and into the dim light of evening he tracked his animal, curbing its frequent attempts to stray and remaining ever ready with a second arrow. Before darkness the poison began to show in the animal's gait, and he dared to press it harder. Now, with the poison working, every mile would count. There was a half moon high in the sky, and he kept on, never looking at it, however, for that would lessen his chances of making the final kill. Close enough to keep in sight of the wounded animal, far enough from it not to cause it to panic and hasten the paralysis, he continued to bend its path toward the encampment where he hoped to find his mate.

Late one morning he saw smoke in the distance. The last few miles were less crucial, but by now his pride had a fine edge on it. So he withheld his hunting knife from the animal's neck until he could hear the voices from his girl's camp. Then he drove it into the kudu's jugular vein, skinned the animal, and packed the skin in a netting bag.

The sun was a little past the top of the sky when he walked into the encampment and said "*Kum bara,*" which is Bushman for "Good morning," though it literally means "I salute the fathers."

Several at once said, "*Cha nam kho?*" (Where do you come from?). !Kun answered in a few syllables and put the kudu skin at the feet of the old man, adding, "There is meat out there."

Silence would mean that the girl's father rejected him. !Kun waited as countless thousands of other young Bushmen had waited in a turmoil of hunger, fatigue, and frustration. And then the father spoke: "We did not see your smoke."

"No signal is needed when one can smell the meat," said !Kun, and the old man's smile told that he knew the boy had been skillful enough to bring the animal into camp. He formally accepted the skin and then, to !Kun's surprise, said, "We are well provided. Make a kaross of it for her."

It remained, however, for !Kun to take her by force because the Bushman word for marriage means "to catch." She would be expected to show resistance. Also, her menfolk would try to hold her, if for no other reason than to flatter her and show the value they put on her. When !Kun took her arm, her brothers and cousins fell upon him with a shower of blows from their knobkerries. These he had to elude or endure, else he would lose the girl. Should she free herself, it might mean that she really did not want him. Once she almost succeeded in doing so, but when he threw an arm around her, he felt her yield and knew that he had won the struggle.

Over the carcass of the kudu !Kun said an invocation to the mantis deity for his success, and then the meat was carried into camp. He permitted one of the old wizards to tattoo a stripe on his forehead and rub the ashes from a bit of the kudu's foreleg into the cut. This would help him see sharply in future hunts.

At the feast his bride wore around her brow and hanging from her neck all the ostrich-shell disks she owned. She also wore a necklace of animal's teeth, among which was a cowrie shell (very rare so far inland) and a shriveled root from a magical herb. Her thighs and buttocks had been decorated with many slanting tattoo lines, and the "peppercorns" of her hair had been uncurled and plastered with fat so that they hung down in a fringe all around her head.

At dusk !Kun saw his bride building a new hut, as was a woman's duty, which would be ready for them after dark, and he thought of the years of cold nights he had shivered alone among the bachelors under a tree or beneath a crude windbreak. Sundown brought a circle of sparkling fires, and they danced till the moon set. !Kun, the young man, was happy that night.

And !Kun, the old man, having relived a year of his life and grown tired in the telling, wants only to get back to his clan, out there beyond the dunes west of Bulawayo, back to the land he knows.

Independent, carefree, impatient of control, and defiant of authority, he is not to be restrained. Overnight he will slip back into the land of long ago.

Now he is gathering his belongings. Monkey-like, he picks up his fire stick with his toes. A little roll of skin contains his only sustenance. Perhaps he will let you see it–a live snake, with its mouth stuffed with grass, which he will kill and eat when he is hungry.

Halfway back to where his people are encamped, out in the Kalahari, he will dig up an ostrich shell he buried, full of water. A few days ago he smelled duiker beyond the dunes in the land that lies toward the sunset. He will creep upwind on the herd, put a poisoned arrow into a straggler, follow it through a land no civilized man would choose to traverse, and arrive among his people with a full stomach. And if he has gained from his visit with the white man, it is apparent in only one way as his silhouette grows smaller against the sky line: he has thrust the keys from several sardine cans through the lobe of each ear.

[illegible]

[illegible]

[illegible]

[illegible]

[illegible]

WHITE ABORIGINES IN EASTERN ASIA

The Hairy Ainus

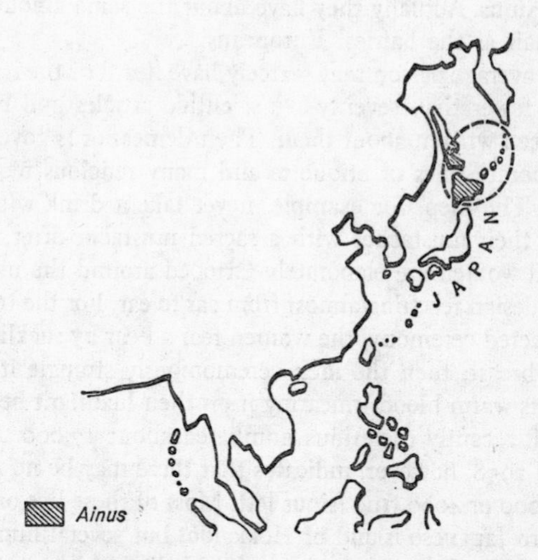

Racially the Hairy Ainus of Northern Japan are a major enigma among the peoples of the world. Despite the fact that they are an ancient Caucasoid tribe, they are separated by thousands of miles from their nearest racial relatives and are surrounded by the most Mongoloid of the yellow peoples. Moreover, their culture displays fascinating customs found nowhere else on earth.

How anomalous they are was summed up by the well-known American anthropologist Carleton Coon when he stood beside an Ainu and remarked that, except for the other man's more widely set eyes and lower nose bridge, they might have been brothers. The Ainus recognize that they are different from the people living near them and call attention to their lack of the Mongoloid eyefold. In fact, when they want to designate a person as being of their own race, they say that he is "of the same eye socket." The word "Ainu" (pronounced Eye'-noo) is their own name for themselves and means "Man." Because early travelers remarked on the abundance of their hair and the habit of the men never to cut their beards, they came to be called the Hairy Ainus. Actually they have about the same amount of body hair as the hairiest Europeans.

The average person may scarcely have heard of the Ainus, yet no fewer than seventy-five scientific articles and books have been written about them. Their demeanor is governed by elaborate rules of etiquette and many religious requirements. The men, for example, never take a drink without raising their mustaches with a sacred mustache-lifter. The married women are elaborately tattooed around the mouth with a design reaching almost from ear to ear. For the tribe's most sacred ceremony, the women rear a bear by suckling it at the breast; then the men ceremoniously strangle it and drink its warm blood, smearing it on their luxuriant beards.

Until recently the Ainus numbered about 17,000. A report in 1958, however, indicates that there may be no more than 3000 or 4000 true Ainus left. Most of these live on the northern Japanese island of Hokkaido, but several hundred are found in the southern half of Sakhalin, which stretches north from Hokkaido for 560 miles. Since Sakhalin comes within a few miles of the Asiatic mainland, it may have been the avenue by which these people reached their present location. A few Ainus also live in the Kurile Islands, which extend like stepping stones from Hokkaido to the tip of the Kamchatka peninsula of Siberia.

Hokkaido is at approximately the same latitude as southern Maine and in area is about the size of Ireland, but the cold Okhotsk Current and mountainous elevations reaching 7500 feet give parts of it a subarctic climate. The average annual temperature is less than ten degrees Fahrenheit above freezing. In parts of the island, snow lies ten to twenty inches deep for six months of the year, and the west coast is often icebound.

The Ainus once occupied a wider territory. The name of the famous Japanese volcano Fujiyama, derived from the Ainus' word for their Fire Goddess, is one of numerous place names indicating that they formerly dwelt as far south as Kyoto. Japanese history tells us that when the Emperor Jimmu Tenno moved into Hokkaido around 66 B.C., he found an aboriginal people who may have been the ancestors of the present Ainus. But most Japanese scholars today claim that the Ainus came from the north not long before their own ancestors arrived from the south.

Expanding Japanese dominion in the first millennium of the Christian era was met by fierce resistance from the Ainus. Ainu women fought alongside their menfolk and even assisted in the taking of slaves and concubines. Most of this warfare occurred before 878 A.D., and the Japanese were able to occupy the entire island of Honshu, forcing the Ainus into Hokkaido. There they lived unmolested for centuries. As late as 1800, the Ainus outnumbered the Japanese in Hokkaido. But around 1868 increasing numbers of Japanese began settling in the island, and the Ainus were forced into narrower territory. Many of them united with the Japanese population, but those in the hinterland remained almost inaccessible until about 1890.

Today the Ainus are a mild-mannered people, and the visitor approaching one of their settlements may be sure of a friendly welcome if he respects their rules of etiquette. Most of their thatched villages are scattered along the coast where there are good opportunities for fishing. However, the Ainus who live in scattered settlements inland are the least altered representatives of their culture. Boat travel is difficult in this area because many of the rivers run swiftly to the sea, while in the well-wooded parts there is frequently an almost impenetrable undergrowth of bamboo from three to four feet high. Through these thickets, narrow trails offer the only passage.

If one's Ainu guide meets an old acquaintance on the trail, both men may quickly squat about two feet apart. They then begin to brush the fingers of each hand alternately back over the opposite palm. While doing this, they talk volubly. Another Ainu gesture of respect, which once may have been more common, consists in raising the hands to the top of the head and bringing them down past the face and beard while uttering a whining noise, which ends in a sharp cry like the bark of a dog.

Anyone entering an Ainu village alone should not go into a hut without first making a noise in his throat. Thereupon someone will pull aside the matting and, if the visitor is welcome, take him by the hand and lead him to the guest's position beside the central fireplace. Shoes are left at the door.

As one enters, the woman of the house puts one hand over her heavily tattooed mouth. If the visitor tactfully recognizes her presence, she will run her right index finger up the palm of the opposite hand and up the arm as far as the shoulder. Then she will draw it from left to right across her upper lip and end by smoothing her hair back behind her ears.

Two Ainu women meeting after a long separation grasp each other by the shoulders, weep copiously on each other's necks, and chant to each other, describing what has happened since last they saw each other. This may continue for as long as half an hour. Men sometimes follow the same custom.

The interior of the hut measures up to twenty feet long and has no partitions. The single window, located at the east end, is sacred, and nothing may be thrown out of it. The hearth must also be treated with respect, for it is the abode of the important Fire Goddess.

The host may offer to fill the pipe of a visitor, and the latter's arrival may be made the occasion for ceremonial drinking of saké, or rice wine. For this, a tray of mustache-lifters is produced. The head of the household then sits before an empty saké cup which has been placed on a stand, strokes his beard, raises the cup with both hands, and bows over it. The saké is thereupon poured into the cup. Before taking any, the man recites a long invocation, dips the mustache-lifter in, throws a few drops of the alcoholic beverage in the fire and a few more over his left shoulder. Then he raises his mustache with his mustache-lifter and takes a drink. Other drops of saké may be flicked toward the sacred east window or toward fetishes massed at the end of the hut. The men often imbibe large quantities; the women have to be content with smaller amounts. The Ainus have long known how to make fermented beverages from rice or millet, but they may originally have learned the method from the Japanese.

The mustache-lifters are about nine inches long and an inch wide. The carving on them, sometimes representing animals, adds to their value for religious purposes. Carving of this sort and distinctive designs on clothing are the chief artistic expression of the Ainus.

When the visitor's eyes become accustomed to the dark interior of the hut, he will see that the Ainus live without any chairs, stools, tables, or other furniture. The inhabitants sit on two layers of matting spread on the earth or board floor. The walls of thatched reed give poor protection against the cold, damp, and snowy winters; yet the only heat is provided by a fire in a depression measuring three by five feet in the middle of the floor. There is no chimney; the smoke stains the rafters with soot and escapes through a hole that is left below one or both ends of the ridgepole. The Ainus kindle fire either by striking a spark or by twirling a stick between the palms. Their practice of wrapping a bowstring around the stick for twirling it may have been learned from other people in more recent times.

The visitor may be served fish that has been smoked on a rack above the fire. A kettle of stew simmers over the embers on an adjustable hook. Unlike the Eskimos, the Ainus do not eat raw meat or fish. Bear or deer flesh is roasted on sticks before the fire. From the pot, the mistress fills the individual wooden cups with stew, which may contain vegetables from her meager garden or some of the vast number of wild edible plants known to the Ainus. When visited by La Pérouse in 1787, the Ainus of Sakhalin did no gardening at all.

The men use chopsticks like the Chinese; the women eat with wooden spoons. Bark dishes are used for solid food and there are stitched containers of thin wood. Chestnuts mixed with fat or fish roe are a popular delicacy. After finishing his bowl, each diner runs his finger around it and licks the inside.

After dark the only light comes from a mussel-shell lamp that burns fish oil, or from a flaming piece of birch bark.

In contrast to the gloomy and primitive surroundings, the robes the people wear are elegant and artistic. Both men and women dress in an embroidered, ankle-length cloak or wrap-around called an *attush*. The cloth is woven from the inner bark of the mountain elm (*Ulmus montanus*) or other tree. Softened in water and split into long threads, the fibers are colored with vegetable dyes and woven. The loom is tied to a post at one end and held taut at the other by a rope around the hips of the weaver, who operates it from a seated position. The Ainus may not have had this device when they first came to Hokkaido. Animal skins are used for clothing in winter. The elaborate designs on the cloaks employing both curved and straight lines, are not woven into the cloth but are done by embroidery. They are reproduced entirely from memory, without patterns.

At night the people recline on planks laid around the edge of the room and cover themselves with pelts of animals. Privacy is obtained by screening the bed off with mats. Generally there are not enough furs to keep everyone warm, and the people tend to sleep huddled together and with their clothes on.

Unmarried men and women enjoy considerable sexual freedom. Many Ainu girls, with their fine teeth and sparkling brown or hazel eyes, are quite attractive. They can also be coquettish. A girl may take the initiative, and she loses no feminine pride by proposing. It is not unknown for the visitor among them to find himself the object of amorous advances. The Ainus show affection not by kissing but by biting, and one traveler describes how one of the girls began gently biting his fingers; presently she extended her affections to his arm, and then his shoulder, and finally put her arms around his shoulders and bit his cheek.

The close proximity of other sleepers may, moreover, provide the comfort of safety, for it is said that rats sometimes scamper over one's body during the night, and snakes have been known to climb into the rafters. Ainu legend has it that the first poisonous snakes were introduced to Hokkaido by a famous Japanese warrior, Yoshitsune, who is believed to have fled there in the twelfth century.

There is evidence that the young people do not fear the consequences of occasional sexual intercourse, for they believe that a relationship must continue for some time to cause pregnancy. Trial marriage is an accepted custom. Sometimes the parents of a young boy will signify his betrothal to an infant girl by adopting her. Or the agreement may involve the exchange of both children by their parents. However, the young couple exercise full freedom and can break the best laid plans when they reach marriageable age, which is fifteen to seventeen for girls and closer to twenty for boys. Nothing like the highly involved puberty rituals practised among some primitive peoples have been observed here, though there is feasting and drinking.

Among the Ainus there is no rule to prevent a man from marrying his first cousin, his niece, or apparently even his daughter.

Some marriages are without ceremony, but the parents like to observe formalities. The boy's father will hand a small sword to the girl's father, who accepts it temporarily, and they both affirm the intended relationship. The two men pray to the Fire Goddess, who is the deity of the hearth, and ask her to guard over the couple throughout life. Offerings of wine sanctify the union, and the general feasting and drinking may go on for two or three days.

The young married man assumes new responsibilities in hunting and fishing, and his bride begins at once to think of a baby. The Ainus call this world the "multiplying world," and believe that childlessness is a sign that the gods are displeased. It is common for a family to have three or four children, and adoption is frequent.

The husband now completes his wife's mouth tattooing, the beginning of which has somewhat the significance of an engagment ring among us. In olden times, the completed design may have had the purpose of labeling a woman as the husband's property. One legend tells how the ancient Ainu fought with certain dwarflike people who dwelt in pits; and archeologists have found such pits in this region. The Ainus in the legend took women prisoners, and in order to prevent them from escaping, tattooed their mouths. Black obsidian knives were formerly used in the tattooing process. The designs are applied by gashing the skin, rubbing in soot, and wiping the wound with a cloth dipped in a decoction of bark.

At first the newlyweds live with either pair of parents, but in due time they build a hut of their own. Before occupying it, they hold a community ceremony to sanctify it. During this, there is so much drunken disorder that the house sometimes catches fire and burns down before the owners have passed a single night in it.

Some time after marriage, the young bridegroom makes gifts for his wife as a kind of second pledging of the vows and a sign of satisfaction. A knife sheath, a spoon, a shuttle, and a loom are given to her, and she in turn expresses her affection and approval of the marriage by making a pair of leggings, a girdle, a necklace, and a headdress for her husband.

Theoretically, Ainu couples are reunited in the hereafter, and when a man's wife dies, he is expected to destroy the house so that it will be conveyed to heaven for her use there. However, since polygamy is permitted, a man may remarry. A widow, on the other hand, is expected to marry her former husband's younger brother or remain single.

Married women play an unobtrusive role in the presence of men. When leaving a hut, a woman is expected to walk backward. Her proper behavior when meeting men on a trail is to step off the path, lower her head, and place her hand over her mouth. It can be assumed that this gesture is related to the tattooing, but it may conceivably be a recent development, resulting from the efforts of missionaries to abolish the mouth tattoo.

Women cannot take part in religious activities. The men are afraid of letting them do so for fear they might "tie them up tightly," which is an Ainu phrase for injuring a person by witchcraft. The wife might do this by hiding the husband's fetishes or burning them, cutting holes in his clothes (presumably with the idea of letting an evil spirit in or causing the soul to flee), by making an image and driving nails into it, or by letting such an image drift out to sea.

Nevertheless a wife is not without honor in her own home. She keeps her own name, and her position is reinforced by the fact that her brother is in some ways the true head of the family. If her husband is unfaithful she may have the satisfaction of seeing him suspended by his hair with only the tips of his toes touching the ground.

When a woman knows she is pregnant, she holds a feast for her husband and parents. Many fetish sticks of willow, each with a mass of curly shavings at the top, are carved and offered to the Goddess of Fire. The people pray for the woman's good fortune, and she refrains from spinning and from eating the flesh of birds and lobsters. She has no intercourse with her husband for two months before the arrival of the child, and for thirty or forty days thereafter.

The Ainus do not hide the facts of childbirth from the children, but when the moment of birth approaches, only female relatives may be present. The woman either squats or lies on her side for delivery. If labor is difficult, the midwives may press her abdomen and massage her with seaweed or a dead bat, or they may bounce her up and down on her feet. After the child is born, some Ainus induce expulsion of the placenta by thrusting a finger down the throat and causing vomiting.

The husband's role at the time of childbirth, as in many

other tribes, is not easy. He becomes sick and morose. He bundles himself up like an invalid before the fire and observes numerous taboos. The Ainu explanation is that while the mother gives the baby its body and life, it is the father who endows it with spirit and intellect. The ordeal exhausts him, and he requires prolonged rest—a custom that anthropologists call the couvade, after the French word meaning "to hatch." The new mother is given a feast and is out of bed in about five days, but the father's indisposition lasts twelve days.

As soon as the child is born, the father or grandfather must go to a river bank and pray. He then carves a personal fetish for the child out of willow—the same wood from which, according to Ainu mythology, the first man was made. The fetish is stuck in a "pillow" made out of a bundle of sticks and is set near the child's sleeping place. It becomes the guardian of the child's growth and remains its protector throughout life. The baby lies on a small litter that has upturned ends and is fitted with a loop of rope at each side so that it can be suspended in the hut or from a tripod or branch in the forest.

The strangest procedure to which the infant boy or girl is subjected is an operation in which the fatty flesh of the thighs near where the legs join is cut. The mother binds the wound with leather-like layers of fungus mycelium taken from under the bark of certain dead trees. The operation is performed without ceremony and is not construed as a modification of circumcision. The women say they do it to prevent chafing between the child's legs and keep the baby from being restless while nursing. Commentators have not ventured to suggest from this that the Ainus may simply have discovered in the use of the fungus a new antibiotic.

The parents may wait two or three years before choosing a name for the child. They will use descriptive words, such as Bright, Graceful, Bird-mouth, or if they run out of more attractive ones, Pot-belly, Saucepan, or even Filthy. The chief of the village bestows the name, and gives the child a small present. The Ainus regard their names as living beings, and if an Ainu gets sick or sees some bad luck sign, he may change his name to better his fortune.

Ainu children are allowed to cry without restraint and are sometimes nursed until they are four or five years of age. When they are old enough, they are taught to respect their elders, and obedience is strongly impressed on them.

Severe tests for guilt or innocence and strict penalties for crimes characterize Ainu society. If a person suspected of wrongdoing can pick a stone out of boiling water or hold a red-hot coal without being burned, he is assumed to be innocent. A verdict may be sought through long deliberation and argument, or by the simple method of throwing a cup over the shoulder and seeing which way it lands. Although the Ainus never inflict a death penalty, they sometimes sever the heel tendons, maiming the individual for life.

Each village has a chief, whose authority is moderated by a council of elders. The office is generally inherited by a son or brother, but sometimes the man who can endure the most severe beating on his bare back wins the position. Village chiefs yield to the jurisdiction of territorial chiefs on territorial issues.

The medicine man is the chief authority when it comes to divination, diagnosis, and control of the weather and hunting. He trains from youth for his profession, and because he is believed to span the real world and the spirit world, he is called "a person with a double life" (*tusu-guru*). His implements are a sacred drum, the skulls of birds and animals, and other fetishes. His seances in a darkened hut bring him into communication with the spirits. The various manifestations that occur, such as spirit drum-playing and the medicine man's ability to escape after being tied up, recall the feats of the Eskimo angakok.

To cure disease, the medicine man goes into a trance; his expression becomes glazed, and he is then supposed to be able to determine the cause of the illness. He may administer herbs or engage in vigorous massage, which may have the purpose of expelling the evil spirit causing the disease.

Wounds are dusted with powder scraped from deer horn or whale bristle and sewn shut with plant fiber. Sometimes a dog is sacrificed as part of the curative ritual. Hunting expeditions are not undertaken unless the medicine man pronounces the time propitious, and various magical procedures are observed to ensure success.

The Ainus are skillful hunters on both land and sea. The use of guns has now greatly reduced the supply of game, but as long as the Ainus hunted with bow and arrow and harpoon, there was relative abundance. One eyewitness, describing the migration of fur seals past Hokkaido less than seventy years ago, estimated that there were 30,000 in an area of only five square miles, throughout which the water was churned as if fish were jumping.

Using oars, the hunters put to sea in 25-foot dugouts. Despite the coldness of the water they are excellent swimmers. When within throwing range, they hurl a forked harpoon with two detachable heads similar to the single-headed Eskimo harpoon. But the Ainus poison their weapon points, using aconite as do the Aleuts. The basic ingredient of the poison is a paste made by rubbing the roots of *Aconitum japonicum* between stones or in a mortar, but other things may be added, including fox's gall, mashed spiders, parts of the water scorpion, and jack-in-the-pulpit. Ritualistic observances accompany the manufacture of the poison, and its strength is tested by touching it to the tip of the tongue. The tongue must be scraped immediately with a knife and rinsed thoroughly or the tester will suffer. Sometimes the poison is buried for a period. The Ainus say that a bear wounded with it will run only 200 meters before falling dead, and that it retains its potency for five months.

The Ainus train their dogs to work as teams in catching fish. Twenty to thirty dogs are divided into two groups about 200 yards apart on the beach. At a signal from their masters, both groups start to swim straight out to sea in single file. When the two columns reach a certain distance from shore, a loud call from the men on the beach causes the right column to wheel left and the left column to wheel right. The lead dogs in both columns come together, and at another signal, the dogs all swim toward shore in crescent formation. The fish, frightened forward by the splashing of the dogs, can presently be seen in the shallows. Each dog, as his feet touch bottom, pounces upon the fish, and in addition many fish are forced ashore. The dogs carry the fish they have caught to their masters, who reward them with the fish heads.

The great importance of the sea as a source of sustenance to the Ainus is shown by the great variety of creatures they take from it. Salmon constitutes their single most important food, but they also take crabs, lobsters, oysters, clams, mussels, scallops, turtles, and seals and in earlier times they may also have hunted walrus and whales. One fishing implement used by the Ainus may be unique: It is a long pole equipped with a curved hook which is on a hinge and which folds out of the way in a groove near the end of the shaft. When the blunt point of the shaft strikes the fish the impact dislodges the hook, causing it to swing down and pierce the fish; the fish is thus pinched between the hook and the end of the shaft.

To attract deer within range of their bows, the Ainus imitate the cry of a troubled or injured animal by means of a curious instrument made of bone and bamboo and having teeth like a comb. They also capture larger deer in pitfalls and fix a bow and poisoned arrow in position so that a passing animal will release the arrow. These devices present some danger to the unwary traveler.

In autumn, the people forage for lily roots, leaves, small fruits and berries, nuts, mushrooms, and other wild foods in wide variety. They hunt game even in the dead of winter, seeking out the hibernating bear in its den by means of the telltale yellow discoloration of the snow made by the animal's warm breath. Here again the dogs are trained to help. But it is a lone man who crawls into the den with his head bundled up against attack. He carries a long knife in case the sluggish animal chooses to fight rather than to escape. Others are waiting outside to kill it as it rushes past.

When they find a young cub, the hunters are likely to seize it and begin the many months of preparation necessary for their most sacred ceremony, the sending of the bear messenger to the spirit world.

All their other rituals are secondary in spiritual and emotional importance to the great ceremony of the bear. To understand the meaning of this singular ritual, it is necessary to examine the spiritual concepts of the Ainus. The most important deity to the Ainus is the mythological tribal hero Aeoina. He is the supreme teacher, who taught the first Ainus all that they know about hunting, fishing, and handicrafts. He is sometimes called "The Person Smelling of Man," because, after coming to earth, he wore an earthly garb and carried it back with him to the spirit realm. He is the guardian of all tradition, the deity who keeps the Ainus dedicated to their ancient ways.

There is a more important deity, however, in terms of prayers and ceremonies. This is the Fire Goddess, Huchi (or Fuji), which means Grandmother or Old Woman. She resides in the family hearth and is the great ancestress of the Ainu race. She must be addressed devoutly on almost all important occasions. Her husband, the Ancestral Governor of the House, is less well defined but is represented by the most important fetish, or *inua*, in the household. This is a pointed stick from a lilac tree, with the usual mass of curly shavings left attached to the top. There are sometimes crude marks on the stick for the mouth and heart. Occasionally, this fetish is brought from the northeast corner of the house and stuck into the floor near the Fire Goddess.

The Ainus perform their bear ceremony to communicate with these and possibly other deities who are regarded as ancestral to their race. The bear is not a sacrifice, but a messenger. It is a carefully nurtured spiritual emissary. Other animals have spirits; even things do. These "souls" are frequently propitiated by offerings of wine or in other ways. But the spirit of the messenger-bear enjoys the most lofty status. It is the pre-eminent ambassador to the gods.

The bear is usually captured as a cub in late winter. One of the women takes it to her breast as though it were a child. It becomes accustomed to human companionship. One may see the bear enter the hut, put a paw on the edge of the millet pot, lift the lid, and scoop out pawfuls of the contents. One, two, or three years may pass, during which time the people treat it like a "spoiled child." When it grows strong, a wooden cage usually has to be built for it.

Finally the time of the ceremony arrives, ordinarily in September or October. The feast is called the *Iomante*, or *Iomande maratto*, which means "Feast of Sending Away." This is a time of almost uncontrollable grief for the woman who has nurtured the bear. All during the preceding months or years, the people have fattened the bear even as they would one of their own children, but only to kill it. Only the most urgent spiritual responsibility could induce such an act, and elaborate care is taken lest the bear misunderstand the ritual. Throughout the ceremony, the people tell the bear how great an honor they are according it and how sad they are to see it leave this world.

Their grief is softened only by the fact that the bear's spirit will, of course, return to earth in another bear. The Ainus believe, as do many other hunting peoples, that the souls of slain animals, after a sojourn in the afterworld, return to earth in the bodies of other animals. And since life itself depends upon success in hunting, it is important that the animals should want to return to earth. This belief explains many of the rites performed over an animal that has been killed. In the bear ceremony of the Ainus this motive is quite conspicuous. Their aim is to prepare an animal that will serve as an especially vocal and enthusiastic emissary. This animal is expected to counteract any evil rumors spread in the spirit world by other animals who may have reported that life on earth was only a miserable affair that quickly ended when a human hunter killed and ate them.

So the men talk at length to the spirit of the sacred bear, reminding it how thoroughly they are honoring it. They tell it that it must visit its father and mother with joy. The women have prepared many cakes and dumplings that will accompany the bear into the spirit world and enable it to invite both the near and the far-away deities to a grand feast. While feasting, they say, "Thou wilt surely say good things about us."

To indicate how deeply they will grieve over losing the bear, the men shave their foreheads and necks as for mourning. They dance before the bear, while the women and children clap their hands and sing songs. This goes on for some time; then the men turn toward the fetishes they have made and worship for a while. After this they address the bear again, impressing upon it how much they hope to see it again. They never question that the bear can return to earth. They only hope that it will want to and that it will bring other animals with it.

The spectators shout and clap and shoot blunt arrows at the bear. Then they tie it to a post, put a block of wood between its jaws and choke it between two poles. Finally they stab or shoot it.

Not one drop of its blood must fall on the ground. The men catch the flow and drink it warm, smearing it on their beards until they present a fiendish appearance.

The east window of the hut is then broken, and the dead bear is brought in through the opening. It is skinned to within an inch or so of its nose. Its head is then severed from its body. The skin is left attached to the nose and is placed on a mat called the "fetish floor." Food offerings of chopped fish and millet dumplings are placed under the bear's snout in the belief that they will serve for its feast in the next world. They even place a mustache-lifter under the bear's nose. The bear is given some of its own meat and broth to "eat," and a little of its own blood.

Then the men put on crowns and dance. The bear is again asked to tell its parents in the spirit land that its Ainu foster parents brought it up free from trouble and harm. It is supposed to tell the spirits, "I have brought cakes, dried fish, and fetishes with me. Let us rejoice." The entrails of the bear are cut up fine, sprinkled with salt, and eaten raw—an unusual practice among people who otherwise always cook their food.

The pelt is then severed from the nose, and the skull is passed out through the east window to take its place among other fetish skulls on a fence, which visitors will do well to treat as sacred. Great quantities of saké are drunk, and the bear, having also been handsomely wined and dined, is sent on its journey.

It should be added that missionaries have now virtually eradicated these ideas and practices.

It is the writer's view that few, if any, primitive people in what can be called the animistic stage of belief entertain any clear idea of reward or punishment after death as a result of earthly behavior. Certainly the main purpose of their worship and their observance of taboo and ritual is to secure comfort and abundance in this life. And the spirit in which they approach death is characteristically free from feelings of remorse or impending punishment. A death-bed scene described by the Venerable Dr. John Batchelor is a good illustration of this. Some sixteen women were sitting around a stricken woman, making clothing in which to dress her as soon as she died. One was embroidering gloves, another making socks, a third a headdress, and so forth. When Dr. Batchelor asked the sick woman whether her apathy indicated that she wanted to die, she replied, "Oh, no, I want to live." She evinced no qualms about where she would go. The Ainus put it simply when they address a person who has died: "You were an Ainu; now you will be a god. Farewell." Actually, the woman in question took a turn for the better, and her friends who had been making the funeral preparations left "giggling like a pack of hysterical schoolgirls." The woman lived on for a number of years.

As an Ainu grows older, he is apt to become preoccupied with religious matters. Occasionally, he may receive a "call to the mountains," causing him to disappear for several days and to live alone in the wilderness. In this way he is "made to know the news;" in other words, he receives divine instruction through meditation.

With such inclinations, it is perhaps no great hardship when the elderly people of the tribe, in accordance with tribal custom, are segregated. Sometimes they are given a small hut remote from other people and kept supplied until they die. The hut is then burned, for this releases it for use in the beyond.

The dead are buried in their finest clothing and given a complete assortment of tools for use in the future world—bow and arrow, pipe and tobacco, fire-making equipment, eating utensils, and, in the case of a man, the indispensable mustache-lifter for use in ghostly rituals beyond the grave. A woman will be equipped with sewing and weaving implements and materials, trinkets, and kitchen utensils. These grave offerings are always "killed" by being broken, torn, or chipped. This releases them for the journey to the realm of the dead.

Food and drink are placed near the body as it lies in the hut, and the Fire Goddess is asked to take charge of the soul. The virtues of the deceased are extolled, and the spirit, like that of the bear-messenger, may be instructed to carry messages to the ancestors. Burial is beneath an upright wooden marker, and a log is laid on the grave. The people do not return to the spot.

Some culture traits of the Ainus link them with peoples on the American side of the Pacific. Their art is thought to show a kinship with that of the Northwest Coast. Their use of poison on weapons and a rudimentary form of mummification involving removal of the viscera suggests some contact with the Aleuts. And in fact, there is an old Japanese record that tells of the Aleuts visiting this part of the world during the Tokugawa period, between 1603–1867 A.D. Other usages point to contacts in the south. By and large, neither their culture nor their language mirrors anything strongly characteristic of Caucasian tradition. Their language is said not to resemble any other either in grammar or vocabulary, and their culture is about as foreign to

European tradition as that of any other of the Palearctic ("old arctic") peoples along the northern Asiatic fringe.

However, the riddle of their unmistakable relationship to the white race in the physical sense is beginning to yield to analysis.

Thus far the evidence favors the belief that the far-flung Mongoloid peoples attained their present numbers only in fairly recent times. Before the very sudden expansion that seems to have brought them to their present prominence, eastern Asia was apparently predominantly Caucasoid. The word "Caucasoid" means "Caucasian-like" and is here used to designate people who would be classed in the Caucasian division although they might not show identity with any of the European types of Caucasians with whom we are most familiar.

These Asian Caucasoids were present at least by the latter part of the recent Ice Age. On the Pacific Coast of Asia, they probably ranged all the way from the Okhotsk Sea in the north to the latitude of Formosa (Taiwan) in the south. The strongest and purest of the Asian Caucasoids of the mainland may have lived in the basin of the Anur River, which flows into the Okhotsk Sea near Sakhalin. For this reason they are called Amurians. They are believed to have been the ancestors of the Ainus.

The physical anthropologist Joseph B. Birdsell, at the University of California at Los Angeles, has contributed substantially to this theory and estimates that these people were probably abundant in east-central Asia down to the end of the New Stone Age, perhaps even into early historical times. In other words, they were there only a few thousand years ago.

An interesting suggestion related to this theory is that some of the closest living relatives of the Ainus are to be found 4000 miles away in Australia. Dr. Birdsell concluded on the basis of field studies in Australia that an Amurian Caucasoid strain is discernible in some of the aborigines there. The present-day aborigines of Australia, according to his studies, represent an uneven blending of three human types. The Amurian is one of these. This is most evident among the people of the Murray River basin, some of whom have a massive, rough-hewn type of countenance reminiscent of the Ainus, and a skin which, though dark, is light in comparison with that of other Australian aborigines. Their hair is extraordinarily abundant on face and body, and is straight or wavy. They also show a tendency to graying and baldness. All these are Caucasoid traits. But in Australia they are somewhat obscured by other admixtures.

So much for the evidence of the southernmost Asiatic Caucasoids. If the Amurians prove also to have spread northward to the region of Bering Strait and if they were in that region something like 20,000 or 30,000 years ago, we may find that the white man, not the Indian, did discover America. No Amurian skeletal remains have yet been found in the New World, but artifacts from 20,000 to 30,000 years old have. It is conceivable that these may have been left by people physically far different from the Indians of today. The people who left them may have become extinct or blended with succeeding migrations. Perhaps the abundant archeological remains that are being turned up will some day include the skull of one of these earliest Americans and enable us to piece together the first chapter in the racial history of America.

A PEOPLE OF THE EASTERN HIMALAYAS

The Lolos

In a labyrinth of mountains and gorges near the headwaters of the Yangtze in far western China lies the stronghold of the Lolos. Half of their territory of 11,000 square miles is almost two and a half miles above sea level, and almost all of it is well over a mile high. It is the region that air-lift pilots of World War II looked down upon when they flew over the mountains between Calcutta and Chungking.

The Lolos do not like to be called Lolos. The Chinese apparently first used this term as a modification of the name of one of the Lolos' chiefs, but it is also the word for a tiny basket in which the ancestral spirits of the Chinese are believed to reside. The Lolos therefore look upon the word as an insult to their own forefathers. The Chinese also call them "I" (spelled "Eye" in some of the literature), a word connoting "foreign" or "barbaric." The Lolos call themselves Nosu or Nersu, which may mean "people of the north."

The land of the Lolos is located between the camel country of Mongolia, the yak country of Tibet, and the elephant country of Burma and Thailand. The inner parts of it remain scarcely better known today than was the more northerly Silk Road across Asia in the century following Marco Polo's traverse. The forefathers of the Lolos were aborigines here when the first Chinese invaders spread to the fringes of their territory 2000 or 2500 years ago. With outlying clans, the Lolos of today have been estimated to number as many as a million persons, but their culture remains pure only in the Great Liang Mountains, near the juncture of the three Chinese provinces of Szechwan, Yunnan, and Sikang.

This has long been considered a dangerous region. In 1909 the British explorer Donald Brooke left Chien-ch'ang with ten persons to explore the mountains of Lolo land, but he was killed by these people and his entourage captured and enslaved. The Lolos have long repulsed the incursions of the Chinese and have provided themselves with a slave caste by capturing them. The people of this class have mostly come to consider themselves Lolos.

Even when China was open to travelers, it was difficult to reach this region. To travel alone was to court capture or murder; and it was almost impossible to procure an escort, because even soldiers dared not enter the Liang-chang Mountains. The traveler could try to buy the protection of each Lolo leader along the way, but the only insurance he could get was of limited duration.

There are no roads in these mountains. Precipitous foot trails mount the steep slopes, and because available horses are used as pack animals, the traveler usually must walk. Icy streams must be forded, and some prefer to wear straw sandals that can easily be removed. The Lolos themselves always go barefoot.

From the higher points in Lolo land, the traveler sees the snowy peaks of Tibet to the west and the northwest. There are no towns here, and after days of exhausting travel up and down the mist-clad slopes, it is a relief to see the scattered huts that mark the closest approximation to a Lolo village.

Fierce dogs may make the entry difficult. If it is summer and the hour is late, the men will be climbing up the long, steep trail from their fields of buckwheat, barley, millet, or rice far below. The women are seen fetching water in heavy wooden tubs, which are carried low on the back by means of a rope across the chest. The distance a bride may have

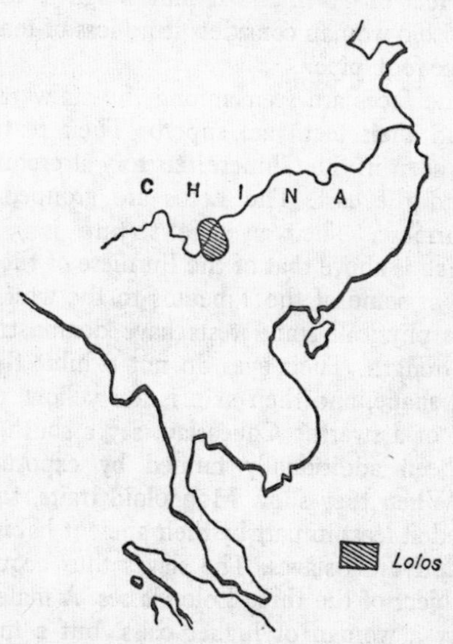

to carry water to her new home is often a crucial factor when she considers a proposal.

The house is a rectangle of wattle and mud, with a roof of rough board or thatching. It has no windows and only one door, and there is no way of determining from its appearance whether it belongs to a nobleman or a commoner, except perhaps by size. The highborn Lolo sometimes builds a simple house through fear of losing it in a blood feud; his enemy may burn it down in lieu of taking his life.

Both men and women wear a dark brown cloak of sheep's wool. Beneath this the man wears enormous trousers, so wide and loose that they look like a skirt. A pointed felt hat with a wide brim tops his attire. The woman fastens her long jacket in front by a brooch of silver or brass, and wears either a skirt or trousers under it. She may display a dozen or more silver chains hanging from her ears. Her enormous headdress is built up in front with as much as a hundred feet of cloth, and it may weigh as much as six pounds. A Lolo woman considers it no loss of femininity to smoke a five-foot pipe.

Handsome faces are seen among the stalwart men and women, and their teeth are superb. Their features differ from those seen in the Chinese territory stretching far and wide toward the east. The Lolos are grouped with the Tibetan-Burmese. Their average stature is 5 feet 6½ inches, which is above that of the Burmese of the south but below that of some of the Tibetans to the west. They are well set up physically, and tests have demonstrated their muscular strength. Their eyes do not exhibit the extreme Mongoloid shape, and their skin is less yellow, resembling rather that of a swarthy Caucasian, say a southern Italian who has been additionally tanned by exposure to the elements. When they show Mongoloid traits, these are to be explained at least in part by their ancient habit of taking Chinese captives as slaves. The slaves thus acquired form the most abject of the three Lolo classes. A male slave can never marry a woman of higher class, but a man of the Lolo "nobility" may on occasion take a slave girl. And on the lower levels of Lolo society there has doubtless been considerable intermixing.

Inside the house, the only light comes from several flaming sticks of dried bamboo about five feet long. These are stuck into holes in the wall and pointed downward so that they burn continuously. The central part of the single fifty-foot room is kitchen, living room, and dining room. A fire, set back from the door, is surrounded by mats and bearskin rugs. There are no chairs or tables, and no sanitary facilities.

The visitor is given a place on the floor away from the door. He is glad to stay near the fire, because in the farther corners the temperature may go below freezing at night. If he wants privacy, however, he is welcome to sleep on a bamboo balcony that is regularly used for storage, but he risks falling through to the floor below. His place in the circle is to the right of his host. Low-caste people and slave girls sit directly across, close to the door. A section at one end of the common room may serve as the master's room and is in rare instances set off by a bamboo partition. The other end is a stable for horses and cows.

The Lolos are a quiet, discreet people. They consider it bad manners to sneeze while eating, and women are said sometimes to commit suicide over the disgrace of having made an offensive noise during a meal.

They work hard and eat only twice a day. The basic dish consists of various grains fried in a pan. The parched kernels are then ground into flour and mixed with water to form a paste or gruel similar to the Tibetan barley *tsamba*. The produce of the fields is augmented by meat obtained by hunting with the bow and arrow and the lasso. Antelope, deer, bear, and various birds are most often hunted; wild asses and panthers are also sought. Wild thrushes, captured and kept in cages, provide them with a popular sport. The birds are not valued for their song but for a special version of cockfighting. Matches are arranged and large sums are won and lost on the outcome.

At such elevations, even the combination of hunting, herding, and farming by no means yields an abundance of food. Summer is the best season; in fall and winter the diet deteriorates from beans to turnips, and by springtime the people may be forced to assuage their hunger with buns made from bitter artemisia plants. Salt is almost always scarce, and as a medium of exchange is even preferred to silver.

As warriors, the poorly armed Lolos have shown unsurpassed courage and have remained undisputed masters of their realm. The wealthier men own horses and become excellent riders, but the warriors fight also on foot with spears as much as thirty-six feet long. They parry the weapons of an enemy with a shield and a trident-shaped implement. They hurl stones with great skill and therefore like to fight from a superior height. Some use homemade muzzle-loaders, carrying their bullets in their mouths and igniting the fuse by means of a smoldering root of the pear tree. Lolo warriors cross the upper Yangtze and strike at the Chinese with great vigor and suddenness, robbing, kidnaping, and returning swiftly to their homes. The Chinese seek to protect themselves against such attacks by taking refuge in towers from forty-five to seventy-five feet high.

The Lolos also fight to some extent among themselves, but less viciously. They fear to remain in the lowlands, apparently dreading disease; but on the other hand they look upon the distant snow-clad peaks of Tibet as the home of spirits who will seize any maiden who passes.

The people of the uppermost class in Lolo society, frequently referred to by outsiders as the nobility, are called the Black Nosu, Black Bones, Heh-I, or Earth Eyes, the latter name referring to the fact that they own the land. At the bottom of the ladder are the slaves, called Wa-tzu, originally acquired through warfare. One Earth Eye may have as many as three hundred or four hundred Wa-tzu. But some belonging to the upper class even farm their own land.

The more talented of the Wa-tzu may be received into the household of the Earth Eye and can even rise to a managerial position. It is not uncommon for a Wa-tzu to live in his master's house and serve as steward or cook. The improvement in social status leading to such a post may require several generations.

The Earth Eyes would consider it beneath them even to be involved in a quarrel with one of the Wa-tzu. The Earth Eye marries his girl slaves off to other men's male slaves; and each master has the power of life or death over his slaves. For example, one runaway slave, who became lonely for the wife he had left, decided to return, but he was decapitated by his master's own hand.

The fact that the upper caste is a fighting caste, ever ready to protect the territory, somewhat mitigates the hardship and injustice endured by the slaves. To an even greater degree is this security valued by an intermediate plebeian class called White Bones. This class is made up largely or entirely of Wa-tzu who have risen from servitude, acquired their own land, and in some instances even taken slaves. Even a low Wa-tzu can capture slaves from the Chinese; such slaves are then called "third-class Wa-tzu."

The Lolos will tell you that in very ancient times a cut tube of fragrant bamboo floated down the Han River and struck the bank, whereupon it exploded and a man named Atsa was created. He married a dog-shaped girl who was sleeping under a pear tree, and she gave birth to the Lolo people. Ever since, the Lolos have worshiped the bamboo and the pear tree, believing that they are descended from them. The bamboo represents the origin and also the future of life. The pine tree is also given an important legendary position. In fact, the Lolos refer to themselves and to the "pine ancestor" by the same name, Atsape.

Each Lolo community has a sacred twenty-foot square of ground planted with fragrant bamboo. At the foot of the bamboo is a circle of five-foot rocks surrounded by a bamboo fence about ten feet high. Each year on the twenty-fourth day of the fourth moon, the people remove the bamboo fence and erect a platform before the fragrant bamboo. Here they pray to the spirit of the bamboo and make animal sacrifices. They believe that any loss of vigor in the sacred bamboo is symbolic of approaching misfortune. In one locality, women who are barren and long for sons go to a certain "bamboo mountain" and pray to a cluster of bamboo.

The spirits of the pine and the pear tree are similarly honored with propitiatory rites. The ceremony that occurs on the third day of the third moon is connected with the initiation of adolescent boys. Each boy is permitted to break off a branch of pine or pear and plant it at the foot of a larger tree. Girls over twelve are barred from witnessing this ceremony.

The rituals of the Lolos represent the primitive religious substratum in this part of the world, unaltered by more highly evolved concepts. In Tibet and China, on the other hand, such beliefs as survive from ancient times are rather heavily overlaid by Buddhism and other philosophies.

The Lolos are haunted by the fear of becoming possessed by evil spirits, which produce illness and death. Their wizards, called *pai-mao,* specialize in casting out demons, and their work is considered extremely dangerous. A chief wizard, in fact, may have to employ another wizard to "cleanse" him after exposing himself to "contamination" during these rites. In order to discover the nature of the offending spirits, the *pai-mao* first plays on a drum and chants. The assembled people may join in from time to time, telling the evil spirit to go away. Gradually the *pai-mao* falls into a trance and in that state acquires information as to the cause of the malady. Another way in which he may "diagnose" the evil is by making the sick person breathe on an egg, then breaking it open and examining the contents. This presumably enables him to identify the evil spirit and determine what sort of sacrifice is needed. In addition to sacrificing a chicken or some larger domestic animal, offerings of tea, wine, and salt accompany the healing rites. The *pai-mao* casts out the evil spirit by constructing a straw figure or a ring of grass as a scapegoat and transplanting the offending demon into it. He brushes this over the body of the patient, then casts it away. Or he may induce the spirit to pass through a rope of grass, which he then cuts to pieces to prevent its return. To keep malevolent spirits from infesting a household, amulets and "door gods" are put at the entrance. The most highly respected of these is the "vinegar and charcoal god," Chiang Tai-kung.

A most surprising element in the culture of these people is a curious written language used by the medicine men. At first glance, the characters look somewhat like highly simplified Chinese, but they are totally different. A circle with a dash in it means "egg." A circle containing an X means "thunder;" a small circle inside a larger one stands for "iron," and a circle containing a cross means "monkey." The characters are read from top to bottom, like Chinese, but the columns run from left to right, which is the reverse of the Chinese method. The manuscripts displaying these strange characters are on bamboo paper and are passed down from father to son. Their content is sacred and to some extent secret. Since the wizards do not divulge their knowledge of the portents and remedies contained in these scriptures, little is known about this sacred language. Witch doctors belong to the Wa-tzu, or slave class, and since this class is at least partly Chinese in origin, it has been suggested that this odd language may represent an early stage in the evolution of writing in the Orient. However, it seems just as likely that it is a more recent improvisation by people who were aware of the power of writing but lacked a mastery of any of the traditional systems.

Legend has it that long ago, when earth and sky were in dark confusion, three priests were sent to earth with the "original books" tied to the horns of cows they were riding. While they were crossing an ocean, the pages got wet and had to be dried out later on the branches of a cypress tree. Some of the pages, alas, got stuck to the branches and were lost. Thus only half of the original scriptures survive today, and cypress branches are used in certain ceremonies to represent the lost pages. For example, when the witch doctor is summoned to cast out evil spirits, he may first plant cypress branches in the ground, along with pieces of firewood sticking up in rows, calling them the tablets for the spirits.

The identity of the animal that must be sacrificed depends upon the date of the affliction. Similarly, the right day for a battle or other important or dangerous undertaking is determined by divination. For this the wizard uses a specially shaped piece of wood about three inches long and partially split. He throws the divining stick on the ground, and the way in which it lands gives the answer to his question. For all his various services, the wizard receives part of the sacrificed animal and sometimes additional remuneration. He is expert in interpreting dreams and omens, seventeen important examples of which are interpreted in his sacred manuscripts.

When all rites fail to cure a sick person and he appears to be dying, he is moved to the door of the house and dressed in his burial clothes. Like many peoples, the Lolos are anxious to get the ghost out of the house and prevent its return. After death, the relatives sacrifice a chicken and place it near the corpse's head.

When the funeral cortege moves toward the burial or cremation ground, two masked devils and several minor ones accompany it, beating drums and making music. Halfway there the procession halts. The masked devils drop out of the procession, and the women mourners discard their mourning robes and squat on the ground. The procession then moves on, presumably taking the ghost with it. Cremation further protects living people from the spirit of the dead, and it is also believed to facilitate the rebirth of the soul in another person. Twice a year, sacrifices are brought to the place where the ashes were deposited.

Lolo girls are sometimes betrothed in infancy. To seal the bargain, a fowl is sacrificed, and each family keeps one of its ribs as evidence. An unmarried girl wears her hair in one plait instead of two like her mother, and she is expected to remain pure until married. Lower-class marriages are generally not ostentatious, but considerable fanfare accompanies weddings among the nobility. Much wealth is pledged by the family of the young man, and the parents of the girl provide her in turn with a substantial dowry.

Most curious are the elaborate hostilities that precede the actual marriage. Partly because the girl's parents cannot expect to see her again for from three to ten years, they resist vigorously the overtures of the go-between who comes to make certain that the girl will be ready on the appointed day. Her parents beat him severely as a token of their daughter's value to them. Negotiations are purposely prolonged, and finally the bridegroom gathers his friends and attacks the house. The bride's people make strenuous efforts to defend their home and their daughter, and the damage to property and person can be considerable. But when the bridegroom's force succeeds in entering, peace is declared and alcoholic beverages and meat are served.

The bride is now heavily veiled and escorted to her new

home, with her brothers in attendance. On arrival, there is another scuffle. Her veil is snatched off, and her relatives try to throw it onto the roof as evidence of the authority that she will command in her new household. Meanwhile the bridegroom's people attempt to trample the veil on the doorstep to prove the opposite. Again, this is not entirely a sham fight; serious injuries may result.

The bride must stay three days in a temporary shelter before entering her new home. The wedding is signalized by a vast amount of eating and drinking, which in one known instance continued for seven days and seven nights. It may be added that the Lolos are primarily monogamous, and there is no prostitution.

Much remains to be learned about these interesting people, whose archaic ways may clarify our understanding of early movements of peoples and cultures in Asia. To the anthropologist they therefore represent an exciting subject of study. But our knowledge of them is scanty, even when we include information from Chinese sources, and it is likely to remain so. Though Lolo resistance to intrusion is proverbial, we cannot be sure that Communist ideology has not reached them. The class system of the Lolos and the impoverishment of the slave class might offer a chink through which Communist agitators could try to introduce some radical changes. If that happens, Lolo culture and social organization may have changed considerably when next we are able to examine them.

[illegible] against [illegible]

[illegible] continued for seven days [illegible]

[illegible] emotional [illegible]

[illegible]

A WANDERING TRIBE OF THE AUSTRALIAN DESERT

The Arunta

The Arunta of Australia are one of the most primitive groups on earth. They do not understand the father's role in parenthood; instead they have built up an entirely different explanation of pregnancy and made it a central theme in their religious system. Moreover, they practice the most painful and horrifying initiation ceremonies in the world. An operation they perform on the urethral canal is so drastic that one wonders how the men are able to perform normal procreative functions thereafter. In spite of this, they increase in numbers up to the limits of their parsimonious environment and formalize the institution of marriage with rules about as complex and rigid as any in the primitive world.

For our knowledge of this tribe we are indebted especially to the studies of Sir Baldwin Spencer, who served as special commissioner for the government of Australia and Chief Protector of Aborigines in the Northern Territory, and to his collaborator, F. J. Gillen, Special Magistrate and Sub-Protector of Aborigines at Alice Springs. Besides these noted co-workers, a considerable number of other field anthropologists, psychologists, and sociologists have contributed to what we know of the Arunta (or Aranda, as they are sometimes called).

They are as perfect an example of a Stone-Age people as we have, and their sexual psychology and ceremonial elaborations present specializations not met with anywhere else in the world. Some of the information concerning their customs and beliefs has only recently been shared even by the experts; it was so sacred that the investigators had to promise they would not divulge it during the lives of the informants.

Physically, the Australian aborigines may be closer than any other to Neanderthal man, who inhabited parts of Europe some 50,000 years ago. Because of the limited resources of their environment and the isolation in which they have lived from early times, their cultural development has been retarded. They lack agriculture, metals, pottery, and the bow and arrow. They do not even have the beginnings of a belief in a supreme deity.

Isolation has also restricted the animal life of their homeland. Only the pouched mammals and the egg-laying monotremes (the platypus and the spiny anteater) represent the mammals in Australia, aside from the wild dog, or dingo, which is believed to have been introduced by man. The poverty of their desert environment has kept the Arunta from increasing beyond a few thousand individuals, though their domain is greater than that of Austria.

The stone knives, spears, and other implements these people make are of the same order as those excavated from the prehistoric encampments of the Stone Age. The Arunta hurl their spears by means of the ancient throwing-stick, which adds leverage to the arm. That they lack the bow and arrow, which even the very primitive Bushmen of

South Africa possess, may be explained by the possibility of their having become separated from the rest of mankind before it was invented. Nor have they ever discovered methods for poisoning the tips of their weapons.

They make up for these handicaps to some extent by skillful use of the boomerang. Strangely enough, although experts in the aerodynamics of the boomerang tell us that many Australian boomerangs are properly shaped to return to the thrower, some of the most reliable anthropological authorities have said that these people did not actually make the boomerang return to them. The explanation for this contradiction probably lies in the fact that earlier observers did not understand the principle of the returning boomerang and mistakenly judged the abilities of the natives on the design of the implement rather than the actual performance. It was thought that twist or beveling was necessary to make a boomerang return, but it is now known that the implement need only have one surface convex and the other nearly flat. Just as an airplane wing of similar cross-section tends to lift, a boomerang with one surface curved tends to twist in flight. The principle of the gyroscope joins with this force to produce curving flight.

The Arunta never analyzed these factors, but they did sometimes construct boomerangs with one surface convex and the other flattish, and there is good reason to believe they knew that such a weapon would return. It is reported by some that they sometimes sent a boomerang right around a tree in order to rouse a flock of birds; they would then bring the birds down with other weapons.

We shall have to describe the Arunta more or less as they were when first studied by Europeans around the turn of the century, for (except in such cases as the Bindibu, with whom contact was made only recently) most of Australia's 47,000 pure-blooded natives have undergone much change. The Arunta, furthermore, probably number no more than a few hundred today.

At the moment when an Arunta woman first realizes that she is pregnant, she takes note of her surroundings, so that she may know which of the innumerable totemic spirits in various landmarks was the father of her child. These spirits are the ancient ancestors of the tribe. Legends describe in detail their wanderings and adventures. They generally inhabit rocks, hills, and trees, but some are said merely to mark certain spots on the featureless plains.

A woman who does not want a child is in danger every time she must pass one of these spirit localities, and she may try to fool the spirit into thinking she is unattractive. She will walk bent over and with a cane and will croak, "Don't you touch me; I am an old woman." The fertility spirits are thought to be especially fond of traveling in whirlwinds, and so when a woman sees a dust column approaching, she is likely to run away from it.

The actual father of the child believes he has had no part in parenthood, except perhaps in preparing his wife for the entry of the ancestral spirit. When she tells him she is pregnant, he consults the old men of the tribe to make sure which spirit has been responsible. They review the myths of the region and decide which totem is the father. This is of the greatest importance, for it determines what religious duties the new member of the tribe will ultimately have.

Since the ancestors were not human beings, but animals, plants, and other things, the spirit-father of the child may be a kangaroo, an insect, a species of tree, or even some such natural phenomenon as water, fire, or a heavenly body. Whatever it is, it becomes the child's totem and imposes on him lifelong religious obligations.

When the expectant mother retires to the bush to give birth to her child, she squats close to the sand, and her female attendants dig a shallow hole to receive the baby. After the baby is born, attendants sever the umbilical cord by giving it a sharp blow between two stones. It may be preserved and worn by the child later as a necklace.

The baby is given two names, one of which is sacred and is determined soon after birth by the older men of the clan in consultation with the natural father. They alone know this name, and it is never uttered except in a whisper and only on the most solemn occasions. The other name is known to all.

Many other subjects relating to religious concepts are so sacred that the Arunta have developed a fairly comprehensive sign language to avoid even whispering during certain ceremonies. By means of gestures and without a sound, the men can converse for hours. The signs resemble our deaf-and-dumb language, but of course no alphabet is involved; each posture of the hand signifies a whole word or even a sentence. In some groups, women in mourning must also speak entirely by signs for as long as a year.

The newborn babe, instead of being dark brown like its parents, is at first a light copper color. Its skin darkens, however, in a matter of days. As the child grows, some of the features that distinguish it from other dark peoples become more distinct. Among grown men, for instance, the nose is sometimes even broader than it is long, the eyes are deep-set beneath prominent eyebrow bones, and the forehead slopes backward more than in many races.

The young women are well proportioned and carry their head-burdens with a stately gait. The teeth of the Arunta, unless damaged by imported foods, remain in excellent condition. The large size of their teeth and the fact that some individuals grow extra molars seem to link these people with earlier human types. The trend since the time of the Java Man (*Pithecanthropus erectus*) and even earlier has been toward fewer and smaller teeth. The spines of the Arunta are straighter and the vertebrae smaller and lighter than those of either Europeans or Negroes. But the lower limbs sometimes bow slightly forward and outward in a deformity known as "boomerang-leg," which may be caused by a dietary deficiency. Their hands are relatively small, the span of a grown man measuring only about six and one-half inches from thumb to little finger.

They use their toes for picking up such things as firewood and also for dragging a spear along in the grass when they do not want an enemy to see it. To climb a tree, they grasp the trunk and hump both feet up, then lift both hands at once, and so on.

It was the evolutionist Thomas Huxley who first drew attention to the similarity of the skull of the Australian aborigine to that of prehistoric Neanderthal man. Various specialists since that time have endeavored to define the Australian's position among existing races. According to Joseph B. Birdsell's analysis, discussed earlier in connection with the Ainus, some of the Australian aborigines show a relationship with the ancient Asiatic Caucasoids as well as with the Oceanic Negritos and a strain called Carpentarian. The Oceanic Negrito was the earliest component in the Australian population, according to Birdsell, and is relatively unimportant today, at least in some Australian groups. The Carpentarian is believed to be related to the so-called Veddoid element in the aboriginal and low-caste populations of central and southern India.

Except under the influence of ceremonial frenzy, the Arunta is reasonably easy to approach. The tone of his voice is baritone or tenor, never bass. It has a melodious quality, which the musicologist E. Harold Davies describes as being suffused with a slight huskiness that adds to its charm. When these people sing, however, they utter a high nasal whine.

Their musical instruments are scarcely more than noisemakers. The Arunta do not even employ a percussion membrane in their tapping devices. One observer reports that they may add to the general hubbub of a ceremony by blowing on a crude panpipe; and a man will sometimes sound a conch in the belief that it has magical power to arouse the emotion of love. But the instrumental accompaniment of their ceremonies hardly contributes in the melodic sense. They do not have the kind of instruments that would enable them to discover the natural octave through experimental production of overtones. It is therefore somewhat surprising that their songs follow the pitch relationships used in the European musical system. If they have not borrowed the scale from other people possessing better instruments, they presumably arrived at it by a direct appreciation of the effective intervals it provides.

As the Arunta infant grows, it learns to expect, as the desert changes, a seasonal shift from subsistence to famine. The worst time is during the two drought-stricken moons at the coldest time of the year, when at night the temperature sinks to 30 or even 20 degrees Fahrenheit. The small family bands are then scattered in ceaseless search for food. At night they huddle by a tiny fire under their only shelter —a simple lean-to made by piling brush against a pole supported at each end.

With hunger and thirst their goad, men, women, and children are up at dawn. In twos and threes, they scour the land for food. Brief respite from the chill of night gives way to a parching sun, and if during the course of the day distant clouds flash with lightning, it is a false promise. The dry wind only raises clouds of dust, limiting visibility and diffusing the sunlight into a lurid yellow glow.

The women are working with their digging sticks, searching for roots and small burrowing animals such as lizards and the lesser pouched mammals. Armed with spear-throwers and boomerangs, the men are hunting for kangaroos and the ostrich-like emu. Noiseless movement and endless patience on the part of the hunter are an absolute necessity, for few of them can kill or disable a sizeable animal at more than twenty yards, even with the added thrust of the spear-thrower. The hunters are famous for their endurance and their skill in reading small clues in the sand or clay, and their memory for geographical details is phenomenal.

When they reach one of the rare waterholes, they refresh themselves and then poison it with a decoction of the pituri plant (*Duboisia Hopwoodi*) in order to catch the emu that may come to drink. After drinking, the bird may wander only two hundred yards or so before it falls. The Arunta have domesticated only the wild dog, or dingo, and it has neither become very valuable in hunting nor been taught to carry burdens.

Being ever on the move, the Arunta must keep their possessions to a minimum. No people on earth have worldly goods that weigh less than theirs. The head of the family carries about twenty-one pounds, consisting of spears, a spear-thrower, a wallet and a pouch, perhaps two boomerangs, a narrow wooden shield for use against possible enemies, a throwing club, a belt, and a stone ax. The spear-thrower and shield double as fire-making equipment. The Arunta do not have the bow drill, nor can they kindle a flame by twirling a stick. They saw the spear-thrower back and forth over the shield until the sawdust starts to smolder and can be blown into a flame.

The woman does all her food gathering and cooking with about twelve pounds of equipment: a pointed digging stick, a long shallow bowl hollowed out of wood, a roll of skin, a bark water vessel, a fire shovel, a water bailer, and a net bag. Neither sex wears any clothing and they have no way of carrying water on their long forced marches over the desert. An Arunta hunter suffering from thirst has been seen to open a vein in his arm and drink his own blood.

Their only narcotic is made from the same plant they use for poisoning a waterhole. Its leaves and small twigs are dried, broken up, and made into pellets, which are carried in their bags. When chewed, the substance, they say, makes them "feel very good." They have never made use of a relative of the tobacco plant, *Nicotianus suaveolens*, though it grows plentifully in parts of their country.

Because sweets are scarce, they dig up the nests of honey ants and bite off the ants' pea-sized, nectar-filled abdomens. For sweetness they also pick the branches of mulga trees that exude sweet droplets of red gum because certain insects have burrowed into them.

The appetite of the Arunta for fat is rarely satiated. As soon as a hunter kills a kangaroo, he cuts a small hole in one side of the abdomen and pulls the intestines out. Any fat that may be present is carefully removed and eaten. The intestines are usually cooked by rolling them around in hot ashes.

Such are the austerities into which the Arunta is born. Then, even before the youth is old enough to understand its meaning, he may be involved in a strange pledge with a girl of his own age. He is betrothed not to her but to the girl child she may some day bear. The father of the girl and the father of the boy arrange this. The two youngsters are taken to the women's camp, and there each mother rubs her child all over with a mixture of fat and red ocher.

Almost two generations thus separate the lad from the outcome of this bargain. But the arrangement assures the boy of an important provision: the girl is pledged to provide him with her own hair for the purpose of making the girdle that a man must wear. When, after the passage of many years, the daughter whom he is pledged to marry approaches puberty and the man himself is middle-aged, he visits her and greases her breasts in a ceremony which is both an expression of his love and a rite believed to make her breasts grow. A man may have more than one child-bride promised to him under this system, but any of the girls he may not care to marry can later be assigned to a blood or tribal brother.

Just before a girl's marriage, her future husband turns her over to certain of his cousins and some other men. They take her into the bush and deflower her with a stone knife; then three or more of the men have the right of *jus primae noctis*. She is then decorated for the wedding. The men are often granted the privilege of intercourse with her once more before the couple are joined. For the wedding, the men assemble and decorate the groom. Meanwhile the young bride may be sitting on her mother's knees, crying. When the bridegroom comes to her, accompanied by his attendants, he goes straight to his future mother-in-law and says, "Give me your daughter." He takes the young girl by her arm, and she pretends to resist. The mother puts the girl's arm into the man's hand, and he squeezes it firmly. This signifies that they are married.

The bride passes her first night with her mother. On the second night, she goes to sleep with her husband, beside the same campfire; but they do not touch each other. Any slight provocation during the next few nights may cause her to return to her mother, but finally the two grow used to each other and become husband and wife.

The Arunta believe that a man can win another man's wife from him by magical means, and suspicion of this causes some of the quarrels that make adult life stormy in this tribe. A man may wear a special magic headband in the presence of the woman he wants in order to cause "her internal organs to shake with eagerness." They believe that shell ornaments and other amulets are effective in arousing love even at a distance.

But a woman takes considerable risk if she yields to the urge to leave her husband. Since she has to make her escape at night, she is exposed, she believes, to various night-prowling spirits specializing in snatching women away. Also, her husband may inflict severe punishment on her for infidelity. On the other hand, a man is not reluctant to lend his wife to a guest.

Quarrels are also caused by the belief that it is possible to commit murder by magic. The chief methods are by pointing a bone at the victim or by hurling a miniature magic spear in his direction. When someone is suspected of having caused death by witchcraft, a relative of the victim sets out to seek revenge. He takes a medicine man with him and sometimes several of his fellows as well. It is important for him to carry the victim's hair girdle. There are various rites en route to preserve the loyalty of his companions. Sometimes the men open their old incisions and squirt blood over each other. Or the man who is leading the party may don special slippers made out of emu feathers and dried blood. But before he can put the slippers on, he has to undergo an operation in which the ball of each little toe is heated with a hot stone until the joint softens; then the toes are dislocated so they stick out of a special hole in the side of each slipper. The slippers are apparently believed to enable the man to perform the most powerful magic. The Arunta have such unshakable confidence in the powers of black magic that when a man has been wounded by a "bewitched" spear, it is said that his fear and despair are sufficient to make a slight wound fatal.

Certain offenses that might not be considered consequential in our society can cause severe reprisals among the Arunta. One of these is the failure of an individual to perform all the requirements of mourning. Such grievances are sometimes settled by formal duels. The offended person will challenge the other by hurling a boomerang into his camp. The duel that follows is a sort of war dance. The adversaries may use boomerangs and shields or they may whack each other with war clubs. Their movements, despite their savagery, are conventionalized and even graceful.

Women are said to quarrel as often as the men. The disappearance of a utensil may be the provocation. Vile epithets are flung back and forth. When one of the women produces her fighting stick, the two approach each other, striking the ground in front of them. As soon as either is struck on the foot, the battle is joined. They take turns, first one and then the other striking at her adversary. The one on the defense tries to protect herself with her three-foot club, which she holds by both ends. Sometimes a woman's fingers are broken; and if she is gashed, she will catch the blood as it flows and throw it in the other woman's face. The other may retaliate by hurling handfuls of hot ashes. Throughout, there is pandemonium among the other women and the dogs; but the men sit around quietly and gloomily, turning their eyes from the scene.

A death in the encampment requires that the shelters be burned and abandoned. The face of the bereaved spouse is smeared with white pipe-clay, and there is much shouting and wailing. Some relatives are not permitted to mention the name of the deceased; and some are required to scarify themselves, particularly on the shoulders. A widow is expected to collect small bones from various animals and attach them to her head in the form of a conspicuous chaplet. After twelve to eighteen months she disposes of this by burying it in the top of the grave. This ends her formal mourning, but she may choose to paint a narrow white band on her forehead to indicate that she is not yet ready to remarry.

The Arunta bury their dead in a sitting posture, knees to chest, facing toward the individual's sacred landmark. The spiritual part of the person, which is called the *Kuruna* and has made possible his reincarnation from an ancestral spirit, is referred to as the *Ulthana* until the mourning period is completed. The dead person's hair is taken, and since his spirit is supposed to hover around the grave and make it dangerous, the spot is abandoned. However, the people may return after a year or so to banish the ghost ceremonially, after which it is believed to return to the sacred landmark.

Many of these beliefs and customs are already known to the young man approaching puberty. But this does not apply to the most important religious mysteries. Thus, when at the age of ten or twelve, he approaches his first initiation ceremony, he is moved by curiosity as well as by a dread of the suffering he knows he will have to endure before he can be admitted to adult status. Year after year he has seen his older brothers led off into the bush to learn the secrets of sex and the mysteries of the spirit world. He knows that some of the rites are horrifying, but he also knows that he cannot avoid them and that these ordeals alone can lead him toward the magical powers that are more valuable than anything else in the world. Unlike a spear or a shield, which are useful only until they are worn out, a man's religious lore remains his precious possession throughout life. Existence as a mature man is unthinkable without it.

With the approach of the hot season, bringing occasional showers, several local groups may have joined to form one encampment. Here they will conduct ceremonies to make the coming season productive, and the youth senses an atmosphere of expectancy. His first indication that he is about to begin the long series of initiation rites, which will continue at intervals until he is thirty years old or more, comes when several of the older men seize him and hustle him away from camp.

The first rite is a simple lesson intended to instill respect for his elders and teach him to share food with the others. The men throw him up into the air repeatedly, and as they do so, one of the others, his maternal uncle, for instance, may strike him with a stick as he falls, shouting, "I'll teach you to give me food." After this is over, they paint him in stripes of red- or yellow-ocher and bore a hole through the septum of his nose. He has thereby passed the introductory ordeal.

The main camp, a noisy and colorful assemblage, is divided into two "halves," or moieties. Every boy is born into his father's moiety but can only marry into his mother's. However, each moiety is divided into two sections, and the boy never belongs to the same section as his father. Within each section, furthermore, there is a pair of subsections. The system is additionally complicated by the fact that the Arunta do not have words for specific relatives, such as wife, father, or mother, but lump whole groups of relatives under one term. Thus the word for "father" (*oknia*) applies also to the brother of the father and to the father's father's brother's son. The details are too complex to explain fully in an account of this length, but it should suffice to say that the regulations governing marriage and social relations in the encampment are so intricate that, for example, one can even be banished or put to death merely for walking into the wrong shelter.

The equivalent of incest rules among the Arunta extends far beyond the blood-ties specified in our own. This is due to the division of the group into moieties and sections and to the extended group relationship terms mentioned above.

The second stage of the boy's initiation, the circumcision rites, may occur any time after he has reached puberty. Not many boys undergo this ceremony at one time, nor do other divisions of the tribe attend. A special ground is prepared by clearing the grass and shrubs from a path forty to fifty feet long and heaping the surface soil up on either side to form a low ridge. Bushes are left at each end. The complexity of the ten-day ceremony leading up to this important event is indicated by the fact that Spencer and Gillen devote twenty-two pages merely to a summary of its parts, without including the songs and texts. Women are excluded from most of the performance and are made to believe that the whirring of the bull-roarers (slats of wood decorated with mystical symbols and whirled on strings) is produced by the totemic ancestor.

The men seize the initiate and hustle him off, struggling. Most of the procedures that follow are enactments of mythical tribal history in which each performer impersonates an ancestor who lived in the Alchera, or earliest times. At one point, two men cut veins in their arms and sprinkle their blood on the performers; and each performer carries on his head and between his teeth a small mass of shavings saturated with blood. Again, eight or ten of the men pounce heavily upon the initiate, who is lying on the ground.

Two are chosen to perform the operation, and they work as a team, one holding the subject and helping while the other uses the stone knife. The blood is caught in a shield and taken to the women's camp; there the elder sisters of the boy and of his mother rub the blood over their breasts and foreheads. The flesh is given to a younger brother to swallow, in the belief that it will cause him to grow tall and strong. In legend, it was the women who performed the operation of circumcision on the boys, and in one tale, efforts on the part of the subject to escape caused him to lose all his parts.

The initiate is now told something about the Churingas, round or oval pieces of stone or wood, which are the most sacred objects known to the Arunta. The smallest ones measure only an inch in diameter, but some of the wooden ones reach a length of six or seven feet. They are often inscribed with mystical designs. Some have a hole in one end, so that they can be whirled on a string like bull-roarers. The Churingas are the dwelling place of the spirits of the ancestors and represent the closest material bond between the people and the powerful totemic spirits. They are ordinarily kept hidden in the sacred totemic storehouses—caves or crevices in the rocks, and most of them must never be seen by a woman. Dreadful penalties are inflicted on anyone who is careless with a Churinga.

The young initiate must wait many years before he actually receives his personal Churinga; he may be anywhere from twenty-five to forty years of age when his father or an uncle who has taken care of it gives it to him. He must be considered fully capable of carrying out all the duties connected with it, which include rubbing it periodically. A man's personal Churinga represents the spirit force of his totemic father and provides all the powers that make existence possible. Women also have Churingas, but less emphasis is placed on theirs. Actually a woman never is permitted to see her personal Churinga, and she never even learns what Churinga name she was given at birth. After the Arunta boy has passed through the ceremony of circumcision, he is set upon by other men, who bite his scalp repeatedly with all their might, until he is howling with pain and the blood is pouring down his face. This is supposed to make his hair grow.

A month or so later he undergoes his second operation, known to surgery as subincision, which is at least equal in importance and much more severe than the first one. With a stone knife, the urethral canal is slit open from underneath in a deep, full-length cut. As the men seize the boy and hold him while the operation is performed, the whirring sound of the bull-roarers is loud enough to be heard by the women, who are completely excluded from the ceremony. The women then assemble, and the boy's mother or her sister cuts some of the other women across the abdomen, including those whose daughters are eligible to marry. While the woman does this, she imitates the whirring sound coming from the men's ceremony.

The boy's blood flows into a shield, and if the pain is more than he can endure, he urinates into embers and allows the steam to rise, which is said to give some relief. The parts that have been cut never return to normal, and after this ceremony the men always squat to urinate. Drastic though it is, the operation does not render the men incapable of having children; if it did, the tribe would die out, for all young men undergo the operation. Nor is there evidence that the practice was developed as a means of controlling population; such an idea would be inconsistent with the Arunta explanation of reproduction.

One such operation might seem enough for anyone, but older men usually come forward a second or even a third time and ask the surgeon to re-do the Arilta operation more thoroughly.

Psychologists have emphasized the possible phallic significance of the Churingas and have liberally applied the terminology and symbolism of Freudian psychology to the emotional background of these rites. At least one investigator has interpreted the subincision operation as being motivated by a jealous desire on the part of the men to simulate the sexual physiology of the women.

Apart from such psychological overtones, the original purpose of these rites is thought to have been to establish a favorable relationship with the tribal gods by virtue of the sacrifice that is implied. Anthropological studies do not bear out the once widely circulated explanation that circumcision was originally motivated by hygienic considerations. The intent most widely observed where practices of this sort are performed is connected chiefly with the spirit forces that primitive people believe reside in blood and cast-off parts of the body. There is scarcely any way in which people have not attempted to mutilate, embellish or distort the body, and circumcision is one of the fairly common ones. Among the Arunta, these operations have remained thoroughly religious in character. There is a deeply devotional mood associated with the rites, which makes them more than a device to keep the women in their place or to assuage whatever envy of women the men may have. These rites are connected with the most sacred concepts of totemic ancestry and spirit power.

The worst of the physical ordeals the young man must go through are now over, unless he lives in such a region as the northeastern one, where certain groups also require that one of the man's teeth be knocked out with a pointed stick and a heavy stone. This is related to rain-making and should perhaps not be regarded as part of the initiation rites. In many parts of the western, northern, and upper southern areas, the initiate has to have his thumbnails removed before he can possess his personal Churinga. One of the natives gave the Australian T. G. H. Strehlow the following description of the operation: "An old man produced a sharp kangaroo bone (*ntjala*). He stabbed my thumb with it and pushed the bone deep beneath the nail . . . the torment was unbearable. . . . When the nail had been loosened, he took a sharp opossum tooth, forced it into the living flesh through the base of the thumbnail, and tore the nail off from behind. . . . The men chanted: 'They rip off the nail, they tear off the nail; blood flows like a river, rushes along like a river.' Then they seized my left hand and removed the thumbnail in a like manner." The initiate had been told that this would make his hand more pliable and enable him to engrave stone and wooden Churingas in later life. Only after enduring it was he allowed to touch his personal Churinga.

The fourth or spiritual phase of initiation goes on continuously for four months. One purpose even then is to reinforce the authority of the elders, but a great deal more instruction in tribal lore is now given the initiate. He learns what the totemic rituals represent and how to perform them. During this period, not a day passes without ceremonial activity. Sometimes there are five or six ceremonies within twenty-four hours. Blood drawn from the arm or from the old ceremonial incision figures prominently as material for glueing feathers on ceremonial objects. As much as half a pint of blood may be drawn off.

A high point in these so-called *Engwura* ceremonies

comes when the initiates must undergo a series of fire ordeals. While the women throw burning grass and sticks on their heads, the men defend themselves with branches. They must also lie down for five minutes on a fire over which green boughs have been laid and kneel for half a minute in the coals of a smaller fire. Firebrands are also thrown back and forth between the men and the women. The Engwura ceremonies end in extreme license.

This four-month series of rites brings to a climax the struggles of the growing man to reach the spiritual maturity which alone can integrate every aspect of his life with the all-powerful spirits. An impression of the intricacy of the final stage of initiation may be gained from the fact that one period of only eight days out of the total of 120 fills twenty-eight pages in the report by Spencer and Gillen. Yet without any written records the people remember and pass all the details down from generation to generation.

When handing a man his personal Churinga for the first time, the elder may say, "This is your body from which you have been reborn. It is the true body of the great Tjenterama, the chief of the Ilbalintja storehouse. The stones which cover him are the bodies of the bandicoot-men, who once lived at the Ilbalintja Soak. You are the Great Tjenterama himself: today you are learning the truth for the first time. . . ." Other initiates become living representatives of lesser spirits, and their personal Churingas, although acknowledged to be man-made and not descended from the most ancient times, are nevertheless very sacred.

The caves and crannies where the religious paraphernalia is kept are approached only with proper ritual. The old man throws a handful of sticks, stones, and pine needles in the direction of the cave to tell the spirits that humans are coming near. No animals must be killed in this vicinity, for it is the place where the life of each man in the totem group originated. It has been his spiritual home ever since the instant when his mother passed near-by and the totem spirit entered her womb. Each man knows that all the propitiatory rites that focus on success in hunting—and therefore on the preservation of life itself—derive their efficacy from the sacred force residing here.

The men soberly pour their blood out upon the ground until the spot of red covers twenty-seven square feet. On the crust that forms they paint a sacred design. Every particle in the rock near-by represents a life-portion of the totem ancestor and is a potential animal of the same species. The men rub the rock with a stone, and the dust drifts off on the dry breeze. The oldest man removes the sacred objects from their hiding place. He chants a song that tells of the wanderings of the totem ancestors. In low, hushed voices his companions repeat the verses with him. The Churingas are unwrapped and spread out side by side. Each has a special chant sung over it. The men press the Churingas affectionately to their bodies, and the emotional stress is so great that their eyes fill with tears.

STONE-AGE SEAMEN OF THE SOUTH SEAS

The Samoans

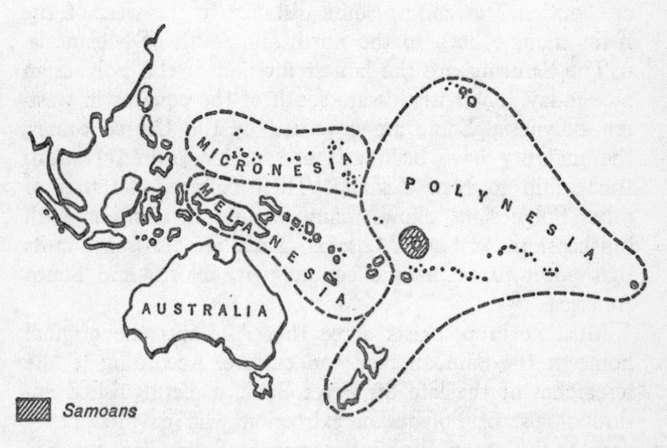

A thousand years or more ago, a group of people whose ancestors had come from Asia and apparently first settled in Micronesia, began to move out into the farther reaches of the Pacific Ocean. They traveled in outrigger canoes and lived out of sight of land for many weeks at a time. Many were lost at sea. Those who survived and discovered new islands colonized them. In time, having become skillful in long-range navigation, these people populated almost every island in what we now call Polynesia. Their well-nigh incredible voyages entitle them to high rank among the greatest travelers and explorers of all time.

Polynesia is a triangular area, approximately 4500 by 4200 by 4000 nautical miles, in the middle of the Pacific, containing more than three hundred principal islands, grouped mostly in ten clusters. At the northern corner of the triangle lie the Hawaiian Islands; its easternmost point is Easter Island, about 2000 miles from the coast of South

America, and its southern corner is New Zealand, geographically separate from Polynesia but racially part of it. The westernmost islands lie about 3000 to 5000 miles from Asia; but numerous intervening islands make the approach from the Asiatic side much less difficult than these vast distances might make it appear. A few Polynesian islands are "outliers" extending some distance to the west of the main triangle both to the north and south of Melanesia.

The Samoans are the largest division of the Polynesian race today. Their islands are south of the equator in western Polynesia. Some are governed by the United States; the majority have been assigned under United Nations trusteeship to New Zealand. Their culture, like that of other Polynesians, shows many features in common with southeastern Asia and Malaysia. There are also some traits that point to prehistoric contact with North and South America.

Most anthropologists agree that Asia was the original home of the Samoan race and culture. According to the researches of the late Sir Peter Buck, a distinguished anthropologist of Polynesian extraction who devoted many years to this study, the ancestors of the Polynesians reached their territory from the northwest by way of the Micronesian islands. According to Dr. Buck, the Polynesians struck eastward through the Carolines for 1700 miles, then down the Gilberts. Their first voyages must have been random ones; but theirs was a highly specialized maritime culture, and as they spread, their knowledge of the Pacific grew and they developed various techniques for making long voyages. They studied the flight lanes of migrating birds, watched for the kinds of clouds that marked the presence of land below the horizon, and made use of the odors that were carried far beyond eyesight from coastal vegetation or tidal flats.

Down the curving Gilberts, atoll by atoll, they drifted, paddled, and sailed. More than 3500 miles from continental Asia they reached the edge of Polynesia. With few exceptions, the islands they passed through on this route were coral atolls, poor in food plants though rich in the products of the sea.

These islands were too low to be seen more than a few miles away, but the boatmen learned to detect slight differences in the color of the water, which enabled them to keep within an archipelago even when they could not see it. As long as they stayed away from the deep blue, they could move about almost indefinitely, confident of regaining land again.

Where bamboo was available, the Polynesians made canteens from its jointed sections. Elsewhere, they drank coconut milk instead of water. Through daylight and darkness, drenched and dry, they cruised, fishing, sleeping, sometimes even giving birth in their canoes.

At first, in the Palaus and Yap, the voyagers found high volcanic mountains affording good supplies of wood for boats. But such resources were not found again until they came to Truk, a thousand miles farther on. Finally once more there were high islands at Ponape, Kusai, and isolated Banaba. Elsewhere the scant coral soil supported only the coconut, the unpalatable three-inch Morinda "apple," and a coarse, inferior brand of taro. A useful staple throughout the volcanic islands of Polynesia, taro is the plant that is grown as an ornamental in the temperate zone under the name "elephant's ear." Its starchy root is its most valuable part. In Micronesia, the voyagers lacked the better varieties of taro. The pandanus, otherwise known as the screw pine, was probably available for weaving the matting for their sails.

Almost all the other plants upon which the Polynesians developed their economy were acquired later, after they had reached the Polynesian triangle. Most were acquired through trade with Melanesian neighbors—breadfruit, banana, plantain, yam, sugar cane, and certain utility crops, such as the paper mulberry tree for making bark cloth, kava for a distinctive Polynesian beverage, the *ti* plant for their kiltlike skirts, and turmeric, an East Indian plant of the ginger family, which was used as a medicine, a spice, and a yellow dye.

The Polynesians also acquired their three domestic animals—the pig, the chicken, and the dog—from the Asiatic side of the Pacific. The Samoans may have been the first Polynesians to acquire the pig, and they tell a quite credible legend of how they smuggled the animal out of Fiji: The Fijians would not part with any live pigs, only slaughtered ones; so the Samoans hid some piglets in the body of a roasted hog, wrapped in *lavai* leaves that were used for flavoring the meat. The piglets reached Samoa alive, and their descendants were traded from island to island. This valuable animal ultimately spread to most parts of Polynesia except New Zealand and Easter Island.

Some of the easternmost Polynesians may have voyaged 2000 miles or more across the open sea to South America. This would explain their possession of the sweet potato, a South American plant. On the other hand, Thor Heyerdahl of "Kon-Tiki" fame favors the theory that Peruvian Indians in prehistoric times brought not only the sweet potato to Polynesia but many other things that typify Polynesian culture. Prevailing winds and currents would have made this easier (as demonstrated by the dramatic raft voyage of Heyerdahl and his companions) than for Samoans to have sailed from Polynesia to South America and back. In navigational skill and equipment, the Polynesians seem to have been more advanced than the Peruvian Indians; and most anthropologists detect many more points of contact with Asia than with America in language, food economy, religion, and other matters.

Heyerdahl (who has published his theories in a comprehensive study entitled *American Indians in the Pacific*) lists many traits that convince him of Polynesia's close cultural ties with the Indians of the Northwest Coast of North America. Here again, the prevailing winds and currents would favor the carrying of people from America rather than the reverse. Some of the Northwest Coast Indians made sixty-foot dugout canoes capable of carrying fifty or sixty persons. Although the distance is about 2200 miles from Vancouver Island to Hawaii, the possibility of such a voyage is certainly not to be ruled out. Even in far-away New Zealand, 6000 miles from the land of the totem pole, there are carved wooden house-posts that may conceivably show a relationship to some of the ancestor-carvings of the Northwest Coast of America. It should be added that the Samoans, and Polynesians in general, show evidence of racial mixing, and it is not possible to determine the region bordering the Pacific from which the principal line of their ancestry came. There is, obviously, great anthropological interest in the origins of Polynesian culture, and exciting results may be forthcoming as more facts are amassed and new techniques developed.

These "Vikings of the Sunrise," as Dr. Buck calls the Polynesians, propelled their outrigger canoes with paddles and used sails of pandanus matting. In later voyages they used boats as much as fifty, sixty or even eighty feet in length. For greater safety in rough weather, they sometimes used crosspieces to join two boats together side by side. They learned to make crude maps showing the known islands in their relative positions. They knew nothing of the compass or of any kind of metal, but they developed a unique method of navigating by the stars.

Harold Gatty, the author of a handbook for castaways entitled *The Raft Book*, believes that the Polynesians discovered what we might call the "overhead-star technique" of navigation. All that they needed to know to reach a given point on the globe was the star that was directly overhead at that point; they could reach their destination by sailing steadily in that direction. This technique would have served them better than a fixed compass course, because the latter does not ensure the shortest, or great circle, route. As the navigator sails toward a given star, the star appears to rise higher in the sky; thus he also has at all times a direct measure of his distance from his destination. When he arrives, the star stands directly overhead.

The one difficulty with this method is that the starry

dome of the sky "rotates" day and night, making the stars appear to rise and set. This problem, according to Gatty, was solved by a fairly well-developed system of keeping time, in which day and night were each divided into six periods of equal length. The Polynesians were able, Gatty thinks, to keep shifting from one star to the next along a known arc in the sky as the stars swung overhead.

The earliest European navigators in the Pacific marvelled at the ability of the Polynesians to voyage back and forth among quite distant islands. It is known that they achieved this sometimes by simply aiming for the particular point on the horizon where a given star or constellation rose or set. This method would not have led them by the shortest route, but in most instances the additional distance would not have been great. The Polynesians could have navigated satisfactorily by this method alone, without the use of the overhead-star.

At first, the Polynesians probably discovered the nearer islands on normal fishing excursions and the more distant ones as a result of being driven by storms. As their knowledge increased they began planned voyages, and some groups, looking for new lands, may have methodically explored all sectors of the sea. It is believed that they had begun to make well-organized and intelligent voyages by about 950 A.D.

Tahiti and Raiatea in the Society Islands may have been the first to be settled within the triangle, although these islands are near the center of Polynesia. From this base, according to Dr. Buck, colonizing parties spread out along seven radiating routes. The Samoan Islands were also among the earliest to receive settlers. One estimate puts the first people in Samoa around 450 A.D., which is considerably further back than local legends go.

The Samoans have not preserved their genealogy so meticulously as have other Polynesians, and they have lost the idea that their ancestors ever lived elsewhere. Most other Polynesian groups can trace their royal families back about twenty generations, or approximately five hundred years, allowing twenty-five years for a generation. Some of the ancestors mentioned in the legends are common to widely separated islands, such as New Zealand, Hawaii, the Society Islands, the Marquesas, Gambia, Cook, the Tuamotus, and the Austral Islands. These groups must have been in contact with one another within the period embraced by the genealogies. The longest genealogical list is a 92-generation sequence memorized by the people of Rarotonga. This would represent something like 2300 years; however, the more ancient names in it do not represent reliable history, the personages being more like gods than human beings. But the more recent names and stories of the Polynesian legends are believed to be accurate enough to serve as a framework of history until more refined methods are developed.

The Samoans must have separated from other Polynesians at a fairly early date, because their customs and beliefs have developed along somewhat special lines. They have been clearly influenced, for example, by Melanesian Fiji, 450 miles to the west. The first people to reach another major Polynesian cluster, Hawaii, may have reached there as early as 450 A.D. These, however, were probably the non-agricultural settlers known in Hawaiian legends as the Menehune. They are described as a dwarfish people who were in the islands when the ancestors of the present Polynesians came. "Pre-Polynesian" settlers are also described as having been found in other parts of Polynesia when the ancestors of the present people got there. A strong contingent of "modern" Polynesians is believed to have arrived in Hawaii about 1100 A.D. Easter Island, which is separated by 1920 miles from the Marquesas, may not have received its "modern" colonists until later. There may have been people in New Zealand by 950 A.D., but the main influx came later, perhaps not until 1350.

A young Philippine servant from north of Manila whom the French navigator La Pérouse had with him in Polynesia in 1787 was able to tell the meanings of most of the words in the vocabularies of Tahiti and Tonga. Subsequent studies have confirmed that the Polynesian language belongs to the great Malayo-Polynesian division, which extends over a wide range from southeastern Asia out through the islands. Study of more than 250 vocabularies has tentatively revealed that the Polynesian dialects relate closely to the languages of northern New Hebrides and Fiji, whose people, however, are Melanesian. This may mean that the Melanesians were numerically dominant when the Polynesians met them and that, although the Polynesians did not intermarry with them extensively, they adopted the existing Melanesian language or were strongly influenced by it. The fact that the Polynesian dialects are much less varied than the Melanesian indicates that they are newer and supports other evidence that the Polynesians have not occupied their islands for long. Polynesian appears also to be related to the Micronesian dialects. With North or South America, on the other hand, we find no such relationships.

In Samoa, the ancestors of the present people found a homeland far richer than the islands they had known earlier. This 270-mile chain includes ten principal islands and totals 1200 square miles. The lush green slopes on Savaii, the largest of the group, rise to a maximum height of 6094 feet. With rich soil and abundant supplies of fish in the offshore waters, the Samoans increased and grew strong. Their idyllic existence was challenged, however, around the end of the eleventh century by the people of Tonga, some three hundred miles to the south. The Tongans conquered the Samoans, according to legend, and were able to settle in the islands. Five generations passed before the Samoan chiefs Tuna and Fata drove them out. A story tells how, as the Tongans drew away from Samoa in their boats, one of the defeated leaders shouted from his canoe: "*Malie tau, Malie toa,*" meaning, "Clean fight, brave warrior." Down to the present day, the descendants of Tuna and Fata, who ruled the district of Tuamasaga in Samoa, have thus used the title "Brave warrior."

The Samoans have also warred almost continuously among themselves. Hollow wooden hand gongs and a loud wooden whistle were sounded to summon the people to attack or defense. To recognize each other in the heat of battle, the warriors wore distinctive headbands and face painting. War clubs, spears, and slings were their chief weapons, and they carried shields made of pieces of bamboo fastened together. The clubs, three to four feet in length and in many shapes, were heavy enough to deliver a crushing blow. People defeated in war suffered the shame of having their hair singed off, and the women were sometimes taken as captives. Tribute was exacted, and changes in the social scale were enforced.

The extremes of friendliness and hostility of which the Samoans were capable were dramatically demonstrated to the first Europeans who visited the islands. Admiral Roggewein, a Mecklenburger in the Dutch service, is credited with discovering the islands in 1722; but he did not go ashore. Neither did the Frenchman Louis de Bougainville, who lay offshore forty-six years later and traded with the natives. The first Europeans actually to land in Samoa were members of a French scientific expedition headed by Count Jean-François de la Pérouse. La Pérouse landed in Samoa in 1787 and was soon to learn that a life of ease and plenty had not deprived the Samoans of the will to fight. Though the Samoan women appeared free with their affections and all went well the first day, tragedy was in the making.

La Pérouse's second-in-command, de Langle, made two mistakes in science which were the cause of the disaster. First, he stubbornly held to the theory that stale water caused scurvy; and second, he forgot that a falling tide might leave his two long-boats stranded within reach of hostile natives. He had found an attractive village a few miles beyond where the expedition's two ships lay, and he asked his commander permission to refill their water casks there.

La Pérouse, however, had detected signs of turbulence among the Samoans. He pointed out to de Langle that the men were tall—five feet nine or ten—and that they had excelled the French sailors in feats of strength. He called attention to the scars of battle that almost all the Samoan men bore. De Langle had no ear for these warnings. His glimpse of the idyllic village obsessed him, and he charged his commander with responsibility for the effect the continued use of stale water might have on the scurvy from which the crew was already suffering. At length, La Pérouse, despite a "secret presentiment," gave in.

Sixty men accompanied de Langle to the village. As the sailors lined up to fill their water casks, two hundred natives gathered. The record states that "a certain number of women and very young girls . . . offered themselves to us in a very indecent manner, and their advances were not universally rejected." Perhaps the men unwittingly violated some taboo at this point.

In the short time that the Frenchmen had been in the islands, they had apparently already witnessed an unusual ritual of Samoan sex mores, though without fully understanding its meaning. Every important community in Samoa had a specially chosen maiden, a ceremonial princess called a *taupou*. In contradistinction to the freedom enjoyed by other Samoan girls, the taupou was most strictly chaperoned. Her virtue was so important to the community that, before her marriage, she had to undergo a public defloration ceremony. Should she fail to pass this test, she would be punished severely, sometimes even being beaten to death by the other women. La Pérouse described what may have been a variation of this ceremony: "The altar was prepared in the best-looking house in the village; all the blinds were let down, and the curious were sent away. The victim was placed in the arms of an old man, who, during the ceremony, exhorted her to moderate her expressions of pain: the matrons howled and sang; and the sacrifice was consummated in the presence and under the auspices of the old man, who served both as priest and altar."

We shall probably never know whether one of de Langle's men violated a Samoan taboo relating to the ceremonial princess of the village, or whether greed for the white men's possessions excited the Samoans to aggressive action. Also, there were many small points of etiquette the breaking of which would have offended the natives. It was proper, for instance, for a visitor to sit cross-legged in the presence of a chief, and not remain standing, as a European might do out of respect. It would have been bad manners to sit with one's feet extended or to lie down in a hut with one's legs pointing toward the center. Elaborate rules surrounded every phase of Samoan social life.

We cannot trace de Langle's actions, for he did not live to tell the tale, but there were vague signs of discord when one of his men, a botanist, De la Martinière, left the beach and went inland in search of specimens. Several Samoans followed him and exacted a bead for every flower that he picked, threatening to smash his skull if he did not pay. While he was gone, the crowd quickly swelled to a thousand or twelve hundred; and the tide fell, stranding the long-boats.

When de Langle ordered his men to try to push the boats off, some of the islanders held onto the grapnel rope, and others began to throw stones at the white men. As a warning, de Langle fired a shot over the heads of the Samoans. It was of no avail. The Samoans attacked in force, five or six hundred of them hurling a continuous shower of two- and three-pound stones at the Frenchmen. Either because the Samoans recognized de Langle as the leader or because they had some grudge against him, they felled him first. He fell into the water, and they beat him to death with clubs. They tied him by one arm to the boat, presumably to loot his clothing later or to exhibit his head in accordance with Samoan custom. Within a few minutes, eleven other Frenchmen were also killed.

Returning to the beach, De la Martinière came upon a scene of slaughter and confusion. Most of the other forty-nine men had been wounded with stones and were trying to swim out to the barges, which had been anchored in deeper water. De la Martinière dashed into the water through a hail of stones and swam desperately toward the barges. In tribute to his scientific devotion, it should be recorded that he reached the barges without letting go of his bag of plant specimens.

European voyagers who followed La Pérouse were inclined to be cautious. But gradually those who became well acquainted with the Samoans learned that they did not always behave as "savages" and that hospitality was, in fact, a solemn duty among them. A visitor who had acted in accordance with Samoan etiquette and brought the prospect of good trade would receive an elaborate welcome, culminating in the celebrated dance of the ceremonial princess.

Let us imagine such a welcome taking place on a November evening. The first winds that herald the rainy season are bending the palms and making their fronds rattle drily. The small boat that brings the visitor ashore reaches the encircling reef, threads the channel, and surges into shallow water. A man from the village wades out knee-deep and clasps his hands behind his back so that the visitor may put his knee into them and be carried ashore.

An elderly Samoan near the water's edge holds up a kava branch and gives a speech of welcome. On cooler ground above the beach, in a circular clearing almost a thousand feet in diameter, stands the village. The air is savory with grated coconut and plantain, turmeric and taro; soon roast pork and the caviar-like palolo worm will add their fragrance. For only four days ago the people saw the land crabs marching down the mountains to breed in the sea, and they sensed in the air the strange aroma that heralds the swim-dance of the palolos. Up from their grottoes in the reefs the worms will come, to squirm and mate and disappear as has been their habit, once in October and again in November, since the days of the ancestors. The Samoans know that the palolos will rise when the moon is nearing its first quarter; only at that time will there be the proper combination of light and tide for the swim-dance.

The sun drops into the sea, and the village grows quiet. All of the morrow will be needed for the preparation of the feast. Inside the huts, the only light comes from candlenuts burning singly, one after another, on thin skewers of bamboo and from the flicker of wicks set in pressed coconut oil. People doze lightly on their mats, for they must be up at midnight, when the tide is ready to ebb.

Then the word goes forth, and young and old hurry out to the shallows with coconut torches and baskets. The surface of the sea comes alive with the frenzied intertwining and undulating of bodies–male palolos brown, females indigo and green. The water grows murky, as they expel their myriad eggs and milt. The people scoop up the palolos by the basket-load and take them to the banquet kitchens. There, others wrap them in leaves and cook them in coconut cream.

Meanwhile, at dawn, another crew has sailed seaward in a large outrigger, swift enough to pursue the shark and the powerful bonito and to overtake the schools of smaller fish that are their prey. Once at sea the fishermen follow the commands of their Fishing Captain, whose authority here supersedes even that of the principal Chief himself. The leader directs them to troll their baited shell rattles to attract sharks. The lures flutter near the surface, resembling food fish. Not a few of the sailors have lost fingers, some a whole hand, because at some crucial moment, a shark, held close in a noose, could neither be clubbed to death immediately nor released.

The men grow alert. The one who is watching the bait has seen some movement and is drawing the line slowly in, attracting the shark closer. Soon the huge fish is visible to all. An assistant with another baited line maneuvers the creature into position for the noose. The man holding the rope awaits his chance, then slips the loop back over the shark's dorsal fin and pulls it tight. A third strikes the fish with a club. The shark snaps violently; it must not be released while its jaws are directed upward. Talking to the shark as much as to one another, the men hold to their purpose and win. The huge creature, finally lifeless, is lashed to the outrigger beams.

A flock of seabirds tells where bonito are chasing their

prey, and before returning shoreward the men hook several of these large fish and many smaller ones. On the homeward journey they are so heavily laden that when they reach the shallow channel through the reef, they go overboard and guide the canoe from the water.

During the day, others on shore have been netting and trapping fish, poisoning them with the seed of the *futu* plant (*Barringtonia asiatica*). Grating the kernels, they thrust the mash into holes in the reefs where the fish are hiding. Divers also carry the poison into deep water. The fish emerge stupefied and are caught. Still others have been fishing with a mass of cobwebs attached to the line in place of a hook. With this they bring in small gar, whose teeth are so firmly entangled that the men have difficulty disengaging them. When he fishes with hook and line, the Samoan thinks nothing of flicking the fish out of the sea and snapping it loose from the hook in midair so that it falls into his canoe.

In clearings back in the forest, trained pigeons are being used as decoys to attract wild birds into nets and cages. The trained birds are skillfully manipulated in flight on the ends of long strings. The wealthier men own dozens of these tame birds. They feed them carefully on nuts and taro, and compete against rivals on other islands in netting contests. Some of the fowlers are maneuvering nets on poles that are as much as forty feet long, capturing birds in flight. Parakeets, rails, terns, doves, and pigeons go into the baskets that are destined for the banquet.

Cooking is progressing in special huts, one of which is just behind the oval guest house. A hollow in the ground lined with basaltic stones forms the oven. Fire is kindled by rubbing a stick in a groove, and the oven is filled to floor level with burning wood or other plant material. In this, fist-sized stones are heated to the glowing point. These are lifted out with tongs made of coconut midribs, and some are then placed inside the bodies of dressed pigs; other hot stones are heaped around leaf packets containing fish of various sizes. The empty oven, with its lining of hot stones, receives other food wrapped in green leaves. Octopus, lobster, crawfish, and crab are baked in a special oven. With the Samoans, eating is a reason for living; and to the delights of gourmandizing are added an opportunity to gain prestige through generosity and the proof of opulence.

The floor of the feast house, for the sake of dryness, is a platform two feet above the ground and is covered with a neat mosaic of stones. An oval of stout posts five feet high supports the rounded roof. Each post signifies the rank of the person who is permitted to sit in front of it. The height of the platform and the number of roof beams in the hut are an exact indication of the owner's rank. Anyone who aspires to a higher rank than his economic status might support is restrained by a powerful builders' "union." The carpenters will not continue to build after the owner of the house can no longer pay; and there are no substitute workmen. The members of the carpenters' union eat and drink only the best, and their guild is sanctified in ancient lore. At every stage of construction, the owner must feast them and pay them with fine mats and other goods. Deep is the shame of a house-builder who has to stop before his roof is fully thatched.

When all is ready, the guest is shown to his proper pillar in the hut, but he must not sit down until a fresh mat has been spread for him. Then, cross-legged and with his back against the post, he waits for his host to arrive. The Chief comes in and seats himself with utmost deliberation. He must be given no sign of recognition until he acknowledges the presence of others. In one district of Samoa, the silence following the Chief's entry may last for several hours; yet no matter how strongly the aroma of roast meat may tempt the visitor to restlessness, he must not move for fear of punishment by death.

The ceremonial princess has not appeared, but a sort of male counterpart, an "heir apparent" known as the *manaia*, comes in and takes an important position in the oval. The heads of family groups also find places. These are the *matai*, the titled men, who convene from time to time as a judicial and regulative council, called the *fono*. They are not born to their titles but must earn them. The untitled men of seventeen years and older, who comprise a social and work group called the *aumaga*, are still helping in the preparations for the feast. So are the corresponding female group, the *aualuma*, which includes girls of thirteen and older, unattached females, and the wives of untitled men. Some of these serve as ladies-in-waiting for the taupou and are now dressing her; others are working in the kitchens.

Finally, the Chief deigns to inaugurate the ceremonial welcome, and the scene that unfolds reveals the Samoans as past masters of oratory in its most subtle and exalted forms. It is not the Chief himself who addresses the assemblage but the Talking Chief, who combines the functions of public relations expert, keeper of titles, master of ceremonies, and even marriage broker. He represents the real Chief in all important situations and preserves the niceties of protocol. He enjoys the unique privilege of building a house which has only one roof beam less than that of the Chief. The real Chief must always be addressed with special ceremonial phrases, and he alone is permitted to eat certain tabooed foods.

The Talking Chief rises and stands with his feet apart, holding in one hand his staff of office with its tip on the ground in front of him. He never moves the lower end of the staff while talking. His other arm is behind his back, and his long hair is gathered up at the nape of his neck. Over one shoulder is draped his ornate braided fly whisk. Standing thus, he addresses the company as a group and as individuals, drawing upon a seemingly endless fund of honorifics and accenting his salutations with flattering references to local genealogy. At times he may seem to be stealing the show from his Chief; but no ruler left to his own modest boasting could create such an aura of dignity and glory around himself as that which the Talking Chief periodically weaves around his leader. In his flow of eloquence, visitor and villager alike are softened by flattery into accepting even the obvious exaggeration.

The Talking Chief is the symbol of gracious intercourse. The community cherishes his eloquence; it is their bulwark in the social rivalry with neighboring groups. If occasionally he manages to usurp his Chief's powers and dabble in politics, it is because he represents an institution without which Samoan social life could scarcely function.

On and on flow the flowery phrases, and still there is nothing to eat. When finally the Talking Chief, showing a nice balance of ostentation and cordiality, refers to the banquet the women are preparing, he makes it seem an all-too-modest expression of esteem for the visitor.

The guest may now have an opportunity to respond, speaking through an interpreter, if necessary. He voices his humbleness in the face of such hospitality and backs his remarks by offering a few contributions of food himself. Presentation of his offering enables him to disavow some of the honor that has been heaped upon him, but if his gift is too flamboyant, he may find himself in a long contest of words. Only the correct blending of condescension and largess on the part of the Talking Chief can resolve this. Everyone else is also given an opportunity to commend the Talking Chief on his eloquence and deliver a few gracious phrases of his own; and finally all is ready for the kava ceremony.

The Talking Chief must supervise the distribution of kava, but the ceremonial princess plays the central role in the mixing of the drink. She enters, bare to the waist, followed by three young male attendants walking single file. She sits cross-legged, and the attendants place before her the kava bowl, the cup, the strainer, and the kava substance wrapped in breadfruit leaves. The princess has spent part of the day chewing the kava root, mouthful by mouthful, and her jaws may still be tired. This duty is so arduous that some taupous yield their title to escape it.

The kava substance is unwrapped and put in the bowl. Holding the tips of her fingers together, the taupou allows one of her attendants to pour water over them from hollow coconut shells. Water is also added to the shallow, eighteen-inch kava bowl, which is carved from a single piece of wood. The earliest kava bowls had only three or four legs, but modern ones are made with as many as twenty-four. Holding her fingers together and moving them in graceful, formal gestures, the taupou kneads the kava into the strainer, a shredded mass of fibers two feet long and four inches in diameter. She then drains out the dull greenish liquid and tosses the strainer over her shoulder to the attendant waiting behind her. He flicks the woody particles out of it with a whiplike motion and gives it back to her. The process is repeated until all the fibrous bits have been removed. Water is again poured over the taupou's hands, and the Talking Chief announces that the drink is ready. The titled persons clap their hands in slow rhythm.

The cup-bearer, seated on the taupou's left and keeping one hand behind his back, palm out, holds a polished coconut shell while the princess squeezes a quarter cupful from the strainer. Holding the cup as high as his head, he sweeps it down to the ground and presents it to the Chief, palm outward. He then steps backward and waits. In serving all the others, he holds the cup with the back of his hand forward. Each person drinks only after the Talking Chief has called out his "kava name," and before drinking, each pours a few drops of kava on the floor as an offering and speaks a short prayer. The empty cup is sent spinning back across the mat-covered floor to the bowl.

Women do not generally drink kava, and it is taboo to the untattooed boys. No child must touch the kava utensils. Kava must be served on every important occasion in Samoan life—at marriages, births, and deaths. It solemnizes every transaction and figures in rites to cure illness, avert misfortune, and prepare for war.

The drink is not alcoholic; in fact, it becomes stale after a few hours and has to be mixed anew. It is variously described as a stimulant and a narcotic, and it is known to stimulate the secretion of urine. The kava plant, *Piper methysticum,* belongs to the pepper family. The stems of this plant have been found to contain a sleep-inducing agent, marindinim. Various ill effects have been ascribed to the long continued use of kava, ranging from unsteady gait to chronic eye infection and a scaly skin disorder; but the afflictions for which kava has been blamed have probably had other causes.

The kava ceremony is followed by the feast itself. The light-brown bodies of the attendants carrying the food in from the ovens are glistening with rain, for sudden squalls, not unexpected at this season, are sweeping in from the sea. The gusts cause the burning candlenuts to flicker, and woven screens are let down between the house-posts. Soon the rain can be heard slashing spasmodically against the hollow-sounding matting and roof-thatch.

The feast begins with a starch soup served in coconut shell cups, flying fish in turmeric sauce, and hot taro dumplings placed before each guest in woven baskets. To these are added diced raw bonito in bowls of spiced sea water, shark flesh and shark stomach, roast doves, and the rare palolos in their leaf dresses. Coconut cream is the sauce for large sections of taro and for ripe-banana *poi*, mashed by the fists of the aualuma girls and served in wooden bowls. An enormous sea turtle has just been captured in the traditional Samoan fashion: a swimmer dove beneath it and flopped it over onto its back, causing it to float helpless at the surface. Its internal parts have been removed and cooked separately in one hundred and fifty leaf packages; the remainder of the animal has been baked in its own shell with a loading of hot stones and lavai leaves. Whole pigs, steaming from their filling of hot stones, are laid in the center of the hut on mats of interwoven palm fronds and breadfruit leaves.

Everyone eats with his fingers, only occasionally improvising a scoop from a piece of uncooked breadfruit or making a fork of a leaf-rib. Some of the coconut wicks blow out in the gale, but the feasting goes on. The storm strikes with fresh violence, and several men leave to heap large palm fronds against the walls and tie ropes around the house to keep them in place. They cover the roof with banana leaves tied in pairs, but it is not enough; the roof, threatening to lift off, has to be weighted with the trunks of banana plants. Yet still they eat; and the guest, though replete and exhausted, must try to continue. Finally the Chief excuses the visitor's small appetite with a patient smile, asks for the wooden finger bowl to be passed around, and calls for the entertainment to begin.

Above the roar of the tropical storm rises the cadence of hollow wooden gongs, sounding boards, and rhythm-beaters made of loose bundles of bamboo. Participants without instruments clap their hands. Three men come forward and sing a plaintive song in harmony; a solo on a bamboo panpipe is almost lost in the wind and the din.

The cacophony ceases, and two rows of girl dancers enter and sit cross-legged. They clap their hands and strike the ground with bunches of split stems, then rise and face each other, stomping, hopping, and jumping. They surge toward each other and away. Their movements become lewd; and an older man and woman, in the shadows, rise to parody their performance. Now and again, a spectator voices his approval of some movement either sensual or ludicrous.

And then it is the taupou's turn. Her body has been bathed and anointed with coconut oil and with fragrant herbs. She is barefoot, and her only garment is a single kilt of soft matting or *ti* leaves. She wears a garland of flowers, and her ankles tinkle with ringlets of shells and bright seeds. The flesh of her throat glows beneath a necklace of whale's teeth interspersed with bits of luminous fungus.

But it is her headdress, her *tuinga,* that dominates all else, defying one to imagine anything more intricate or spectacular. The princess cannot get into the house without bending over. The towering ornament of bleached human hair is gaudy with red parrot feathers and plaques of blue nautilus shell. Half a year of treatment with coral lime, sea water, and sunlight has been required to produce this tawny fluff. To support it, five radiating rods fan upward from the mother-of-pearl forehead band, carrying the diadem to a height of nearly two feet. Tortoise shell and bark cloth have been worked into its construction, and five separate pieces must be assembled and taken apart every time it is worn. So that the headdress will not slip during her dance, it is bound so tightly to her head that she will probably suffer severe headache and may possibly faint before the performance is over.

There is a lull in the wind, and she takes a central position, a haughty expression on her face. A new cadence issues from the orchestra. At first her body seems scarcely to be moving to the rhythm. The tempo rises, and she responds without effort. Soon she is setting the pace and the mood. Her movements suggest subtle longing as she lightly touches her ankles, her thighs. The Talking Chief exercises his privilege and rises and dances beside her. He faces her, matching her movements, but she pays no heed. Nothing can ruffle her proud composure. He seeks to attract the audience's attention by less delicate counter-movements, but the taupou permits only an occasional trace of impudence to alter her expression of hauteur. Her dance quickens and comes to a climax in a frenzy of sensual gestures. The spectators call out their approval and demand an encore.

She is the people's symbol of grace and beauty. Within the group, she is the living emblem of virtue and continence in a culture that recognizes few inhibitions. In social rivalry with neighboring communities, she epitomizes local prestige. Her dance can be a veiled insult or a token of highest honor.

When her performance is finished, she retires to the protection of her chaperones. She sleeps always with an older woman at her side and is not allowed to leave the hut. She is more highly honored than the Chief's wife, but her life is one of formalities and denials, with always the periodic duty of kava chewing.

The taupou is expected to marry outside the village. So great is the prestige attached to such a union that communities vie with one another to secure the honor for one of their own sons. Public sentiment sometimes heavily overclouds the romantic aspect of the taupou's love life, and she may then run away with someone altogether different from the husband-elect. But if her marriage follows the more formal pattern, enormous amounts of property change hands and the event has social repercussions far and wide.

Marriage ends her career as a taupou. Another must then be chosen, usually from among the relatives of the Chief's sister or of his father's sister. A chief's daughter can also become a taupou.

Samoan girls generally receive proposals through a go-between called a *soa*. This is usually a brother of the boy who is pressing his suit or the girl's own sister acting for her suitor. When the girl accepts a suitor's gifts of food, it is a sign that she is willing. The marriage must be formally validated by the exchange of presents–houses, canoes, and other equipment from the boy's father, and mats, bark cloth, fans, and coconut oil from the family of the girl's mother. But it may be secretly consummated before that. The Samoans believe that pregnancy is possible only through continued intercourse with the same person.

The first missionaries landed in Samoa in 1830. Instead of shooting birds out of the air as had the *papalagi*, or "sky-bursters," as the first European visitors were called, they preached peace. This concept was foreign to Samoan culture, as was the idea that sex is wrong except under rigid marital regulations. There began a long and difficult period of adjustment for the Samoans.

However, they proved surprisingly willing to espouse many features of the new religion. Their own religion had not been as strong as the polytheistic pantheon of other Polynesian groups. Myths and legends, to be sure, were told in great variety in explanation of the origins of things, but religious ceremonies were few and unimpressive. Family priests officiated in minor ways, but the kind of raised stone platforms that were used for religious functions elsewhere in Polynesia had chiefly political significance in Samoa.

In the first nine years of missionary effort, 12,500 converts were claimed in the large islands of Western Samoa alone. Massive stone churches began to spring up among the thatched huts, and the former life of impulse and indulgence gave way to a rigid Sabbatarianism. Hymns became the accustomed music amid the rustling palms, and the tattooing which in La Pérouse's time made a naked man look almost dressed began to disappear. Formerly the youth of fourteen to eighteen had to endure weeks of pain while comblike instruments made from the pelvis of a slain enemy were struck with a mallet over much of his body. Soot from the candlenut was rubbed in for coloring, and the massive inflammation that sometimes resulted could endanger his life before the final design around the navel ended the ordeal. The women's tattooing, which was less extensive than the men's, likewise fell out of fashion as the loose calico dress known as the "Mother Hubbard" began to mark the civilized Samoan.

Customs that had served the Samoans when their society was contained in a sort of idyllic vacuum could not survive in contact with world commerce. A number of diseases that had been unknown before the coming of Europeans sprang up to plague them: tuberculosis, influenza, and measles and other childhood illnesses. Sexual laxity helped to spread venereal infections, but seemingly with less shocking results than among certain other Polynesians. Dietary changes, including the introduction of artificially sweetened beverages in place of coconut milk and kava, ushered in another unfamiliar disease, diabetes, or, as they call it, "sugar sickness."

From a population roughly estimated at between 40,000 and 80,000 before 1850, their numbers dropped sharply. But as the people gained a greater capacity to withstand the effects of civilization and improved health measures were introduced, they began to show fresh vitality. Between 1921 and 1945 there was a sharp increase in their population, so that by 1947 the inhabitants of the Samoan Islands numbered about 83,000. Europeans comprised only about half of one per cent, at least in Western Samoa. Since the Samoans have mixed freely with peoples of other cultures and are generally accepted by Europeans as being scarcely different from themselves, it is surprising that there has not been more intermarriage. But persons of mixed Polynesian and Caucasian parentage aggregate only about seven per cent in Samoa.

Since the day when La Pérouse's men were mowed down by the stones and war clubs of the Samoans, other wars have shaken the islands of the Pacific. On occasion it has been the Samoans who have shown the greater spirit of humanitarianism. When the foreign powers were warring over the islands in 1888 and Bismarck's forces were shelling helpless villages, warships were sent by the United States to halt the destruction. At that juncture a typhoon roared across Apia harbor, sinking three German and three American warships. The Samoans, without hesitation, swam to the rescue of both sides alike. The affection and admiration they showed for so gentle a personality as Robert Louis Stevenson, who passed the last years of his life in Samoa, gave additional proof of their transformation.

Though difficulties have attended their adjustment to civilization, they have exhibited more patience than might have been expected of so daring a people as the "Vikings of the Pacific" who discovered and dominated a larger section of the earth's surface than has any other aboriginal group. Many changes have taken place in their mode of life, but the Samoans have retained the niceties that made their hospitality distinctive and famous among the far-flung islands of the South Seas.

INDEX

DOLPHIN BOOKS AND DOLPHIN MASTERS

The bold face **M** indicates a Dolphin Master. Dolphin Masters are Dolphin Books in the editions of greatest importance to the teacher and student. In selecting the Dolphin Masters, the editors have taken particular pains to choose copies of the most significant edition (usually the first) by obtaining original books or their facsimiles or by having reproductions made of library copies of particularly rare editions. Facsimiles of original title pages and other appropriate material from the first edition are included in many Masters.

FICTION

JANE EYRE Charlotte Brontë	C5
THE SCARLET LETTER Nathaniel Hawthorne	C7
KIDNAPPED Robert Louis Stevenson	C8
THE RISE OF SILAS LAPHAM William Dean Howells	C9
UNCLE TOM'S CABIN Harriet Beecher Stowe **M**	C13
THE PRAIRIE James Fenimore Cooper	C14
THE PICTURE OF DORIAN GRAY Oscar Wilde	C15
THE WAY OF ALL FLESH Samuel Butler	C16
THE RED AND THE BLACK Stendhal	C17
PERE GORIOT Honoré de Balzac	C18
MADAME BOVARY Gustave Flaubert	C19
THE VICAR OF WAKEFIELD Oliver Goldsmith	C20
THE MILL ON THE FLOSS George Eliot	C21
JUDE THE OBSCURE Thomas Hardy	C22
MANON LESCAUT Abbé Prévost	C29
IVANHOE Sir Walter Scott	C31
A TALE OF TWO CITIES Charles Dickens	C32
NORTHANGER ABBEY and PERSUASION Jane Austen **M**	C34
THE MOONSTONE Wilkie Collins	C35
FRANKENSTEIN Mary Shelley	C44
THREE MEN IN A BOAT Jerome K. Jerome	C46
TALES OF THE GROTESQUE AND ARABESQUE Edgar Allan Poe **M**	C50
HIS MONKEY WIFE John Collier	C53
LOOKING BACKWARD (2000–1887) Edward Bellamy	C55
MOLL FLANDERS Daniel Defoe	C56
BARCHESTER TOWERS Anthony Trollope	C57
CRANFORD E. C. Gaskell	C60
THE RED BADGE OF COURAGE Stephen Crane	C61
ADAM BEDE George Eliot	C62
JOSEPH ANDREWS Henry Fielding	C63
A CHRISTMAS CAROL Charles Dickens	C65
VILLETTE Charlotte Brontë	C66
MOBY DICK Herman Melville	C70
TREASURE ISLAND Robert Louis Stevenson	C72
PRIDE AND PREJUDICE Jane Austen	C74
FAR FROM THE MADDING CROWD Thomas Hardy	C75
THE LOG OF A COWBOY Andy Adams	C77
BLACK BEAUTY Anna Sewell	C78
GULLIVER'S TRAVELS Jonathan Swift	C86

A HAZARD OF NEW FORTUNES William Dean Howells C88
QUENTIN DURWARD Sir Walter Scott C89
ALICE'S ADVENTURES UNDERGROUND and ALICE'S ADVENTURES IN WONDERLAND Lewis Carroll M C94
THE ADVENTURES OF HUCKLEBERRY FINN Mark Twain C98
ROBINSON CRUSOE Daniel Defoe C103
TRISTRAM SHANDY Laurence Sterne C104
BURIED ALIVE Arnold Bennett C105
WUTHERING HEIGHTS Emily Brontë C107
PORTRAIT OF A MAN WITH RED HAIR Hugh Walpole C108
THE MARBLE FAUN Nathaniel Hawthorne C110
AUTOCRAT OF THE BREAKFAST TABLE Oliver Wendell Holmes C111
MANSFIELD PARK Jane Austen C113
HARD TIMES Charles Dickens C114
THE DAMNATION OF THERON WARE Harold Frederic C116
THE RETURN OF THE NATIVE Thomas Hardy C119
THE EXPEDITION OF HUMPHRY CLINKER Tobias Smollett C120
THE HISTORY OF HENRY ESMOND, ESQ. William Makepeace Thackeray C121
EVELINA Fanny Burney C123
THE DAY OF THE TRIFFIDS John Wyndham C130
THE PRIVATE PAPERS OF HENRY RYECROFT George Gissing C131
THE ADVENTURES OF TOM SAWYER Mark Twain C133
THE WARDEN Anthony Trollope C134
TRILBY George du Maurier C135
TESS OF THE D'URBERVILLES Thomas Hardy C138
NEW GRUB STREET George Gissing C139
RODERICK RANDOM Tobias Smollett C140
DAVID HARUM Edward Noyes Westcott C146
EUGENIE GRANDET Honoré de Balzac C147
THE HOUSE OF THE SEVEN GABLES Nathaniel Hawthorne C148
EMMA Jane Austen C149
SILAS MARNER George Eliot C151
RESURRECTION Leo Tolstoy C152
THE MAYOR OF CASTERBRIDGE Thomas Hardy C153
ELSIE VENNER Oliver Wendell Holmes C154
SISTER CARRIE Theodore Dreiser C160
TWENTY THOUSAND LEAGUES UNDER THE SEA Jules Verne C167
AROUND THE WORLD IN EIGHTY DAYS Jules Verne C168
THE PATHFINDER James Fenimore Cooper C173
SENSE AND SENSIBILITY Jane Austen C174
BEN-HUR Lew Wallace C175
GREAT EXPECTATIONS Charles Dickens C181
OLIVER TWIST Charles Dickens C182
OMOO Herman Melville C183
KING SOLOMON'S MINES H. Rider Haggard C188
THE FANCHER TRAIN Amelia Bean C197
THE SKETCHBOOK OF GEOFFREY CRAYON, GENT. Washington Irving M C206
THE SPY James Fenimore Cooper C207
NANA Emile Zola C208
SHE H. Rider Haggard C210
THE LAST OF THE MOHICANS James Fenimore Cooper C211

POETRY AND DRAMA

THE DIVINE COMEDY OF DANTE ALIGHIERI: THE INFERNO
Translated by Henry Wadsworth Longfellow M — C1
LEAVES OF GRASS Walt Whitman M — C3
LYRICAL BALLADS William Wordsworth and
Samuel Taylor Coleridge M — C4
POEMS OF KEATS AND SHELLEY (1820) M — C11
INVITATION TO POETRY Lloyd Frankenberg — C24
archy and mehitabel don marquis — C26
RUBAIYAT OF OMAR KHAYYAM Edward FitzGerald, translator — C28
SHAKESPEARE'S SONNETS M — C33
THE GOLDEN TREASURY OF ENGLISH SONGS AND LYRICS
Francis Turner Palgrave M — C45
THE DRAMATIC WORKS OF SHERIDAN
Richard Brinsley Sheridan M — C47
THE DIVINE COMEDY OF DANTE ALIGHIERI: PURGATORIO
Translated by Henry Wadsworth Longfellow M — C51
THE DIVINE COMEDY OF DANTE ALIGHIERI: PARADISO
Translated by Henry Wadsworth Longfellow M — C52
DON JUAN Lord Byron — C64
PARADISE LOST John Milton — C73
MEN AND WOMEN Robert Browning — C136
THE PLAYS OF OSCAR WILDE Oscar Wilde — C137
H. M. S. PINAFORE, AND SIX OTHER SAVOY OPERAS
W. S. Gilbert — C155
THE MIKADO, AND FIVE OTHER SAVOY OPERAS
W. S. Gilbert — C158
IDYLLS OF THE KING Alfred, Lord Tennyson — C165
EIGHT DRAMAS OF CALDERON
Edward FitzGerald, translator M — C169
PLEASURE DOME Lloyd Frankenberg — C190
SIBYLLINE LEAVES Samuel Taylor Coleridge M — C195
SONNETS FROM THE PORTUGUESE AND OTHER POEMS
Elizabeth Barrett Browning — C209

HISTORY AND BIOGRAPHY

THE BERNAL DIAZ CHRONICLES
Albert Idell, editor and translator — C25
OUR FRIEND JAMES JOYCE Mary and Padraic Colum — C27
GIANTS OF GEOLOGY Carroll Lane and Mildred Adams Fenton — C36
MR. LINCOLN'S ARMY Bruce Catton — C37
BATTLES THAT CHANGED HISTORY Fletcher Pratt — C38
TEACHER Helen Keller — C39
THE LIFE OF CHARLOTTE BRONTE E. C. Gaskell M — C48
COMMON SENSE and THE CRISIS Thomas Paine M — C49
THE FOUR GEORGES William Makepeace Thackeray — C54
TWO YEARS BEFORE THE MAST R. H. Dana — C76
SEA FIGHTS AND SHIPWRECKS Hanson W. Baldwin — C84
THE AUTOBIOGRAPHY OF BENJAMIN FRANKLIN M — C87
LIVES OF THE POETS [Cowley to Prior] Samuel Johnson — C91
LIVES OF THE POETS [Congreve to Gray] Samuel Johnson — C92
THE MAN WHO KILLED LINCOLN Philip Van Doren Stern — C101
LIFE OF NELSON Robert Southey — C112
THE LIFE OF SIR ARTHUR CONAN DOYLE John Dickson Carr — C117
TONGUE OF THE PROPHETS Robert St. John — C118
AN AUTOBIOGRAPHY Anthony Trollope — C128

AUTOBIOGRAPHY OF BENVENUTO CELLINI Benvenuto Cellini C129
THE PELOPONNESIAN WAR Thucydides C150
VENERABLE ANCESTOR Harry Hussey C157
BENT'S FORT David Lavender C159
BALBOA OF DARIEN Kathleen Romoli C162
THE CONQUEST OF PERU William H. Prescott C166
EXPERIMENT IN REBELLION Clifford Dowdey C171
THE AUTOBIOGRAPHY OF JOHN STUART MILL
John Stuart Mill C179

PHILOSOPHY AND RELIGION

WALDEN Henry David Thoreau C10
THE REPUBLIC AND OTHER WORKS Plato C12
THE LIFE OF JESUS Ernest Renan C59
THE MEDITATIONS OF MARCUS AURELIUS
Translated by George Long C68
THE VARIETIES OF RELIGIOUS EXPERIENCE William James C71
ON THE NATURE OF THINGS Lucretius
Translated by H. A. J. Munro C80
THE RATIONALISTS Descartes, Spinoza, Leibniz C82
THE EMPIRICISTS Locke, Berkeley, Hume C109
THE SECRET SAYINGS OF JESUS
Robert M. Grant with David Noel Freedman C163

ESSAYS AND LETTERS

THE CONDUCT OF LIFE Ralph Waldo Emerson M C2
THE ESSAYS OF ELIA and THE LAST ESSAYS OF ELIA
Charles Lamb M C6
LECTURES ON THE ENGLISH COMIC WRITERS
William Hazlitt M C30
HAWTHORNE Henry James C58
THE ESSAYS OF FRANCIS BACON C67
THE SPIRIT OF THE AGE William Hazlitt C79
ON HEROES AND HERO-WORSHIP and REPRESENTATIVE MEN
Thomas Carlyle and Ralph Waldo Emerson C83
LIFE IN MEXICO Frances Calderón de la Barca C93
THE NATURAL HISTORY OF SELBORNE Gilbert White C96
CONFESSIONS OF AN ENGLISH OPIUM-EATER and SUSPIRIA
DE PROFUNDIS Thomas De Quincey M C97
THE COMPLETE ANGLER Izaak Walton C102
THE NEXT MILLION YEARS C. G. Darwin C106
AN ALMANAC OF LIBERTY William O. Douglas C115
LETTERS FROM AN AMERICAN FARMER
J. H. St. John Crèvecoeur C164
FABIAN ESSAYS IN SOCIALISM Edited by G. B. Shaw C170

MYSTERY

BLACK PLUMES Margery Allingham C41
THE MAN IN THE GREEN HAT Manning Coles C42
THE BELL IN THE FOG John Stephen Strange C43
THE PEOPLE AGAINST O'HARA Eleazar Lipsky C122
A STUDY IN SCARLET & THE SIGN OF FOUR
Sir Arthur Conan Doyle C124

ADVENTURES OF SHERLOCK HOLMES
Sir Arthur Conan Doyle C125
MEMOIRS OF SHERLOCK HOLMES Sir Arthur Conan Doyle C126
THE HOUND OF THE BASKERVILLES
Sir Arthur Conan Doyle C127
POOR HARRIET Elizabeth Fenwick C185
THE WHISPER IN THE GLOOM Nicholas Blake C186
THE LADY AND HER DOCTOR Evelyn Piper C187
A HERO FOR LEANDA Andrew Garve C189

MISCELLANEOUS

A HANDBOOK TO MARRIAGE Theodor Bovet C23
SEX AND FAMILY IN THE BIBLE AND THE MIDDLE EAST
Raphael Patai C40
THE EXECUTIVE LIFE Editors of FORTUNE C69
ZAPOTEC Helen Augur C81
CONVERSATIONS WITH TOSCANINI B. H. Haggin C85
AMERICAN WAYS OF LIFE George R. Stewart C90
THE ABC OF CHILD CARE Allan Fromme, Ph.D. C95
THE AGE OF FABLE Thomas Bulfinch C132
THE LIFE AND DEATH OF CELLS Joseph G. Hoffman C156
MARRIAGE EAST AND WEST David and Vera Mace C161
THE ORIGIN OF SPECIES Charles Darwin C172
PRIMITIVE PEOPLES TODAY Edward Weyer, Jr. C200

DOLPHIN REFERENCE SERIES

POEMS TO REMEMBER John Kieran, editor C99
100 GREAT OPERAS AND THEIR STORIES Henry W. Simon C100
THE FAMILY HANDBOOK OF HOME NURSING AND MEDICAL
CARE I. J. Rossman, M.D. and Doris R. Schwartz, R.N. C141
THE COMPLETE BOOK OF CHESS TACTICS Fred Reinfeld C143
THESAURUS OF ANECDOTES Edmund Fuller C191

DOLPHIN HANDBOOK SERIES

THE FINE ART OF MIXING DRINKS David A. Embury C177
HOW TO SAY A FEW WORDS David Guy Powers C178
HOW TO BE A CONSISTENT WINNER IN THE MOST POPULAR
CARD GAMES John R. Crawford C180
COOKING WITH A FRENCH TOUCH Gerald Maurois C184
BEER AND GOOD FOOD Myra Waldo C196
CREATIVE COOKING Nicholas Roosevelt C213
A NEW WAY TO BETTER ENGLISH Rudolf Flesch C214
IT'S EASY TO INCREASE YOUR VOCABULARY William Morris C215